# THE POLITICAL CAREER
## OF
# FLOYD B. OLSON

# THE POLITICAL CAREER
## OF
# FLOYD B. OLSON

GEORGE H. MAYER

With a New Introduction by RUSSELL W. FRIDLEY

MINNESOTA HISTORICAL SOCIETY PRESS • ST. PAUL • 1987

Borealis Books are high-quality paperback reprints of
books chosen by the Minnesota Historical Society
Press for their importance as enduring historical
sources and their value as enjoyable accounts of life
in the Upper Midwest.

Minnesota Historical Society Press, St. Paul 55101
Copyright © 1951 by the University of Minnesota Press
New material copyright © 1987 by the Minnesota Historical Society

*International Standard Book Number 0-87351-206-5*
Manufactured in the United States of America

10 9 8 7 6 5 4 3 2 1

Library of Congress Cataloging-in-Publication Data

Mayer, George H., 1920-
The political career of Floyd B. Olson.

(Borealis)
Reprint. Originally published: Minneapolis : University of
Minnesota Press, 1951. With new introd.
Bibliography: p.
Includes index.
1. Olson, Floyd Bjornstjerne, 1891-1936. 2. Minnesota--
Governors — Biography. 3. Minnesota — Politics and government.
I. Title.
F606.0484 1987      977.6'052'0924 [B]      86-33332
ISBN 0-87351-206-5 (pbk.)

To
*George M. Stephenson*
Scholar, mentor, and friend

# Contents

# Cartoons

# Illustrations

(between pages 150 and 151)

# Introduction to the Reprint Edition

FIFTY YEARS after his death in 1936, the mystique surrounding Floyd B. Olson shows no sign of diminishing. In August of 1986, over three hundred people flocked to the State Capitol in St. Paul for commemorative ceremonies including the rededication of the Olson statue on the capitol mall and the opening of an exhibit, "Floyd B. Olson: The People's Governor." In 1964, when the Minnesota Historical Society asked thirty-two teachers of Minnesota history and politics to evaluate all of the governors of the state and name the five most outstanding, Floyd Olson emerged as far and away the first choice. In the words of Arthur E. Naftalin, professor of public affairs at the University of Minnesota and producer of a public television series on Minnesota governors between 1931 and 1979, "The governorship of Floyd Olson remains a golden memory in Minnesota history."[1]

In bringing *The Political Career of Floyd B. Olson* back into print, the Minnesota Historical Society Press makes available a rich source on Olson and the turbulent years through which he governed Minnesota. Begun a decade after Olson's death and published thirty-six years ago, this biography comprises a faithful account of the sixty-eight month governorship of the Farmer-Labor

---

[1] Naftalin, "Minnesota Governors: Floyd B. Olson," videotape produced for the Hubert H. Humphrey Institute, University of Minnesota (Minneapolis: University of Minnesota Media Resources, 1981); *Minneapolis Tribune*, October 23, 1966, p. 2C. Twenty-three of the thirty-two teachers returned their evaluations; the other four governors named, significantly behind Olson, were John S. Pillsbury, Alexander Ramsey, John A. Johnson, and Harold E. Stassen.

party leader. Highly readable, full of insight into the man and Minnesota during a period of the utmost social and economic stress, the book takes the reader on an absorbing adventure in Minnesota politics and government on which Olson left a permanent stamp.

Foes and followers have provided ample testimony to the extraordinary abilities that won Olson his place in the pantheon of Minnesota political heroes. Republican Harold E. Stassen, who in 1939 ended the Farmer-Labor party's eight-year control of the governor's office, commented, "There's no doubt that he had a tremendous personality. He had an impact on the state, and if you're speaking in terms of significant political leadership. . . . you would have to and should rate him as a very significant political leader of that whole rising-out of the distress of the depression years and the third party movement—he would loom large." Stafford King, long-time Republican state auditor who was elected to his first term the same year (1930) as Olson, considered him a genius as a political leader presiding over and holding together a tenuous coalition that ran across the political spectrum from left to right. King described Olson as the most outstanding of the ten governors with whom he served between 1931 and 1967. Olson's rapport and popularity with students impressed the young Eric Sevareid, a leader in the early 1930s of the Jacobins, a left-leaning student organization at the University of Minnesota. Sevareid considered the governor a better speaker than Franklin D. Roosevelt. Others praised Olson's first-rate intellect and emphasized his empathy with people.[2]

Standing six-feet-two-inches tall, blue-eyed, handsome, virile, aggressive, gifted with a quick wit, a man of good cheer, Olson had the common touch with persons from all walks of life. Comfortable in extending a warm greeting to a mob of thousands of desperate

[2]Interviews of Stassen by the author and Arv Johnson, May 9, 1963, of King by the author and Lila M. Johnson, June 26, 1968, tapes in the Minnesota Historical Society (MHS) audio-visual library; Sevareid, *Not So Wild A Dream* (New York: Atheneum, 1946), 54; interviews of George A. Selke, July 9, 1957, and Theodor S. Slen, October 11, 1971, notes in the author's possession.

farmers marching on the State Capitol and disarming their anger with stirring oratory and an uplifting message of hope, he was equally at home at a labor rally, a college convocation, or in the company of wealthy friends or foes—with whom he frequently consorted at country clubs and summer resorts.

George H. Mayer provides a comprehensive and incisive account of Olson's political career, beginning with his rise to prominence during the 1920s as the increasingly visible and successful Hennepin County attorney. A Democrat in an overwhelmingly Republican government, he earned a reputation as a compassionate friend of the common people and as a tough prosecutor of racketeers and public officials who violated the law. His successful handling of Ku Klux Klan leaders in 1923 brought an end to the growing influence of that organization in Minneapolis. During 1928-29 he received statewide recognition for his investigation of graft in city government, culminating in the successful prosecution of three Minneapolis aldermen for bribery.

For reasons not entirely clear, Olson remained aloof from the newly forming Farmer-Labor party, which had enjoyed only marginal success since its founding in 1918. Instead, he flirted with the Democratic party, a doubtful vessel for reform, as the best alternative to Republican dominance. (A sharp turn to the right during World War I weakened the prewar progressive coalition that had united the Republicans and carried their party to a long string of victories.) Caution and preoccupation with building his law practice seemed to temper his rebellious convictions; in 1918 and 1920 Olson filed for the Democratic nomination for the fifth congressional district seat, although neither of these bids attracted sufficient support to secure him the party nomination. By avoiding the label of radical, Olson later opened himself to the charge of carpetbagging when, in 1924, he wrested the Farmer-Labor nomination from the old Nonpartisan Leaguers and founding Farmer Laborites.

Olson went down to defeat as the Farmer-Labor party's

FLOYD B. OLSON

standard-bearer for governor in 1924. In the author's words, "From the discouraging election of 1924 Floyd B. Olson extracted some valuable lessons. He learned that the average voter had a limited capacity for radicalism and could absorb even small doses of it only in time of depression. He also learned that political organization outweighed personal energy and spectacular oratory in deciding elections, and he decided to build a statewide personal organization" (page 37).

Worsening economic conditions favored the strategy he fashioned over the next six years. Plummeting agricultural prices, skyrocketing farm foreclosures, a severe drought, bank failures, widespread unemployment, and labor unrest became all too familiar during the early 1930s. By 1930, as Farmer-Labor candidate for governor, Olson forged a broad coalition of farmers, workers, socialists, isolationists, and progressives. Aided by an internal struggle within the Republican party, the deteriorating economy, and a brilliant campaign stressing moderation and the restoration of good government, Olson won the election by nearly 200,000 votes.

With the newspapers of the state overwhelmingly opposed to him, Olson became the first Minnesota governor to make extensive and effective use of radio and the lecture platform. He was a virtuoso speaker, and his powerful voice, theatrical delivery, searing sarcasm toward opponents, clear analysis of the issues, and satirical humor captivated audiences. The usually unfriendly *Minneapolis Journal* described an audience of over 2,000 listening to Olson: "Those standing stood like statues from start to finish; those sitting sat forward on the edges of their chairs, intent not to miss a word."[3]

For the next six years, Olson led the Farmer-Labor party to its greatest victories. He exerted intense personal pressure and orchestrated public opinion to force a hostile legislative majority to enact

[3]*Minneapolis Journal*, March 28, 1936, p. 8.

remedial social legislation. He secured large appropriations for relief, a two-year moratorium on farm foreclosures, an old-age pension law, a statute prohibiting injunctions in labor disputes, and the state's first income-tax law. By 1933, he emerged as the unquestioned spokesman for midwestern farmers, calling upon the federal government to fix agricultural prices. Extending an encouraging hand to labor, he unsuccessfully supported the passage of unemployment insurance, urged workers to organize, personally settled the Hormel Company strike of 1933, and refused to use the National Guard to break strikes.

Mayer accurately portrays Olson as a political realist who generally advocated moderate reforms. As party leader, he was never far from controversy and conflict, but he maintained a tight control over party affairs, platforms, and conventions throughout his first two terms. Although he criticized the American economic system and, on occasion, referred to himself as a "radical," Olson's rhetoric usually outran his performance. He frequently disappointed left-wing leaders of his party with both his moderation and his refusal to appoint only Farmer Laborites to public office. By the 1934 party convention, however, his ability or desire to curb the growing numbers and influence of the left wing declined. Unlike preceding conventions when Olson had carefully organized the agenda, passed on the nominees, and actively shaped the platform, the governor seemed disinclined to do so or to perform the critical task of party mediator at which he had proven so masterful. Instead he delivered an electrifying keynote address, abandoning his written notes that called for caution to proclaim: "I am what I want to be. I am a radical." Immediately thereafter he departed for Washington, D.C., leaving the left wing in control of the convention.

Olson was reelected to a third term in 1934, but by the narrowest margin of his three victorious campaigns for governor. This time he marshalled strong support from urban labor and reform forces but less enthusiasm from farmers who were alienated by the new party platform. This startling document proposed public ownership of industry, banking, insurance, and public utilities and the formation of a "cooperative commonwealth." In the face of widespread hostility, Olson adroitly managed to distance himself from the more inflammatory planks of the platform, but his final term was marred by strikes, intraparty fights, increasing party patronage, and a virtual deadlock in the legislature.

*The Political Career of Floyd B. Olson* remains the best and most comprehensive work to date on Olson and his career. In the decades since the book's original publication, however, a significant amount of primary-source material has become available. Olson, among all Minnesota governors, has been the subject of the most research — published and unpublished. These resources will enable future biographers to formulate new or revised interpretations of Olson's life and political career. Mayer used only four collections of personal papers: Olson's and those of his secretary, Vince Day; Henry G. Teigan, editor of the *Farmer Labor Leader*; and E. G. Hall, president of the State Federation of Labor in Olson's era. Many more sets of related papers are available today, and numerous oral history projects have studied the Farmer-Labor party, especially the 1920s and 1930s and the life and career of Floyd Olson.

Research subsequent to Mayer's illuminates several areas in which the author's conclusions bear rethinking. Among these are Olson's boyhood, family life, and education; his wanderings and experiences through the American West, in Alaska, and Canada; his early involvement in the Democratic party; his membership in the Committee of 48, a group that in 1919 organized to convince Robert M. La Follette of Wisconsin to run as a third-party candidate for president; Olson's association with labor organizations; his role in labor disputes other than the well-documented 1934 truck drivers' strike; his ability to keep a foot in both camps — for example, his closeness to management and labor in the Hormel strike of 1933; and his relationship with Franklin D. Roosevelt, including his support and criticism of various New Deal programs.

Mayer artfully delineated Olson's complex personality and various moods and stances. "Olson rarely spoke of his inner life," he wrote, "but on one occasion he told Leif Gilstad, political writer for the *Minneapolis Journal*, how the memory of his humble origins both sobered and heartened him. 'I find now and then when I get smug with position and perhaps inclining to forget — or if my spirits are low — I go down into the Gateway and bum around a bit. It brings me back on my feet, and puts new fight in me.' Behind the flintlike facade of the political realist was the warm heart of a sentimentalist who fought in his own faltering and sometimes unethical way for the day when the meek would inherit the earth. It was this spirit of Christian brotherhood that gave a fleeting touch of greatness to the Olson administration" (page 122).

Yet in this "political biography" Mayer avoided dealing with an unexplored area of Olson's complex personality: his alcoholism and rumored liaisons with a number of women outside of his marriage. Mayer states that "to assess the degree of truth in the stories" about his "wild carousing" is "beyond the scope of this political biography" (page 5). But the record on Olson's alcoholism is extensive, including lore about his alleged affairs and attraction to women. Mayer wrote before the "sexual revolution" and reflected the restraint biographers of his era exercised in examining certain facets of their subjects' private lives, yet Olson's apparently unconventional life style deserves assessment. The extent to which it shaped his personality and contributed to his final illness needs to be examined.

A second area inviting more research is that of Olson's relationship to the Farmer-Labor party, the Farmer Labor Association, and the national third-party movement. Three important works that offer fresh interpretations of these subjects are John E. Haynes's and Millard L. Gieske's books on the Farmer-Labor movement and Harvey Klehr's volume on American Communism. Recent scholarship also increasingly questions Mayer's uncritical acceptance of the view that left-wing elements of the Farmer-Labor party coerced Olson into appointing Elmer A. Benson to fill the unexpired United States Senate seat vacated by the death of Thomas D. Schall in December, 1935.[4]

A third area, and perhaps the one in which contemporary scholars consider Mayer's biography weakest, is his failure to examine the political strength of the "Popular Front" faction that emerged during the last year of Olson's governorship. At this time the Farmer-Labor party presented itself as Minnesota's New Deal party. In 1936, as the war clouds gathered in Europe and Farmer Laborites were increasingly drawn toward the national and international arenas, American Communists shelved their revolutionary rhetoric, ceased their attacks on Olson, and adopted a new strategy, generally called the Popular Front. This stance advocated an alliance of liberals and radicals against the threat of Fascism. Olson and other key Farmer-Labor leaders accepted this shift and allowed Communists to enter their party. This element then became a major force in the party under Governor Elmer Benson. Again, the studies by Haynes and Klehr are basic sources for understanding the volatile and shifting political currents in the Farmer-Labor party during Olson's declining months.

Mayer also neglected to discuss Olson's impact on the national scene, as evidenced by his appearances in the popular periodical literature and film of his day. Minnesota's flamboyant governor attracted attention in magazines such as *The Nation* and *New Republic* and became the subject of several laudatory articles. A chapter entitled "Olsonville" in Sherwood Anderson's book *Puzzled America*, published in 1935, relates the governor's observations on various depression-ridden regions of the country. Olson also became a familiar and eloquent spokesman for midwestern governors in numerous newsreels that were shown in neighborhood theaters across the nation.

[4]Haynes, *Dubious Alliance: The Making of the Minnesota DFL Party* (Minneapolis: University of Minnesota Press, 1984); Gieske, *Minnesota Farmer-Laborism: The Third-Party Alternative* (Minneapolis: University of Minnesota Press, 1979); Klehr, *The Heyday of American Communism: The Depression Decade* (New York: Basic Books, 1984).

# INTRODUCTION

As one reads the inaugural addresses of Minnesota governors, the three by Olson and the one by Benson are set apart from the others in their urgent call for government, both state and federal, to enlarge its role to relieve human misery brought on by the Great Depression. "We are assembled during the most crucial period," observed Olson in 1933, "in the history of the Nation and of our State. . . . Just beyond the horizon . . . is rampant lawlessness and possible revolution. Only remedial social legislation, national and state, can prevent its appearance."[5]

Floyd B. Olson led the most successful third party in American history to its greatest victories, drawing strength from and enlarging upon Minnesota's sturdy populist tradition. When asked "How much of the success of the Farmer-Labor party was due to Floyd Olson?" Harry H. Peterson, Olson's attorney general, replied, "About 99 percent." A political foe, Republican state senator Charles N. Orr of St. Paul, summed up Olson's response to the crises of the 1930s a year after the latter's death: "His was a new voice ringing across the state with a new and singular appeal, and the people listened. Coming upon the scene when many of our citizens were distressed and restless, he had the foresight to sense unerringly the trend of the times and the eloquence and ability to swing the great mass of the people to the support of changes which he deemed essential. Floyd Olson fitted into the times better perhaps than any other man in public life today."[6]

At his death from cancer at the age of forty-four, there was an unparalleled outpouring of grief by the people of Minnesota. An estimated 200,000 filed by his bier in the State Capitol; the Minneapolis Auditorium was packed to capacity at his funeral; and thousands more listened at loudspeakers outside the building to Wisconsin Governor Philip F. La Follette's eulogy.

[5] Olson, "Second Inaugural Address," January 4, 1933, p. 3, copy in the MHS reference library.

[6] Interview of Peterson, June 20, 1974, notes in author's possession; Orr, in "In Memoriam, Governor Floyd B. Olson," March 18, 1937, [p. 10], copy in the MHS reference library.

# FLOYD B. OLSON

Olson offered hope to the victims of the Great Depression and championed a larger role for government, a political philosophy in retreat today. Many thought he was destined for the White House, and his untimely death invites endless speculation on what his future might have been as war loomed and the wartime effort replaced the ebbing reform crusade of early years of the depression. The Farmer-Labor party he fashioned and led brought widespread citizen participation in political affairs and produced a number of courageous leaders who crusaded for social justice. Its legacy — and Olson's — is a strong orientation toward social concerns and education, progressive reforms, high taxation for a high level of public services, and, above all, the issue-oriented and independent political tradition for which Minnesota is known.

The ability and charisma with which Floyd B. Olson energized and expanded the office of governor remains the standard by which the performance of his predecessors and successors is judged to this day. The tenuous political coalition he forged and led that embraced radicals, moderates, and conservatives scored its greatest victory at the polls ten weeks after his death but rapidly fell apart in the succeeding two years. The Farmer-Labor period remains an exhilarating and fascinating era in Minnesota history for anyone interested in successful political reform movements. George H. Mayer's excellent biography of the central figure in this exciting story does much to explain Minnesota's continuing political behavior as that of a maverick among the fifty states. Its republication is a welcome event.

RUSSELL W. FRIDLEY

# Acknowledgments

THIS biography of Floyd B. Olson has been prepared with full knowledge of the shortcomings inevitably involved in research so soon after the occurrence of the events under consideration. It is my hope that the deficiencies stemming from lack of perspective and the absence of sources which the passage of time may coax from their hiding places will be counterbalanced by the testimony of contemporaries whose insights might otherwise be permanently lost in an age prone to make unrecorded decisions in personal interviews or over telephones.

So many people gave their unselfish help in furthering this project that the ensuing list of acknowledgments hardly does justice to the numberless contributions made. I want to thank Mrs. Floyd Olson and Mrs. Vince A. Day for making available to me the manuscripts in their possession. I also want to express gratitude to Mr. Carl Weicht and Senator Thye, who gave me permission to examine the Olson Papers in the State Capitol. Without the generous help of General Ellard Walsh, Morris Hursh, the late Maurice Rose, George B. Leonard, and Ann V. Egan the elusive many-sided personality of Olson would have defied recapture.

I am likewise indebted to C.F. Gaarenstrom, John Bosch, Robley D. Cramer, Lynn Thompson, R. C. Lilly, Gil Carmichael, Judge William C. Larson, Judge Levi Hall, Helen Notesteen, Charles B. Cheney, Leif Gilstad, Kenneth Haycraft, David R. Arundel, Emil Regnier, Hjalmar Petersen, Elmer A. Benson, C. D. Johnston, Herman Aufderheide, R. S. Wiggin, and Billy Williams

FLOYD B. OLSON

for filling many gaps in my knowledge of Olson and Minnesota politics. I am grateful, too, to Mack Rose of Beverly Hills, California, for his permission to reproduce some of the Olson pictures in the scrapbook kept by his brother, Maurice Rose.

Finally, I should like to acknowledge my debt to the staff of the history department at the University of Minnesota, especially to Dr. George M. Stephenson, under whose direction my initial work on Olson was done for a doctoral dissertation; to Professor V. L. Albjerg of Purdue University, who read the manuscript; and to a succession of sweet-tempered typists, including my mother.

GEORGE MAYER

*Lafayette, Indiana*
*November 1950*

# THE POLITICAL CAREER
## OF
# FLOYD B. OLSON

*Chapter I*     MORE REBEL
THAN RADICAL

W<small>HEN</small> a pancreatic cancer abruptly cut short the career of Floyd B. Olson on the eve of the 1936 election, his political star was so definitely in the ascendant that not even the presidency seemed beyond his reach. Although barely forty-five, he had already served ten years as Hennepin County attorney in Minnesota, won three terms as governor of Minnesota, and made careful preparations to campaign for election to the United States senate.

At an age when most political aspirants were still doing menial jobs for their local organizations, Olson had remodeled the old Nonpartisan League into a militant and successful Farmer Labor party, through which he ruled the state. His sponsorship of farm legislation far more sweeping than the Agricultural Adjustment Act and his employment of state troops to protect the workers during the memorable Minneapolis truck drivers' strike gave Olson a national reputation and endeared him to the more impatient reformers, who clamored for his entrance into the 1936 presidential campaign on a third-party ticket.

A streak of realism unusual among radical politicians, an ability to tame angry men, and a flair for improvising programs wide enough to win support from diverse groups made Olson one of the most formidable leaders of the 1930s. From time to time rumors circulated that he had received bids to join the Roosevelt cabinet. Advanced New Dealers even suggested that the mantle of the chief New Dealer might descend to him in 1940. In retrospect such speculation seems unrealistic, but it gives some measure of the contemporary enthusiasm for Olson's political prospects.

When Floyd B. Olson first ran for governor in 1924, he already possessed many of the characteristics that were to make him such an important political figure a decade later. His physical appearance was striking. He stood well over six feet with broad shoulders and a powerful frame. A pair of restless, half-defiant blue eyes dominated a handsome masculine countenance. The cheeks had a touch of heaviness, lending maturity to an otherwise youthful appearance. His forehead was crowned with a profusion of dark, reddish-brown hair that generally looked well groomed. The lines of his face, suggesting vitality and determination, registered faithfully the various moods of a mercurial personality. Admirers likened him to an ancient Viking — a description to which he sometimes alluded with considerable satisfaction.[1]

Coupled with physical grace was a winning platform manner. Olson habitually captivated audiences with a mixture of eloquence, earnestness, and clarity of expression. Contemporaries, marveling at the way he could thaw out indifferent or hostile groups, compared him to John A. Johnson, renowned orator and Minnesota reform governor of the Progressive era.[2]

Even the rural press, which was notoriously suspicious of urban candidates, could not resist Olson's charm. On one occasion, the *Hawley Herald* reported that "Mr. Olson, in spite of his being a lawyer by profession, made a favorable impression on his audience." Grudgingly it conceded that "he spoke convincingly and did not make a lot of promises which would be impossible of fulfillment."[3]

The secret of Olson's success on the platform lay in an intuitive grasp of what his auditors wished to hear. He performed with the effortless skill of a virtuoso, invariably striking an appropriate note and eliciting the maximum response. A native warmth and friendliness enabled him to avoid the metallic quality so typical of the politician's cultivated heartiness.

Olson liked people of any age or economic level. He enjoyed talking to them, trading yarns, and listening to their problems or grievances. A gregarious streak colored his relations with even casual acquaintances, frequently converting them into devoted friends. Long after he became the most famous alumnus of North High School, Minneapolis, Olson faithfully attended the reunions, renewing old contacts with undisguised zest and whirling Miss Georgia Burgess, his old Latin teacher, around the dance floor at a flattering but unacademic speed. His door was always open when he was county attorney. The Jewish people among whom he had spent his boyhood days would always insist on seeing him when they had business at the courthouse, and his invariable reply was "Send 'em in." [4]

Close friends saw a mischievous, fun-loving side of Olson that escaped the general public. He loved to spend weekends with a few choice spirits at the Gull Lake cabin of Bill Stewart, later his fish and game commissioner, swimming, fishing, and trading practical jokes. Olson was an inveterate prankster, and the tricks he thought up were lusty and earthy — sure to embarrass new arrivals at the Stewart camp.

In Olson, strands of energy and sloth, ambition and carefree gaiety, were woven together to create a complex, contradictory personality. At times he slipped over the line of reasonable recreation into irresponsible indolence. He sang, danced, played cards, and told dialect stories with a gusto that was enhanced by social drinking. His frank, unashamed pursuit of good fellowship sometimes violated traditional standards of social behavior to such a point that it gave rise to much whispered gossip about the "wild carousing" in his private life. To assess the degree of truth in the stories told is beyond the scope of this political biography, but there can be little doubt that the facts were often deliberately exaggerated and broadcast by his opponents for campaign purposes.

His enjoyment of conviviality could make Olson unaware of the passage of time, and consequently less systematic in the discharge of obligations. His unwillingness to carry a watch indicated his aversion and contempt for an orderly, routine regime of hard work. George B. Leonard, pioneer Minneapolis labor lawyer, recalls an automobile trip with Olson, the ostensible object of which was attendance at a Minnesota State Bar Association meeting at Duluth. The pair left the Twin Cities on a Tuesday afternoon, planning to reach Duluth the same night, but just out of Minneapolis Olson suggested a slight hundred-mile detour to the lake country around Brainerd for the evening. When Leonard demurred, Olson promised to make an early start Wednesday and reach Duluth in time for the first session.

On the strength of this promise, Leonard allowed himself to be driven to Breezy Point on Pequot Lake, one of Olson's favorite relaxation spots. The resort, owned and operated by Captain Billy Fawcett and his wife Annette, who were also the owners of the popular magazine house called Fawcett Publications, was a rendezvous for many celebrities in the world of sports and motion pictures. Olson enjoyed their company. On this visit he and Leonard encountered a noisy crowd centering around Sinclair Lewis, then at the height of his fame. Leonard's weak protests failed to dissuade Olson from introducing himself and joining the party. Eventually it moved to Sinclair Lewis' cabin, where Olson exchanged yarns with the novelist for some hours. Lewis was working on *Elmer Gantry* at the time, and the convivial evening ended with the singing of hymns.

When breakfast was over the next morning, Olson remarked that the opening sessions at conventions were always dull and proposed a further detour to another resort he liked, promising his companion the best chicken dinner in Minnesota. By this time Leonard's resistance had been worn down, and he agreed to go provided Olson would drive him past some lake property he had purchased sight unseen ten years earlier. Olson enthusiastically accepted the bargain and they spent Wednesday in the resort country.

Once again, at Leonard's insistence, plans were made to leave for Duluth early Thursday morning, but Olson fell asleep while reading the paper after breakfast and napped for more than two

hours. For the third successive day he coaxed Leonard into stay-
ing at a lake resort, slowly driving the latter to the realization
that he had never intended to reach Duluth. The comedy reached
a fitting conclusion on Friday, when Olson promised to deliver
Leonard at Duluth in time for the final banquet but turned back
toward the Twin Cities after a summer thunderstorm had made
the roads dangerous.

As usual Olson made a conquest. Although Leonard as an
officer of the Bar Association was seriously concerned about the
failure to reach Duluth, the companionship and infectious good
humor of his tempter blotted out all feeling of resentment.

So much emphasis has been laid on youthful poverty as the
motivation for Olson's later championship of the common man
that the economic circumstances of his family deserve close examination. Both parents were immigrants from Scandinavia who
met in Minneapolis, married, and moved to the heavily Jewish
north side, where Paul Olson found employment as a checker
for the Northern Pacific railroad. Like so many other workers,
he lost his job during the panic of 1893, but regained it as soon
as business activity revived. Steady employment thereafter enabled him to provide an adequate living for his family. The
Olson home was plain and simply furnished, but it compared
favorably with other dwellings in the district. In fact, Abe Harris,
one of Olson's boyhood friends, remembered that the gang enjoyed visiting there because occasionally Mrs. Olson passed out
some kind of treat. The legend of grinding poverty simply does
not square with the facts.

Floyd Bjerstjerne Olson, an only child, was born into this
household November 13, 1891. From his father he inherited deep
blue eyes and thick, wavy hair; from Ida Maria Nelson Olson,
his mother, who possessed a strong homely face, he received high
cheek bones and firm, sharp features.

The Olson home was never a particularly happy one for young
Floyd. His father came from poor Norwegian peasant stock and
lacked the ambition to rise in the economic scale. He was a

pleasant, easygoing man with a cheery smile and a liking for beer. His constitutional sluggishness dismayed and irritated his wife, who had received an eighth-grade education in her native Sweden and aspired to better things. She wanted young Floyd to be a white-collar worker and was always annoyed when he accepted a job at manual labor.

Her spartan sense of duty and determination to push Floyd into a genteel profession made Mrs. Olson extremely critical of her husband's habits. She nagged at Paul for laziness, complained about his drinking, and refused to let him smoke except in the basement. Inevitably, Floyd sympathized with his affectionate, tolerant, and henpecked father. They became partners in crime, stealing pipefuls of tobacco behind the furnace and furtively drinking a stein of beer together. While still a teen-ager, Floyd acquired a taste for the more conventional vices.

The austere and quarrelsome atmosphere of the Olson home drove him elsewhere in search of warmth and fellowship. He found much of the congenial family life he was seeking in the Jewish households of his neighborhood. As a frequent visitor, he learned their language and customs, made friends with their children, and developed genuine concern about their problems. He loved to take part in their religious services, lighting the altar candles on Holy Night when the Jews were forbidden by Mosaic law to do any work. They reciprocated with an affection, trust, and loyalty that grew almost fanatical when the mature Floyd went into politics. Several of them eventually occupied strategic positions in the Farmer Labor party. Abe Harris, for example, became editor of the party newspaper, publicity director for the state Conservation Department, and political adviser extraordinary.

Another way young Floyd found excitement and comradeship was to work at odd jobs. After a couple of years selling newspapers, he got a job peddling candy at the old Metropolitan Opera House in Minneapolis. Late at night when most thirteen-year-olds were in bed, he watched wide-eyed while the great actors and actresses of the period performed on the stage.

One of his most delighted moments came when DeWolf Hopper gave his famous rendition of "Casey at the Bat." Olson promptly learned the poem from beginning to end, and offered it in a high school oratorical contest. Unfortunately the judges disqualified the poem as being too "low brow," but this minor setback did not chill Floyd's growing enthusiasm for oratory. He became a member of the debate team at North High School, taking the activity so seriously that he neglected sports and social functions. His performance as a debater gave little indication of the brilliant public-speaking career that lay ahead, but it launched a hobby and gave Olson the confidence to tackle selling jobs. One summer he sold religious books for the Vir Publishing Company in southern Minnesota, often occupying the pulpit and preaching Sunday sermons to convert waverers. Another time he peddled farm machinery in Canada with the same convincing earnestness.

After graduation from high school, Olson put in a restless and unproductive year at the University of Minnesota — a year punctuated by quarrels with the authorities for refusing to participate in compulsory military drill and quarrels with seniors for wearing a derby in defiance of campus traditions. Bored nonetheless, and eager for adventure, he then embarked upon a *Wanderjahr,* working as a salesman, fisherman, miner, and longshoreman. His erratic movements carried him from the grain fields of Alberta to the gold fields of Alaska and finally to the docks of Seattle. Here for the first time, Olson encountered life in elemental rawness. He saw gambling, carousing, fighting, and killing on a scale far greater than in the Minneapolis slums. He rubbed shoulders with people who lived in conditions of squalor and misery beyond the range of his previous experience.

It is probable that Olson first felt the stirrings of crusading zeal for the common man during this year of hardship. Without analyzing the forces that produced wealth and poverty side by side, he groped his way to the pragmatic conclusion that no society organized on such a basis had a right to exist. This outlook was reinforced when he joined the International Workers

of the World in Seattle and absorbed something of their smoldering indignation against capitalistic exploitation of the workers.[5]
Even then Olson seems to have been more a rebel than a radical. The "wobblies" won his admiration because of their defiance
of the existing order. There was something breathtaking in the
resolute challenge issued by these lowly dock workers, and it
caught the imagination of the nineteen-year-old youth. Their
truculence and militant protest against exploitation excited him
far more than their blueprints for a new social order. Behind the
professional radicalism of young Olson lurked the accumulated
resentment of a little boy who had always rebelled against the
domination of a strong-willed, arbitrary mother. Olson never
overcame his dislike for order and authority. The college student
who refused to participate in military drill and bought an over-
size derby to defy the seniors grew into the adult who objected
to carrying money in a particular pocket and who strewed
clothes, newspapers, and toilet articles around hotel rooms.

Olson's political beliefs were always inwardly confused by his
ingrained habit of superimposing radicalism upon rebellion. It
would not be fair, however, to say that he espoused the underprivileged simply because of a grudge against authority and
tradition. His concern about human suffering was a very real
thing. He could never turn a panhandler down, and on one occasion when his chauffeur, Maurice Rose, remonstrated against a
handout to a particularly unworthy recipient, Olson replied that
he had once been refused money in Seattle when he was very
hungry. On another occasion, he stunned a dinner companion at
an elaborate party by gazing reflectively into his champagne
glass and observing that a family of five could be fed for a week
on the money he had just swallowed.

Olson's humanitarian instincts found a vague doctrinal basis
in the philosophy of Jefferson and Lincoln, for whom he had
developed a boyhood admiration. Nevertheless, he always bewildered his radical followers by his seeming uncertainty as to
where he was going. Opponents dismissed the matter easily by
labeling him a self-seeking opportunist. Others believed that he

moved slowly because of political necessity and would throw off the mask at the proper time. What his adult associates could never see was the youthful Olson who admired rebellion for its own sake and fought virtually all manifestations of the status quo because it represented authority.

In 1913 Olson returned permanently to Minneapolis. His mother had always wanted him to be a bookkeeper, but he chose the law — partly, no doubt, because it gave him an opportunity to exercise his growing powers of persuasion. Years later he jokingly told Billy Williams, receptionist at the State Capitol, that a straight right he had received in the stomach at a local boxing match had convinced him it was safer to take up law. This offhand explanation fails to carry conviction, but it was characteristic of Olson to drift into decisions rather than plan carefully for a distant goal.

At all events, Olson went to work as a clerk in the law office of George Nordlin and took his training at the Northwestern Law College, which was a night school. He rode a bicycle each day the entire distance from Minneapolis to Nordlin's law office in St. Paul.

Shortly after his graduation in 1915, he was admitted to the bar and sought a position in the law firm of Larrabee and Davies. This proved difficult to get not only because he was inexperienced but because the elder Larrabee was extremely temperamental and had to be approached at just the right time. Eventually Olson succeeded through the intervention of his lifelong friend William C. Larson, later a judge on the Minneapolis municipal bench, who had dabbled in the film business with the Larrabee children and managed to enlist their help.

Olson started work at the modest salary of ten dollars a week, but quickly earned a reputation as a capable trial lawyer. In his first case he was pitted against the formidable Walter H. Newton, later congressman from Minnesota and secretary to President Hoover. Olson was defending a man charged with first degree assault and managed to get him off with third degree assault — a

11

real victory for a young lawyer. Had he been willing to settle down, he would doubtless have built up a comfortable practice. But he was too restless for an orderly, secure mode of life. Before long he began to dabble in politics.

At the time Olson was trying to work his way into the firm of Larrabee and Davies, he married Miss Ada Krejci of New Prague. They had become acquainted sometime earlier at the Savoy, an old nickel theater in Minneapolis where Olson ushered and his future wife played the piano.[6]

From the standpoint of Olson's future career, the marriage could hardly be termed an ideal one. Ada Olson possessed only the mildest interest in politics. She looked upon public appearances as something of an ordeal and avoided them whenever she could. Her interests were those of a homemaker who sealed off politics at the front door. Although Olson was doubtless grateful that she made no effort to influence him in the appointment of public officials or the formulation of policy, he must have missed the counsel and encouragement which a more politically conscious wife would have provided.

Olson's first exploratory gestures toward a political career are curiously shrouded. Years later he told friends that he had decided to embark on a political career by way of protest against what he considered to be the unfair conviction of James N. Peterson, a fellow member of the firm of Larrabee and Davies, who was tried and sentenced for a book he had written criticizing the United States' participation in World War I.[7]

It may be true that this incident affected Olson in a deep, personal way, indicating to him that nothing short of political action could conquer the forces of intolerance and ignorance standing behind the conviction of Peterson. But we must reject the notion that he was suddenly overwhelmed by a great vision like Saul on the road to Damascus; Olson had been too persistently a rebel against the status quo for any story of so rapid a conversion to be plausible. The most the conviction of Peterson could have done was convince him that the time for action had arrived.

Probably his unselfish wish to serve got mixed up with a desire to play the fascinating game of politics. For a reformer Olson pursued a somewhat baffling course. A logical step would have been to join the Working People's Nonpartisan League, which was then organizing a militant campaign against the injustices most objectionable to him. Instead Olson retained his membership in the Democratic party, a somewhat dubious vehicle of reform. It fused with the Republicans to beat the Nonpartisan League and drove off Scandinavian radicals by vesting control in the Catholic politicians of St. Paul, St. Cloud, and Mankato.

Probably caution tempered Olson's convictions. Unfriendly propaganda represented the Nonpartisan League as a roosting place of dangerous radicals, and during the conflict with Germany it had been widely denounced in Minnesota as an unpatriotic organization. The fact that Olson had not been able to enter the armed forces suggested an elementary prudence. Also, it is entirely possible that he disapproved of the antiwar position attributed to the League. Despite his chronic opposition to compulsory military training, Olson was neither a professional socialist nor a professional pacifist. He had joined the National Guard before the war and had contracted in training the hernia that disqualified him for army service. His later attacks on the Wilsonian crusade seem to have grown out of the revelations of the Nye munitions investigation rather than from youthful conviction.

Such considerations help to explain Olson's early aloofness from reform politics. Momentarily he escaped the label of dangerous radical, but he laid himself open to the charge of being a carpetbagger in 1924 when he snatched the Farmer Labor gubernatorial nomination out of the hands of old Leaguers who had suffered persecution during the war.

His first successful political maneuver gives substance to later charges that Olson lacked partisan conviction. Although he had sought the Democratic nomination for congress in 1918 and 1920, he remained on good enough terms with the regular Republicans of Hennepin County to receive an appointment as assistant county attorney in May 1919. Eighteen months later the Republican board of county commissioners appointed him to fill the unexpired term of County Attorney William M. (Bud) Nash, who was ousted for misconduct.

The official explanation of this extraordinary selection hinted that Olson had slipped through as a compromise candidate because the leading aspirants were deadlocked. However, this did not account for the decision to co-opt a rank outsider into the Hennepin County clique of Republican jobholders. Olson's subsequent conduct gave little ground for thinking he was under improper obligations to the commissioners, leaving only the conclusion that his appointment demonstrated an uncanny ability to sell himself. Had the Republican leaders been willing to open the way for further political preferment, it is entirely possible that Olson would never have enlisted in the reform movement. Particularly in these early days, his political convictions seemed to have a chameleonlike quality difficult to square with his later professions of left-wing orthodoxy.

After the initial boost from the county commissioners, Olson quickly built up a political following that enabled him to win re-election twice as Hennepin County attorney. The post tested his shrewdness and resourcefulness, because Minneapolis was one of the chronically corrupt cities in the United States. Rackets of various sorts flourished, and cheap, ephemeral scandal sheets like the *Saturday Press* maintained a precarious existence by alternately blackmailing petty crooks and condemning county officials for laxity. The air was so full of charges and countercharges that Olson did not escape criticism for slackness in the prosecution of lawbreakers. The *Saturday Press* accused him of conniving at corrupt conditions,[8] and one Harold Birkeland repeatedly filed petitions for his removal from office on the ground that he had deliberately quashed an investigation into the mysterious death of Birkeland's father.[9]

These charges of laxity did not affect Olson's standing with members of the legal profession in Minneapolis. He had a reputation for preparing his cases with great care, and the vast majority of criminal lawyers endorsed him for re-election as county attorney in 1926.

He also won general applause for his effective prosecution of grafting Minneapolis businessmen. He started an investigation in 1928 on the basis of vague rumors that aldermen were granting licenses and purchasing municipal equipment in an irregular manner. For nearly a year he painstakingly accumulated evidence. Many witnesses were examined before the grand jury, and Olson persuaded a number of these to waive their constitutional immunity, incriminating themselves and others. He secured such overwhelming proof of corruption that in January 1929 the grand jury voted indictments of three aldermen and nine prominent businessmen.

As county attorney Olson saw much evidence to strengthen his conviction that crime grew out of an unfortunate social environment. Often his irritation against the existing order showed through the web of legal argument. Abe Harris recalled an occasion when Olson was expected to prosecute a young bank teller for embezzlement. In his preliminary investigation he discovered that the hapless youth had misappropriated funds because his salary of ninety dollars a month did not permit him to maintain the social position of a white-collar worker. So instead of seeking a conviction, Olson asked the judge for probation, insisting that "the bank was far more guilty of a criminal offense in this case than the youth who is facing you." [10] Even though such pleas often lacked a firm legal basis, Olson seldom hesitated to request leniency for society's misguided children. He was particularly sympathetic toward the mistakes of youth and tried to avoid the role of hard-boiled prosecutor where they were involved.

Native canniness enabled Olson to follow a serpentine path through the temptations of Hennepin County politics without being corrupted. He frequently showed leniency to the petty gamblers because he sympathized with their struggles to make a living. If they ran honest games and played square with him, Olson was inclined to wink at their minor infractions of the law. However, he spared no effort to expose the big racketeers and public officials who robbed the common people. To his admirers he seemed like a kind of modern Robin Hood, dispensing rough and ready justice that conformed with the spirit if not the letter of the law. He refused to break lances over lost causes, but in a cautious and pragmatic way sought to improve the tone of municipal government.

Ten years of public service as county attorney gave Olson an indispensable training in practical politics. He saw at close range the influence of business on government, gaining insight into the mentality and the methods of realistic leaders. He took great pains to find out where the venal interests were most vulnerable and discovered how to concentrate irresistible pressure on them. He also mastered the techniques of accommodation and compromise. These lessons were invaluable when, with unabashed self-confidence, he set out to capture the leadership of the Minnesota reform movement.

# Chapter II THE FARMER LABOR MOVEMENT

THE Farmer Labor party, which became the vehicle of Olson's political ambitions, was the apostolic successor to the Grangers, Greenbackers, and Populists. The reform movement of Minnesota underwent frequent rebirths, attesting to the prolonged distress that accompanied the transition from a simple frontier community to a complex, interdependent economy.

Generally speaking, the intensity of political agitation varied almost directly with the condition of agriculture. From 1873 until nearly the end of the century farm prices were depressed and farmers were on the warpath. Populism, which represented the protest of the Minnesota wheat farmer, achieved great strength in the state and did not subside until wheat prices began an almost steady twenty-year climb following the memorable McKinley-Bryan election of 1896.

Unfortunately, neither the increased cash return for crops nor the upward trend in land values gave the farmer more than an illusion of relief. Profitable years were exceptional, and usually his efforts barely sufficed to stave off debt. The farmer blamed his woes on the railroads, the banks, and the terminal grain elevators. They did exact a disproportionate tribute for their services, but a more basic cause of the wheat farmer's distress lay in his insistence on remaining exclusively a wheat farmer after economic changes made diversification imperative.[1]

The continuous cropping of virgin prairie soil, unrelieved by rotation or fertilization, had gradually reduced the yield and

17

stimulated weed growth, increasing the overhead costs of labor thirty-six percent between 1900 and 1910.[2] This development, coupled with the increase of land values, doomed straight wheat farming because profits depended on frontier conditions of minimal labor costs, simple methods of cultivation, and cheap land. The farmer was slow to recognize these trends and slower still to adjust to them. Innate conservatism plus a strong dislike of the increased work in dairy farming or crop rotation led him to resist diversification.

The oldest wheat lands in southeastern Minnesota succumbed first, and by 1900 the worst of the transition to livestock and dairy products was over in that area. Southwestern Minnesota diversified shortly thereafter, turning from wheat to corn and hog production.[3] The discomfort accompanying this agricultural revolution found expression in the insurgency of 1912, when Minnesota cast her presidential vote for Theodore Roosevelt, the Bull Moose candidate.

Climate and geography prevented the pattern of corn-hog and dairy culture from being established in the north of the state. The short growing season in the Red River Valley made profitable diversification difficult,[4] and as a consequence the farmer there made a final stand against the economic compulsions which had forced adjustments farther south. Convinced that the Twin City banks and terminal grain elevators, rather than the crumbling frontier economy, were principally responsible for his distress, the Red River wheat farmer enlisted in the Nonpartisan League, a new protest movement containing strong elements of agrarian socialism.

First organized in North Dakota, the League quickly won supporters on the Minnesota side of the Red River. Its indictment of prevalent business practices echoed the charges of Grangers and Populists that the marketing system was designed to milk farmers of their just earnings. Middlemen and bankers came under particularly heavy fire — the former because of exorbitant tolls in the storing and grading of grain, the latter because of conservative lending policies and high rates of interest. The

League also condemned the existing system of taxation, which weighed heavily upon tangibles and land but overlooked corporate profits as a source of revenue.

Its program called for legislation to correct these abuses and to eliminate the supposed manipulations that resulted in wheat prices below the cost of production. Specifically the 1916 League platform in North Dakota proposed: (1) state ownership of terminal elevators, flour mills, packing houses, and cold storage plants; (2) state inspection of grain grading and dockage; (3) exemption of farm improvements from taxation; (4) state hail insurance on the acreage basis; (5) rural credit banks operated at cost.[5] This was an amazingly frank public ownership program, which cleverly blended native radicalism and European collectivism. Its extraordinary appeal lay in the ability of the drafters to camouflage socialistic principles while playing up the orthodox features of agrarian reform.

The organizational structure of the Nonpartisan League did not conceal its socialistic features so well. Primarily the brain child of A. C. Townley, former socialist propagandist and bankrupt flax farmer,[6] the League was wide open to charges of authoritarianism. Members were obligated to participate actively and to pay dues of sixteen dollars for two years, the latter provision tending to ensure compliance with the former. A staff of trained organizers circulated through the rural areas expounding the League gospel and signing up members, who pledged adherence and support to the League platform. Principles and policies were dictated by Townley, who kept an autocratic grip on the organization, while sustained favorable publicity was secured through a sixteen-page weekly newspaper, the *Nonpartisan Leader*. This served as the official organ of the League, waging a spirited propaganda warfare with the opposition press. All these techniques were socialist contributions to political organization, and they worked so well that within a year of its inception in 1915, the League counted nearly forty thousand dues-paying members in North Dakota.[7]

Such spectacular success encouraged Townley to reach out for control of state politics in 1916 by entering League candidates in the Republican primary. The advantages were threefold: domination of the Republican party would ensure control of the state; farmers could vote for the League candidates without deserting their traditional party label; and radical proposals could be presented under a conservative label.

The Townley strategy, coupled with effective organizational work, paid impressive dividends at the polls. League candidates captured the Republican nominations for state offices, gained control of the state central committee, and wrote the platform. They won the general election in 1916 and again in 1918, getting rid in the latter year of a hostile state senate which had held up the enactment of League legislation.

This success in North Dakota led Townley to extend League operations to neighboring states. A national headquarters was opened at St. Paul, Minnesota, early in 1917, and crack organizers were sent out to solicit new members.

Economic conditions in the Red River Valley favored the League. Despite the rapid rise of agricultural prices during the war in Europe, Minnesota wheat farmers slowly lost ground. Crop yields fell off in 1916 and remained below normal during the next three years.[8] Those who attempted to recoup their losses by expanding production into marginal areas saw their profits evaporate in high overhead costs and interest charges. Mortgage indebtedness doubled ominously in Minnesota between 1916 and 1920,[9] and wheat farmers of the Red River Valley accounted for a higher percentage than any other area of the state. Frustration, anger, and self-pity drove large numbers of them to join the Nonpartisan League.

Unfortunately rebellious farmers could not assure League victory in Minnesota as in North Dakota, where the population was ninety percent agricultural and campaigns could be based on a single theme. Some formula broad enough to win support among the urban masses of the Twin Cities and the class-conscious laborers on the Iron Range seemed essential. To find such a formula was a difficult task at best, but the League worked under an additional handicap because opponents injected the war issue into the campaign.

There was no obvious connection between the reform of agricultural conditions in Minnesota and the war being fought against the Central Powers, but there was bound to be suspicion of people who were urging comprehensive economic changes at a time when public opinion considered the war in Europe to be the first concern of patriotic citizens. Reform agitation was poor taste if nothing else. Also, despite Townley's effort to evade the war issue and to emphasize concrete measures of aid for agriculture,[10] a highly vocal minority in the League insisted on charging that the conflict was nothing more than a selfish struggle of international capitalists for control of world markets. Such statements discredited conscientious Leaguers and encouraged a vague popular impression that they were disloyal to their country.

The situation invited a smear campaign. Behind a barrage of disloyalty charges, the reform program of the Nonpartisan League could be discredited without any debate on basic social and economic questions. Minnesota Republicans, who had a well-deserved reputation for capitalizing on public fear of social and economic change, began a systematic attack along these lines during the fall of 1917.

Spearheading the campaign was the Public Safety Commission, a wartime organization designed to combat disloyal and seditious activities. Top-heavy with zealous Republicans, it encouraged summary action by local authorities to crush the League. Consequently, when Townley's organizers began appearing in the towns of western Minnesota, patriotic officials denied them permits to hold local meetings and occasionally threw them in jail, on the ground that pro-German and disloyal elements had to be eliminated. Townley protested against this treatment, denied that the war was really an issue, and confined criticism to the government's refusal to conscript wealth as well as human beings.

The interaction of Republican tactics and war hysteria seemed likely to discredit the new reform movement before it could be given an adequate hearing. And the League helped to seal its own fate by a series of political blunders. Foremost of these was the selection of Charles A. Lindbergh to make the gubernatorial race. A sincere western progressive with a decade of experience in congress, Lindbergh nevertheless stood for all the things that made the League suspect. His antagonism toward the great corporations had been a political asset during the Progressive era, but the general retreat of rationality during the war made people antagonistic toward even mild proposals to tinker with the economy. Even worse, Lindbergh had conspicuously associated himself with the noninterventionist group in congress and had supported various proposals to keep the United States out of the war. His record seemed to confirm Republican assertions about the real attitude of the League.

As a result of the hysteria campaign, coupled with the League's own errors, Governor Burnquist won renomination over Lindbergh in the 1918 Republican primary by more than 50,000 votes, the latter developing real strength only in the Red River Valley and the predominantly German counties of the south.

Notwithstanding their overwhelming victory, the Republicans drove the protest vote from the party. By pinning the charge of disloyalty on patriotic farmers who favored the Townley program for agriculture, they created a hard core of bitterness that persisted long after the demise of the League. Thereafter western Minnesota could be counted upon to enlist in reform movements.

An even more important by-product of the 1918 primary was the forging of an unusual alliance between farmers and workers. The defeat of Lindbergh convinced Townley that the League had to broaden its political base by courting organized labor. This decision came just when the wartime trend toward unionization was strengthening the hands of labor leaders and encouraging them to intervene in elections. The urban workers had nothing to lose by backing farm legislation, and Townley agreed to splice labor proposals for an eight-hour day and old age pensions onto the League program.[11] Delegates representing the Minnesota State Federation of Labor and the Nonpartisan League ratified this arrangement at a conference in St. Paul, August 24, 1918, and nominated David Evans of Tracy for governor and Tom Davis of Marshall for attorney general. To satisfy legal requirements both candidates filed as members of a Farmer Labor party. The designation was adopted solely to get on the ballot; the party had no independent existence. Both sides considered the coalition a marriage of convenience. No effort was made on the platform or elsewhere to contend that farmers and laborers had similar interests. In fact, both Townley and E. G. Hall, president of the State Federation of Labor, assured critics of the cooperation policy that there would be no merger, that the groups were simply pooling their resources to achieve specific legislative objectives. This initial arrangement deserves emphasis in view of the glowing statements subsequently made about the identity of interests beween farmer and laborer.

The eleventh-hour union of forces did not produce victory in November 1918, but it laid a firm foundation for cooperation two years later. In fact, delegates to the 1919 annual convention of the Minnesota State Federation of Labor organized a Working People's Nonpartisan League along lines similar to the farm organization. The high point of the coalition was reached in the 1920 Republican primary, when the farmer and worker organizations came close to victory despite the fact that the regulars accused them of advocating atheism, communism, and free love. The election was also noteworthy in that it launched Dr. Henrik Shipstead, the Glenwood dentist, on his long political career.

After 1920 the Nonpartisan League fell on evil days. Because of the break in agricultural prices, farmers could no longer pay the dues necessary to keep the League operating. Misfortune also tended to accentuate the conflicts over policy between the two wings of the reform movement. Townley preferred to use the declining strength of the Farmers' Nonpartisan League to endorse candidates of the old parties that stood behind the League program for agriculture, whereas the Working People's Nonpartisan League wanted to convert the Farmer Labor organization from a legal shell into a genuine third party.[12] With some justification, Townley argued that genuine farm relief would have to come through national action and that isolated third-party representatives would be without influence in congress. His more optimistic colleagues overruled him in the 1922 elections and ran a full ticket under the Farmer Labor label. The candidates for state offices fared badly, but Shipstead was elected to the national senate and Knud Wefald and O. J. Kvale to the lower house.

The modest success of the third-party ticket hastened the resignation of Townley. Accustomed to absolute obedience from subordinates, he could not brook the criticism and opposition which grew more vocal as League power waned. Nor could he acquiesce in the attempt by the Working People's Nonpartisan League to swallow up his farmers' organization. Preoccupied from the outset with the problems of agriculture, he considered organized labor nothing more than a tail to the farmers' kite. A master campaigner in rural areas, Townley never got onto the mental plane of the workingman and never made any real effort to understand his aspirations. From Townley's standpoint, a reversal of roles in the partnership was unthinkable. So when the third-party advocates followed up their 1922 election victory with a drive to merge the two leagues, Townley severed his connection with the reform movement. Thereafter the disintegration of the Farmers' Nonpartisan League proceeded rapidly and it was officially disbanded in March 1924 to make way for the new Farmer Labor Federation.

Despite its limited success at the polls and rapid postwar disintegration, the Nonpartisan League left a residue of solid achievement behind. The six-year agitation in Minnesota gave the farmer a basic education in politics. League newspapers and orators had tirelessly instructed him in the fundamentals of economic policy and in the value of organization to obtain a redress of grievances. These lessons provided the foundations for a stronger reform movement in the future.

The breakup of the Farmers' Nonpartisan League in 1923

shifted the center of gravity in the reform movement to the Working People's Nonpartisan League, which had always collected modest dues and had held its following virtually intact because of faith in state legislation to improve working conditions. However, the trade union leaders did not immediately fill the vacuum left by the resignation of Townley. This was partly because his autocratic disposition had discouraged energetic and imaginative colleagues, but also because the labor movement had produced no leader of the required stature.

It was during this uneasy interregnum that Floyd Olson made a bid for power in the reform movement.

No dark horse candidate emerged from political obscurity more rapidly than the young county attorney. A virtual stranger to reformers in 1922, operating in a sphere removed from the more conspicuous manifestations of party politics, he captured first place on the Farmer Labor ticket two years later.

His availability as a candidate was dramatized by his outspoken defense of Minneapolis workers in a case involving the dynamiting of a contractor's house. The principals were the Citizens' Alliance, an association of businessmen dedicated to the maintenance of the open shop, and Dan Mahady, a former union official. The Alliance wanted to frame Mahady because he had refused to give information about the dynamiting to a stool pigeon. Since Mahady was somewhat impressionable, members of the Alliance believed he could be incited to blow up a safe, and they turned the job of involving him over to a local detective named Gleason.

With singular ineptness Gleason selected for contact man Fred Myers, generally regarded as a dope fiend, and after putting him in touch with Mahady became so fearful of the consequences that he had the two men shadowed and arrested for stealing dynamite. Then, apprehensive lest the pair talk, Gleason tried to secure their release the next day without consulting the authorities. But the matter came to the attention of Olson, who decided to examine Myers and Mahady. Under his adroit questioning the whole story came out, and the trail led right to the door of O. P. Briggs, president of the Citizens' Alliance.

Since no crime had been committed, expediency dictated a suppression of the facts. But Olson was deeply sympathetic with labor's faltering efforts at organization and anxious to expose the tactics of the Citizens' Alliance, which outraged his sense of fair play. Heedless of possible retaliation, he condemned its activity in the strongest possible language: "The irresponsible dope fiend Myers and the drunkard Mahady are certainly not guilty of any moral wrong, and it would be a travesty on justice to hold them guilty of any technical or legal wrong unless the names of Gleason and Briggs are also included in the charges against them. To my mind it was a dangerous, dastardly act to incite these two irresponsible men to gain possession of explosives because there was nothing, nor no one to restrain either or both of them from committing a serious crime."

After this blistering indictment, Olson went on to condemn employers' use of stool pigeons in dealing with labor: "It is not difficult to see why the breach is continually widening between these two classes. It is surprising that intelligent business men will allow themselves to be preyed upon by private detective agencies, who, because of fees paid them, render false reports with the view of terrorizing the employer and increasing his animosity to organized labor."

Olson concluded by paying his respects to the Citizens' Alliance: "If private organizations — no matter what kind they may be — which undertake to enforce the law without cooperating with the duly constituted authorities, and in disregard of the police, are not wiped out, this country will soon reach a condition where faction and class violence will be the rule and not the exception." [13]

The forceful denunciation of the Citizens' Alliance had far greater repercussions than Olson could have anticipated. Followed by his grand jury investigation of the rapid rise in coal prices, which caused the Interstate Commerce Commission to rescind a freight rate increase on coal shipments, it made him something of a hero in Twin City labor circles. During the last month of 1923 trade union leaders like Robley D. Cramer, editor of the *Minneapolis Labor Review*, and I. G. Scott, Farmer Labor alderman in Minneapolis, began urging his nomination for governor.

Olson did all he could to help the boom along. He accepted speaking engagements everywhere and appeared at all meetings where he could widen his contacts. Although few could deny his political appeal, a number of prominent Minnesota radicals who had served labor unselfishly for years considered Olson a presumptuous youngster and resented his efforts to assume leadership of the party. When he sounded out George B. Leonard, prominent Minneapolis labor lawyer and long-time socialist, on the nomination, Leonard bluntly told him he should serve a period of apprenticeship in the ranks before seeking such high preferment from the Farmer Labor party.[14] Others questioned his motives and good faith. They saw a kind of crude opportunism in his espousal of reform policies just when election prospects looked so favorable; old Leaguers suspected that he was joining the Farmer Labor party because the Republican bosses had blocked the more attractive avenues to advancement.

The greatest single handicap to the Olson candidacy lay in the fact that he was virtually unknown to the farmer wing of the reform movement. His nomination depended upon securing the endorsement of the Farmer Labor convention, where labor delegates would outnumber those from the rural areas. So the Olson managers laid careful plans to dominate the St. Cloud convention.

Their calculations were completely upset by a compromise designed to unify the reform movement. All the efforts of the Working People's Nonpartisan League to swallow up the old Townley organization in 1923 had proved abortive because farm leaders objected to joining a homogeneous third party which they could not dominate. During the winter, labor leaders managed to round up enough pro-fusion candidates in rural areas to control the St. Cloud convention, but they were afraid to be too dictatorial in their tactics lest they produce a bolt and ruin excellent election prospects. So they made a deal: the Farmers' Nonpartisan League would disband and enter the new Farmer Labor Federation, and in return the convention would endorse no candidates, permitting farmer aspirants for political office to contest nominations in the open primary in June.

This agreement not to endorse candidates practically destroyed Olson's chances of nomination. The *Minneapolis Journal* predicted that the convention's action would end his candidacy, and apparently Olson took the same view because he was silent and inactive for more than a month.[15] During this period seven candidates filed for governor on the Farmer Labor ticket, but the county attorney gave no hint that he would make the race.

Then on April 24 the Hennepin County Farmer Labor central committee endorsed Olson for governor, and four days later Charles A. Lindbergh, who was dying of a brain tumor, announced that he would withdraw from the race and throw his support to Olson. This dramatic development improved the county attorney's chances immensely in rural Minnesota, especially in the Red River Valley and the German counties, where Lindbergh was very popular. The same day that Lindbergh withdrew, Olson, buoyant and optimistic once again, announced his candidacy with the fighting statement: "I am going out to win the nomination." [16]

He had a long, uphill fight ahead of him. The decision of the St. Cloud convention to refrain from endorsements had given Tom Davis of Marshall the advantage in the gubernatorial race.[17] Davis possessed many assets as a candidate. He was one of the original Nonpartisan Leaguers and had run for attorney general on the first Farmer Labor ticket in 1918. Unlike Olson, who had been on a farm only once or twice in his life, Davis came from western Minnesota and knew rural problems at first hand. For a lawyer he had gained unusual popularity among farmers because of his spectacular success in prosecuting their claims against the railroads for fires started by locomotive sparks. His political technique was antiquated but effective. He cultivated the appearance of an old-fashioned statesman, wearing shaggy hair, a broad-brimmed hat, and a frock coat, and his florid oratorical style entertained even if it did not convince.

His wide support among farmers was supplemented by strong backing from old League leaders who resented subordination to the new federation and believed that Davis would restore their power. Trusted Townley lieutenants like George Griffith, O. M. Thomason, and A. B. Gilbert aggressively pushed the Davis campaign. Only Henry Teigan, former secretary general of the Nonpartisan League, broke with his old friends to support Olson.[18]

Although seven men had entered the gubernatorial contest, it quickly narrowed down to a race between Olson and Davis — and political developments favored the county attorney. The Lindbergh managers proved to be more active in his behalf than had been expected. Dr. L. A. Fritsche of New Ulm unexpectedly filed for governor, cutting into the "wet" support of Davis. And Olson won new supporters in hitherto hostile farm counties by mixing effective oratory with well-planned personal contacts. In fact, he made so much progress after two weeks of campaigning that Charles B. Cheney, political editor of the *Minneapolis Journal*, retreated from his prediction of a Davis victory and forecast a close election.[19]

The Davis forces tried to discredit Olson by casting doubt on the authenticity of his radicalism. Pointedly they asked him what he was doing in 1918 and 1920 when members of the League had suffered imprisonment as well as social ostracism for advocating the reforms currently so popular. They exposed his affiliation with the Democratic party, hinted at unsavory flirtations with Hennepin County Republican bosses, and denounced him as an opportunist who sought to reap credit for work done by others.

These telling thrusts drove Olson to extravagant affirmations of radicalism. He called attention to his membership on the Committee of 48, a group organized in 1919 for the purpose of coaxing Robert M. La Follette to run on a third-party presidential ticket, and claimed authorship of several radical planks in its statement of principles.[20] He also made a blanket endorsement of the St. Cloud platform, although he carefully avoided specific statements about its sweeping public ownership proposals which would alienate the more conservative farmers. He sought to counterbalance statements of radical orthodoxy by emphasizing a moderate four-point personal platform for tax reduction, farm credit, unemployment relief, and investment of Minnesota money within the state. Olson carried out his straddle so effectively that the *Minneapolis Journal* in a pre-election roundup referred to him as "an excellent prosecuting attorney" while condemning Tom Davis as "a man of extreme views not at all adapted to the upbuilding of Minnesota." [21]

Nonetheless, the primary outcome was very much in doubt when the voters went to the polls. It was still in doubt four days later, although on the basis of unofficial returns Olson had topped Davis by 113 votes. The closeness of the election and rumors of foul play produced a tension between the candidates that boded ill for party unity. Davis brought the quarrel into the open by securing a court order for a recount in Hennepin County, the Olson stronghold. However, the recount was stopped by his own motion on July 11, when it had increased Olson's margin to 435.[22] The same day the two rivals smoked a peace pipe in the county attorney's office, and shortly thereafter Davis announced his support of the entire Farmer Labor ticket.

The nomination of Olson was a blow to the Townley lieutenants. George Griffith and A. C. Welch accepted subordinate positions in the new Farmer Labor Federation, but A. B. Gilbert and O. M. Thomason bolted to the Republicans. A few bitterenders tried to carry on in the western counties until 1926, but were buried under an avalanche of votes. Thereafter control remained in the urban wing of the party until its sudden collapse fourteen years later.

When Olson won the primary contest, he was optimistic about his chances for victory in the general election, but by midautumn the situation had changed materially. The reform movement as a whole, and Olson with it, lost support steadily between August and November — owing in large part to developments beyond the candidate's control.

For one thing the Republicans not only polled twice as many primary votes as the Farmer Laborites, but nominated their ablest leader, Theodore Christianson, to replace the unpopular Governor Preus at the head of the ticket. In personal charm and oratorical ability Christianson was no match for Olson, but his dignified bearing commanded respect and his sober manner inspired confidence if not enthusiasm. A Phi Beta Kappa key and a scholarly, reflective mind set him apart from the typical candidate for high office. As speaker of the state house of representatives he had built up a reputation for efficiency and hard work, and he had endeared himself to the farmers by persistent advocacy of economy and tax reduction.

Besides facing such a formidable opponent, Olson had to contend with the disruptionist tactics of communists whose efforts to infiltrate the Farmer Labor party partially discredited it. The communists saw a chance to enter the reform movement when Henry Teigan, William T. Mahoney, and other Leaguers called a regional conference of radicals for October 23, 1923, to consider a third-party presidential ticket for the coming election. Teigan noted the presence of a "few communistically inclined fellows" at this inconclusive session,[23] and when a second convention was called in March 1924 still more of them appeared. Some delegates questioned the right of the communists to participate, but after a stormy debate they were admitted and joined in the call for a national third-party convention to be held at St. Paul on June 17.

Although the Minnesota Farmer Labor Federation originally had no direct connection with the left-wingers who did the spade work for the St. Paul convention, the public assumed a close relationship because reform leaders like Henry Teigan and William T. Mahoney played an active role in both organizations. This impression was strengthened at St. Cloud when the federation, through its legal instrument, the Farmer Labor party, endorsed the forthcoming St. Paul convention.

No maneuver could have played more directly into the hands of Minnesota Republicans. Just as the hysteria campaign had begun to lose effectiveness, the Farmer Laborites gave it a new lease on life by officially blessing the communist-infiltrated third-party organization. Nor did it help when the intended candidate, Robert M. La Follette, publicly repudiated the St. Paul convention two weeks in advance and urged his friends to stay away from it because of the communist participation.[24] The convention accomplished little because of La Follette's intransigent attitude, but the quarrels over communist infiltration received generous publicity in Republican newspapers.

Unfortunately Olson refused to take the communist issue seriously. He took no part in the St. Paul convention, but he permitted communists to support the Farmer Labor ticket without explicit protest. He did bestir himself sufficiently to write his erstwhile opponent, Tom Davis, an open letter stating that he was not a communist, but he did not follow it up with an emphatic repudiation of communist aid. The official party organ reflected his unconcern by observing that "anybody has a right legally and morally to vote any party ticket he wishes."[25]

If Olson expected to pick up votes by this ambiguous stand, he was mistaken. Although he doubtless retained the support of a small and highly vocal communist group, his losses among middle class voters more than counterbalanced it. The communist issue alone was not enough to tip the scales against him in 1924, but it was a constant nuisance during the campaign. In retrospect Olson recognized his error, because he never repeated it in subsequent elections.

The communist issue caused trouble on still another front: it destroyed the solidarity between the Minnesota reform party and the national third-party organization of Senator La Follette. Originally the Farmer Labor Federation had planned to link the fortunes of La Follette and the state ticket in a unified campaign. But after condemning the St. Paul convention, La Follette could not afford to run in Minnesota under the Farmer Labor banner. So he filed as an Independent Progressive and set up a separate campaign headquarters. This created considerable friction, especially over the collection of funds. The La Follette managers sent out solicitors without bothering to notify the state leaders, leaving the federation with the thankless task of extracting a second campaign contribution from indigent radicals. It issued such a truculent protest against these tactics that La Follette, unwilling to risk an open rupture with Minnesota left-wingers, agreed to a compromise whereby the national organization received two thirds, and the state organization one third, of the funds collected by either group.[26]

In midsummer the Olson candidacy received still another blow when the United States Steel Corporation, which controlled the mining companies on the Mesabi Range and the livelihood of several thousand Minnesota workmen, decided to support Christianson.

Normally the decision of Big Steel to support Republican candidates was not news. But on this occasion it had considered backing Olson because he favored a substantial public works program which would expand the market for steel, whereas Christianson, the economy advocate, opposed even highway construction. A representative of U.S. Steel actually sounded out Olson, but the negotiations broke down because the latter courageously refused to abandon his program of heavy corporation taxes.[27] His rejection of the tempting bid convinced U.S. Steel that Olson was just as menacing as any of his predecessors and it threw what might have been a decisive weight against him.

In spite of these multiple handicaps, Olson waged a clever and aggressive campaign that brought him within range of victory. A few days on the campaign circuit confirmed his fear that the St. Cloud platform with its far-reaching proposals for the nationalization of basic industries had alienated the average voter. If the lost ground was to be retrieved, he would have to disassociate himself from the St. Cloud platform without actually disavowing it. But he dared not run on a personal platform, and he did not have sufficient prestige and power to enforce a common strategy on the ticket. Before the campaign had lasted two weeks, he awoke to the realization that his fortunes were inextricably tied to those of the senatorial and presidential candidates, who frequently stressed the public ownership issue. The laws of political logistics made him a helpless tail to the La Follette kite.

The best Olson could do was to remind the voters constantly that since the St. Cloud platform explicitly called for the public ownership of railroads and utilities, the issue did not belong in the state campaign. Whenever opponents made efforts to smoke him out, he shrouded his position in Delphic phrases such as: "I believe in state ownership of some things. I don't believe in interfering with legitimate business." [28] His campaign leaflet of October 4 interpreted the St. Cloud platform very freely, representing the Farmer Labor party as standing for "conservation of water power sites, mineral deposits, timber, and other national resources through the power of taxation and eminent domain for the benefit of the people." [29]

Olson's efforts to abandon the advance outposts of radicalism indicated his acute sensitivity to public opinion — to the gradual ebb of reform sentiment. Just as the improvement of economic conditions in 1896 was disastrous to the prospects of William Jennings Bryan, so the price revival of 1924 ruined the prospects of Olson.

The upward trend, which started early in the year, continued without a serious setback until after the election. The gains of agricultural commodities were particularly impressive. Wheat jumped from 98 cents a bushel in April to $1.32 in November, and hogs from $6.20 to $9.10 a hundred pounds.[30] As farm prices went up, rural unrest subsided. Agrarian radicalism had always been a rebellion against low prices rather than against the capitalist system. And in 1924 prosperity was an invisible campaigner who won more votes for the Republican ticket than its best orators.

With sound political instinct, Christianson sought to capitalize on the steady rightward drift of public opinion. He charged Olson with spearheading a public ownership drive as the prelude to a socialist state. He also played up the charge that the communists had failed to run a gubernatorial candidate because they were satisfied with Olson. Indiscriminately Christianson branded prominent Farmer Laborites as outright communists or as fellow travelers susceptible to communist wishes.

Deprived of effective economic issues by the returning prosperity, Olson could do nothing but deny his radicalism and make the challenger's usual criticism of incumbents. He tried to claim convincingly that the real issues were Republican connivance in the sale of worthless securities, mismanagement of the Rural Credit Bureau, and failure to reduce taxes. Occasionally he hurled Populist thunderbolts or decried the use of state troops to break strikes, but most of the time he sounded like a politician rather than a crusader.

The reform press, which had bubbled with optimism in early August, grew noticeably gloomy as the campaign progressed. Even such a strong Olson organ as the *Minneapolis Labor Review* made an oblique reference to imminent defeat in an editorial scoring Farmer Labor overconfidence as "a silent working enemy that undermines success."[31]

The pessimism was justified. Olson lost the governorship to Christianson by 43,000 votes out of approximately 865,000 cast, but he ran 26,000 ahead of the presidential vote for La Follette, who made public ownership of railroads a leading issue.

Olson's post-election statement did not conform to the accepted pattern of political sportsmanship. Far from conceding that Christianson had won fairly, he charged the Republicans with spreading false rumors and spending vast amounts of money to defeat him: "Manufacturing plants, factories, and mines were shut down; and the workers were virtually told to return to work after the election only in case of a Republican victory. Farmers were threatened that their loans would be pressed: Business men were told that a financial panic would result from Republican defeat: Travelling men were given orders for merchandise, the delivery of which was conditioned upon a Republican victory." [32] This extraordinary indictment expressed more than mere frustration and chagrin; Olson felt the election had been stolen.

The documentation of such charges was beyond his resources. In the first place, if these tactics were systematically practiced, the Republicans would not have issued such instructions in written form or taken note of the matter in their newspapers. Even the silence of the labor press suggests fear of libel suits rather than a complete lack of evidence. R. S. Wiggin, Olson's campaign manager, felt certain that the steel company had put pressure on Iron Range workers to vote Republican.

The results in Minneapolis put the Olson charges on a firmer basis. Wards like the Tenth that habitually produced Farmer Labor pluralities of 3500 mustered only 1500 in 1924, supporting his contention that three hundred workers were employed to ring doorbells and spread lies about him. State Senator William F. Brooks, the Republican leader in Hennepin County, admitted as much in a friendly post-election encounter with Olson at the Minneapolis Athletic Club. [33] There was also some evidence that groups like the Citizens' Alliance spread wild charges about Farmer Labor intentions in order to encourage voting by normally apathetic citizens.

Whether the Republicans went beyond accepted campaign practices to defeat Olson is hard to determine. Even the magnitude of their whispering campaign cannot be accurately measured. Olson thought it decisive and his immediate supporters reached the same conclusion, but many observers on both sides blamed other factors. Henry Teigan thought it was the tie-up of the local party with the presidential candidacy of Senator La Follette that dragged the state ticket down to defeat, and Charles B. Cheney put the blame on the communist issue. [34]

Probably all these elements took their toll. But one development stood out above all others: the revival of prosperity and the conservative reaction that followed in its wake. Olson had been the prophet of rebellion, and for the moment rebellion had lost its appeal.

# Chapter III   VICTORY IN 1930

From the discouraging election of 1924 Floyd B. Olson extracted some valuable lessons. He learned that the average voter had a limited capacity for radicalism and could absorb even small doses of it only in time of depression. He also learned that political organization outweighed personal energy and spectacular oratory in deciding elections, and he decided to build a statewide personal organization. Shortly after the election he confided his intention to an old friend and predicted that the job would be completed in six years — a remarkably accurate forecast.[1]

But for the moment the most urgent task was the reorganization of the reform movement. The communist infiltration had so completely discredited the Farmer Labor Federation that its dissolution was essential to the survival of the movement.[2] Accordingly a harmony conference of Minnesota radicals gathered at St. Paul on March 20, 1925, to replace the federation with a brand new organization known as the Farmer Labor Association.

The constitution of the association prohibited communists from membership but reaffirmed the socialistic doctrines of Townley's Nonpartisan League. The declaration of principles stated that "every person is entitled to an opportunity to earn a living, and should be secure in the enjoyment of the fruits of his or her toil."[3] To implement these rights, the following steps were advocated: (1) a union of "all persons in agriculture and other useful industry" to promote the economic welfare of the wealth producers; (2) the abolition of private monopolistic privilege and its replacement by a system of public ownership to increase the total wealth of society and abolish unemployment.

The structure of the new association, likewise, reflected orthodox socialistic doctrines of political organization. The primary unit was the local Farmer Labor club, which consisted of active reformers in the village or township who were willing to pay annual dues of three dollars.° This provision was intended to protect the association from an influx of carpetbaggers and to vest authority in the most militant and politically conscious citizens. Once a local club was chartered it represented the reformers in the area regardless of its geographical relationship to regular ward and precinct divisions.

The constitution also permitted economic organizations such as local labor unions or farmers' cooperatives to affiliate with the association upon payment of a two percent per capita tax. Like the Farmer Labor clubs, they were entitled to participate in county conventions. These in turn endorsed candidates for local office, passed resolutions advising the parent body of rank-and-file sentiment, and selected delegates to the biennial convention of the Farmer Labor Association, which stood at the apex of the pyramid.†

As the supreme organ of reformers, the biennial convention was empowered to endorse candidates for state offices and for United States senator, draft the association platform, amend the constitution, and appoint the executive committee. The omnipotence of the convention meant that effective control of the reform movement rested with the dues-paying members of the association. Even though state law permitted all registered voters to enter the Farmer Labor primary as candidates or electors, the

° The dues were to be divided as follows: 50c to the local; 25c to the county; 75c to the state; and $1.50 to the official newspaper, the *Farmer Labor Advocate*. (*Advocate*, March 25, 1925.)

† From the outset there was considerable agitation to allow affiliated organizations of trade unions and farmers' cooperatives to send delegates directly to the meetings of the association. The constitution was modified in 1930 to permit this procedure. However, the delegates sent by affiliated organizations did not increase the voting strength of the county, which was apportioned as follows: one delegate at large and an additional delegate for each thousand votes cast for the Farmer Labor gubernatorial candidate in the preceding general election. (*Minneapolis Journal*, March 12, 1934; also Teigan Papers, Teigan to N. Bruden, January 25, 1932.)

party remained in fact a legal shell. Only on rare occasions did a candidate secure the nomination without endorsement by the association convention. This arrangement undercut the direct primary and re-established the undemocratic convention system which progressive legislation had sought to outlaw.

The leaders of the association justified their closely knit organization on several grounds. William Mahoney felt that the great educational campaign to unite wealth producers drew its strength primarily from an enthusiastic, disciplined, and class-conscious nucleus of reform leaders who could not function effectively if subjected periodically to the whim of the voters. So he defended the undemocratic features of the association as insurance against an ouster of genuine reformers by opportunists and spoilsmen.[4] Regardless of what faction won the Farmer Labor primary, the reform leaders were beyond the reach of disruptionists. This view reflected an exaggerated fear of raids, stimulated no doubt by Nonpartisan League success in raiding Republican primaries, and also by the Farmer Laborites'. unhappy experience with a wide-open primary in the 1924 campaign.

The role played by Olson in launching the new association is not clear. He must have approved of it, because he accepted a place on the executive committee and agreed to participate in organizational work during the summer of 1925,[5] but shortly thereafter he retired from the center of the stage and took no active part in the 1926 state election. The revival of prosperity doomed reform candidates to defeat, but a more probable reason for Olson's withdrawal was preoccupation with his own campaign to secure re-election as Hennepin County attorney. Prudence dictated the concealment of party affiliations in the contest for a nonpartisan office.

Olson's victory in the election contrasted so sharply with the demoralizing defeat of the Farmer Labor state ticket that he was being mentioned for governor in the next election before the official returns had been certified.[6] But when the 1928 convention of the Farmer Labor Association endorsed him for governor, he studied the question for three weeks and then decided to refuse the endorsement.[7]

The reasons he gave were personal. His investigation of grafting aldermen was a valid excuse for abstention from state politics, since premature disclosure of his activities might have permitted culprits to escape and effective prosecution could not be conducted amid the distractions of a political campaign. But probably his real reason for refusing to run was a conviction that the gubernatorial nomination was worthless. Not only did the association intend to concentrate its resources on the re-election of Senator Shipstead, but the enervating atmosphere of Coolidge prosperity militated against the success of reform candidates. And for all his crusading enthusiasm, Olson did not care to become the permanent champion of lost causes.

The election results fully justified his prudence. The association threw all its weight behind Shipstead, who won a second term as United States senator while the state ticket suffered overwhelming defeat.

Notwithstanding his refusal to run for governor in 1928, Olson retained an exceptional standing in the reform movement. Not only did he keep his political fences in good repair by repeated personal contacts with local Farmer Labor leaders, but he assiduously courted key politicians of the major parties as well. The periodic meetings of Minnesota county attorneys gave him an excellent opportunity to make such contacts and to gain insight into local political conditions.

At such gatherings Olson's striking personal qualities were an invaluable asset. His pragmatic approach to problems melted the hostility of hard-headed conservatives, while his persuasive friendliness converted suspicion into open enthusiasm. An hour's conversation often won Olson a lifetime friend. Operating on an entirely informal basis, he gradually built up a coterie of key political supporters outside the Farmer Labor party. The McGowan brothers of Appleton, John Foley of Wabasha, and C. F. Gaarenstrom of Fairmont were typical of the influential regional leaders devoted to Olson.

A more complex organizational problem faced Olson in his own Minneapolis bailiwick. There a compact Republican machine ground out huge majorities with monotonous regularity. But like most prosperous political organizations, it suffered from periodic internecine struggles. All through the 1920s, State Senator Brooks and Ed Smith fought for control of the machine. Their rivalry was Olson's opportunity. As county attorney he occupied a good position to intrigue in the Republican civil war, and the hostile attitude of Senator Brooks during the 1924 campaign gave him the incentive to do so. In fact, he was on such good terms with Ed Smith that Ray Chase, the Republican candidate for governor in 1930, charged the county attorney with membership in a rump faction of G.O.P. politicians. Whether Olson intervened to get even with Brooks, to win a key position in the Republican party, or to encourage factional fights, the end product was an open intraparty quarrel in the summer of 1930, foreshadowing the eclipse of Republican supremacy in Minneapolis.[8]

The wooing of Hennepin County was also carried on in less devious ways. An afternoon on the golf course and a chat in the locker room enabled Olson to extend his range of contacts. Often he took lunch at the Minneapolis Athletic Club, where he rubbed shoulders with members of the business and professional group. Both sides were pleasantly surprised by the experience. In the flesh Olson seemed much less formidable and demagogic than he had been pictured by the newspapers. His immaculate clothing and respectful demeanor reassured suspicious businessmen. In turn, the county attorney was impressed by their intelligence and realism. Informal conversations with these active members of the community enabled Olson to sift or rework his reform proposals in the light of practical experience. He never lost his hostile attitude toward capitalism, but he learned to respect the opinions of businessmen, often winning their support in the process.

Olson also made a number of conquests among those who were associated with him through the county attorney's office.

Mrs. Jean Wittich, lifelong Republican and a prominent member of the Minnesota League of Women Voters, became his enthusiastic supporter after serving on the grand jury that heard his evidence in the case of the grafting aldermen. His seemingly effortless magnetism, operating simultaneously in so many directions, enabled Olson to build up a personal political machine unique in the annals of the state.

It has been commonly supposed that Olson selected 1930 for his re-entry into state politics because of the depression, and he encouraged this view with later assertions that his success depended on hard times. But chronology does not bear out the contention. Olson had indicated his willingness "to serve the party in any way it demands" at a Farmer Labor conference a month before the stock market crash in October 1929 and had begun to campaign actively before the Wall Street panic translated itself into an agricultural price break the succeeding May.

In view of the reassuring statements made repeatedly by President Hoover and many prominent businessmen after the crash, it is exceedingly doubtful that Olson foresaw the depression or counted definitely on it. He was relying on tangible things like personal contacts and political organizations when he made his declaration of availability.

The terms of both governor and senator expired in 1930, leaving Olson some freedom of choice. Reform leaders were unanimous in their desire to have him run for governor. The party already had one Farmer Labor senator, who was a lone wolf in Washington, valued more for his prestige than for his accomplishments. A second senator would be an insupportable luxury, whereas a governor would control the state administration and could dispense jobs to the faithful.

As early as October 1929 Teigan was assuring county newspapers that the matter was settled.[9] Other party leaders followed him at regular intervals, expressing confidence that Olson would run for governor. However, they could not smoke out the county attorney. He maintained an inscrutable silence until

January 2, 1930, when he issued the abrupt statement that "several public and private matters will have to be cleaned up before I can decide what office to file for, or whether I should file at all." [10]

This served clear notice on the party that Olson was considering the senatorship. He had frequently expressed a preference for this post in private,[11] but in earlier elections either Henrik Shipstead or Magnus Johnson had carried the party banner. With no Farmer Laborites to bar his path in 1930, Olson felt a great temptation to take the plunge.

The principal drawback was the necessity of making a decision before the designation of the Republican senatorial candidate. The incumbent, Thomas D. Schall, appeared to be less formidable than Governor Christianson, who also sought the G.O.P. nomination for senator. Olson had already tested the mettle of the latter and was not anxious to try conclusions with him again in 1930.

The possibility remains that Olson feigned interest in the senatorial contest to extract concessions from the Farmer Labor leaders who wanted him to run for governor. His unchallenged control of the March convention and subsequent dictation of the party platform reinforces this hypothesis.

Whatever Olson's motive, he played the game in realistic fashion. On February 10 he alluded publicly to the possibility of an Olson-Christianson race for senator[12] and then resumed his silence until two weeks before the convention, when he bowed to the wishes of party leaders and accepted the role they had cut out for him.

When the Farmer Labor Association convened its biennial meeting at St. Paul on March 27, 1930, one fact overshadowed all others: the complete domination of the deliberations by Floyd B. Olson. He addressed the delegates, guided the debates, and supervised the drafting of the platform.

Olson's ascendancy did not depend on control of the political machinery, or on steam-roller methods. He scrupulously avoided the crude, overbearing tactics of the party boss, resting his claim to leadership on a masterful handling of men. He guided them by a mixture of logical argument, cajolery, firmness, and flattery, all applied in just the right proportions. He led without coercing and dominated without offending. He had the flexibility to yield when necessary and to compromise where details rather than principles were involved. In fact, he ran the convention with such finesse that the delegates hardly knew they were being bossed.

Olson's determination to supervise the convention grew out of his desire to avoid the mistakes of 1924, when extravagance of doctrine and intemperate oratory weakened the reform ticket. Believing the party could win only by denying interest in spoils and disclaiming its traditional radicalism, he wrote an open letter to the convention which served notice that if nominated and elected, he would not make appointments to office "on the basis of political affiliation or professional political activity." [13] This ultimatum was accepted without open dissent.

To ensure a platform that would not lay the party open to charges of radicalism, Olson sat in with the committee and helped draft important planks. Under his direction, the more inflammable resolutions of the county conventions were sidetracked. He succeeded in eliminating labor-sponsored planks for unemployment insurance, the forty-hour week, and a state income tax, as well as miscellaneous proposals for government ownership of key industries and recognition of Soviet Russia.

Consequently, the document that emerged from the committee embodied none of the socialistic principles expressed in the constitution of the Farmer Labor Association. It avoided the controversial words "public ownership" entirely, calling instead for "protection" of natural resources and a constitutional amendment to give the state "control" of water power. A tinge of radicalism could be detected in the planks calling for public works to relieve unemployment and for a state-owned printing press, but the heart of the platform was a series of platitudes that appealed to a majority of all Minnesota parties. These included the St. Lawrence waterway, the McNary-Haugen Bill, the reduction of taxes on homes and personal property, and a blanket primary law.

After blocking platform amendments from the floor of the convention, Olson defended the work of the committee with a few explanatory remarks: "As I regard the political situation in Minnesota it is not up to the Farmer Labor party to introduce new and unique ideas of government. It is up to this party, as I see it, to restore the fundamentals of good government." [14] This was a retreat from the old concept that the party was primarily an educational force. By advocating a sharp break with the past, Olson indirectly acknowledged the political axiom that victory is the first objective of a party. The postponement of social reform was bitter medicine for some of the old party wheel horses but they reluctantly acquiesced in his strategy.

The colorless Olson platform went far toward removing the stigma of radicalism from the Farmer Labor party. It possessed all the calculated ambiguity that characterized major-party platforms and enabled them to attract voters of diverse faiths. Henry Teigan thought it "the most practical ever adopted by the party" and exulted over the fact that it was "free from visionary proposals that have often made political parties and organizations subject to unjust attack by the enemy." [15]

Left-wing newspapers that did not reflect official opinion were considerably cooler. The *Minnesota Union Advocate* criticized the platform for "prolixity and vagueness" and regretted the omission "of several matters for which the movement stands." [16] The *State News* thought many radicals were disillusioned and despaired of "a new order of things in Minnesota." [17]

Jeers from the right mingled with thunder from the left. The *St. Paul Pioneer Press* expressed mock concern over the abandonment of principles by the Farmer Labor party. It likened the convention performance to a reversal of John Brown, where "the body of radicalism goes marching on, but the soul lies mouldering in the grave of forgotten political philosophies." [18]

Despite the criticism and ridicule of the press, Olson had

scored a strategic victory in endowing the Farmer Labor party with a new respectability. Whatever cynical Republican politicians might say, many people believed the change was permanent. The very glumness of extreme radicals confirmed this fact. Almost from the adjournment of the convention, there were indications that Olson would make inroads into economic and political groups that had never voted for a left-wing candidate. Herbert Lefkovitz° noticed that even hardened conservatives were losing their fear of the Hennepin County attorney.[19]

Independent Olson supporters, unwilling to affiliate formally with the Farmer Labor party, organized a volunteer committee to work on a nonpartisan basis. Their first prepared statement presented Olson to the electorate as "one of the country's outstanding men engaged in law enforcement" and commended him for sweeping the Farmer Labor party clean of "untried economic theories."[20] It emphasized his nonpartisanship and competence — a theme that was to be reworked with endless variations throughout the campaign.

Although the independent committee materially aided the preprimary boom for Olson, the major burden necessarily fell on the Farmer Labor Association. It had launched a formal drive to recruit fresh members and extend organization to new townships and new counties in October 1929. O. D. Nellermoe worked among the farmers of western Minnesota, and Guy Alexander headed the Twin Cities campaign. George Griffith, former Townley aide and a seasoned politician, became the contact man between the association and the local Farmer Labor clubs. He circulated through the state, establishing precinct and ward clubs in many of the southern counties where no organization had hitherto existed.[21]

Inasmuch as the entire metropolitan press and most of the county weeklies consistently followed a conservative line, the Farmer Laborites needed a major newspaper to present their

° Herbert Lefkovitz of the *St. Paul Pioneer Press-Dispatch* changed his name in June 1940 to Herbert Lefkovitz Lewis.

case to the voters. There were numerous precedents for the establishment of an official party organ. During the heyday of the League, Townley had published a weekly *Nonpartisan League Leader* to keep all dues-paying members informed of official policy and to counteract the propaganda of the conservative press. He had also encouraged League members to pool their resources for the purchase of rural newspapers, setting up a special arm of the League called the Northwestern Service Bureau to offer local stockholders technical help and to provide sympathetic publishers with a press service.

Subsidies kept League publications afloat in the early 1920s, but they eventually collapsed because circulation could not be built up on a staple of political news articles unrelieved by comics or sports. Disregarding this unsatisfactory experience, the Farmer Labor executive committee voted to start a new official organ, the *Farmer Labor Leader*, which appeared for the first time on January 15, 1930.

The selection of Henry G. Teigan as editor of the *Leader* was a guarantee that it would be run like old League newspapers. His editorial training dated back to the *Iconoclast*, the first socialist newspaper in North Dakota. When Townley started the Nonpartisan League, Teigan became its secretary general and handled many of the problems connected with its publications. After these passed into bankruptcy, he served two years as Senator Magnus Johnson's secretary, returning to Minnesota in 1926 to edit a Farmer Labor press service for county weeklies.

A small, wiry man, a chain smoker electric with nervous energy, Teigan was almost ascetic in his devotion to intellectual pursuits and produced a paper full of analytical articles on social and economic problems. Since he possessed the temperament of a teacher rather than that of an agitator or propagandist, his columns lacked the breezy, colorful style that sells partisan viewpoints to the public. Yet his didactic tone often revealed a disarming idealism and a settled conviction that Farmer Labor policies would create a better world. Teigan always seemed uncomfortable and out of place among the machine politicians who gave him the Third District congressional nomination in 1936.

To meet publication costs he revived the old subsidy system. Campaign dues from party members were supposed to carry the *Farmer Labor Leader* through the election, but by September this original allotment was exhausted and Teigan was forced to call on all candidates for fifty-dollar contributions. Like its League predecessors, the *Farmer Labor Leader* was chronically in debt and appeared at irregular intervals. But it had a wider circulation than any of the county weeklies that were supporting the party.

While the Farmer Labor Association grappled with the prosaic problems of organization and publicity, Olson made a series of short speaking tours, swinging through the Iron Range country in April, covering the Twin Cities in May, and winding up with a whirlwind visit to western Minnesota in June. Everywhere he found attentive audiences and keen interest in economic problems.

Most of his speeches were in the old Populist tradition, containing indictments of monopoly, chain banks, and the concentration of wealth. Whenever he ventured into the field of social reform, it was in a temperate and restrained manner. He urged an old age pension law not only as the most humane way to take care of elderly people, but because "its provisions can be carried out at less cost than the present county poor farm laws." [22] Olson presided over this shotgun marriage of social reform and economy with his usual success. He managed to please radicals without terrifying conservatives.

But Olson's favorable reception did not generate a large primary vote for the party. Not only his independent supporters but bona fide Farmer Laborites were lured into the Republican primary by the exciting Schall-Christianson senatorial race. The blind incumbent, who masqueraded as a progressive of the 1912 vintage, received the enthusiastic support of Tom Davis and his admirers. Other radicals also cast Schall votes simply for the perverse pleasure of opposing Governor Christianson. The result was a stunning upset victory for Schall, and also a Republican total of 477,816 votes as compared with a meager 75,050 for the Farmer Laborites.*

A more damaging by-product of the mass exodus to the Republican primary was the Farmer Labor nomination of Ernest Lundeen, who was running against the convention-endorsed senatorial candidate, Knud Wefald. Lundeen's victory upset careful plans for informal cooperation between Democrats and Farmer Laborites. The Democrats were to back Olson for governor in return for Farmer Labor support of Einar Hoidale, their senatorial candidate,[23] but consummation of this secret deal between Olson and Joseph Wolf, the Democratic national committeeman, obviously depended upon each party's nominating a straw man for the office which it did not plan to contest. Wolf held up his end of the bargain easily, but Olson found himself embarrassed by inability to deliver.

Otherwise the primary went as expected. Olson, who was unopposed, polled practically the entire Farmer Labor vote. The Republicans nominated Ray P. Chase, former state auditor, while the Democrats chose Ed Indrehus, the Wolf candidate, who was not expected to give Olson any real contest.

When the 1930 campaign got under way in late August, a political revolution was brewing. The almost effortless predominance of Minnesota Republicans since the Civil War had gradually built up an immunity to the fears that assailed lesser parties, and the results of the primary gave them no particular cause for alarm. Even if the estimated 80,000 Farmer Laborites who intervened in the Schall-Christianson contest were deducted from the Republican total, the party appeared to have a margin in excess of 200,000.

Nevertheless, leaders experienced in reading political portents grew increasingly uneasy. Reports from the rural areas were

* The primary vote of the Farmer Labor party was 98,000 in 1928, and 155,000 in 1926. Cheney estimated that 80,000 Farmer Laborites voted in the Republican primary (*Minneapolis Journal*, June 27, 1930). Art Jacobs put the figure as high as 100,000 (*State News*, July 1930).

particularly disquieting. Normally a vast majority of Minnesota farmers voted the straight Republican ticket, but during the summer of 1930 their allegiance seemed to be shifting. The late spring break in agricultural prices produced widespread unrest. Even more ominous was a general disposition to blame Herbert Hoover for the trouble. He had been unpopular in Minnesota as wartime food administrator because of his decision to fix the price of wheat at $2.25 per bushel,[24] and his opposition to the McNary-Haugen Bill further alienated Minnesota farmers. Cheney noted their spiteful mood in the early summer, reporting that "the Hoover administration is at a low ebb in Minnesota and has no champion on the hustings."[25]

Rural rebellion foreshadowed further defections among small town merchants and businessmen whose livelihood was tied to agriculture. Dwindling profits and increasing competition from chain stores increased their discontent. Such desertions had to be counted as absolute losses since the Republicans had little hope of recouping elsewhere. The unemployed could be counted upon to deal roughly with incumbents, while organized labor stood solidly behind Olson.

On top of these afflictions, the ancient feud between the Smith and Brooks factions of the Hennepin County Republican machine reached the penultimate stage when the second-generation leaders, Fred Dickey and Ward Senn, split openly after the June primary.[26] Dickey threw his wholehearted support to Senator Tom Schall, who had won renomination, while Senn and Governor Christianson, the unsuccessful candidate, declared that they would back the state Republican ticket only. The *Minneapolis Journal* swung in behind them, and Minnesota was treated to the unusual spectacle of the leading Republican newspaper supporting Einar Hoidale, the Democratic candidate for senator.

The Senn faction's declaration of war on Schall tempted Dickey to undercut the Republican state ticket and encouraged Olson to fish in the troubled waters. He had always been on good terms with the Smith faction of the county organization which Dickey had inherited, and he hoped to capitalize on its resentment against Chase. No formal understanding was needed, but on the eve of the fall campaign political observers believed that interparty Olson-Schall and Chase-Hoidale combinations had formed.[27]

Apparently the help that Olson received from the Schall Republicans came without reciprocal obligations, because the Democratic leadership continued to support him. Wolf would never have strung along with Olson if the latter had intervened in the senatorial contest to the detriment of Hoidale. Whatever the exact pattern of interparty relations, Olson emerged from the factional fights with all the benefits and none of the disadvantages.

The outlook for the Republicans was not improved by their choice of Ray P. Chase to oppose Olson. Chase had been Republican heir apparent since the fall of 1929[28] and had received the gubernatorial nomination after twelve years of continuous service as state auditor. He was a perennial favorite at county fairs and commencement exercises, particularly in rural areas. His dignified appearance and conscientious manner created an agreeable impression, and he had the commonplace, plodding qualities that seem to appeal to the voters except in a time of crisis.

These neutral qualities were offset by the unfortunate impression Chase had made on reformers and Germans during the war. As manager of the bitter campaign against Shipstead in 1920, he had drawn up the wildest conceivable indictment of the Nonpartisan League, charging it with designs against "private property rights, religious freedom, the marriage ties, and the home."[29] Even choicer slanders had appeared in the editorial columns of the *Anoka Herald,* published by his brother Roe Chase, and these now provided the Farmer Laborites with handy campaign documents.[30]

During the prosperous 1920s when the Republican label conferred invincibility on a candidate, Chase would undoubtedly have been elected governor. As it was, the party needed every vote and could ill afford the luxury of a standard bearer with such a controversial past.

The accumulation of Republican misfortunes enabled Olson to start the campaign as a heavy favorite. His strategy called for endless repetition of two themes: moderation and good government. Throughout the contest he posed as a sane, practical reformer.

Committees modeled on the preprimary organization of nonpartisan Olson supporters sprang up everywhere as if by magic. Mrs. Wittich formed an "all-party" volunteer unit in mid-August, and shortly thereafter an "Independent Merchants' Committee" was organized. A group of Minneapolis women prominent in church, fraternal, and civic organizations arranged to mail out five thousand letters in Olson's behalf. Even conservative Twin Cities attorneys organized a "non-political" testimonial dinner for him. Henry Teigan exulted over the fact that Olson was able to spend a week addressing "overflow meetings" arranged by businessmen and other persons not connected with the Farmer Labor party, and newspapermen who attended Olson rallies noted that Democrats and Republicans were among his most enthusiastic supporters.[31]

Chase was so alarmed by the success of Olson's tactics that he adopted them himself. For the first time in state history a Republican candidate issued campaign cards and posters which omitted his party designation.[32]

To hold his heterogeneous following Olson carefully avoided controversial topics. He promised to purge political hacks from the public payroll and pledged himself to select public officials without regard to party affiliations. In the same breath he assured state employees that they had nothing to fear from the Farmer Labor party if they maintained a high standard of public service. He even promised farmers and farm organizations a hand in the selection of the commissioner of agriculture.

Olson made every effort to reassure conservative supporters that he sponsored no ill-digested social reforms. He told a luncheon meeting of insurance men that the Farmer Labor party no longer supported state insurance. He also circulated a personal platform that diluted still further the limited reform proposals adopted by the Farmer Labor convention. Specifically omitted were the plans calling for a state printing press, the abolition of injunctions in labor disputes, the blanket primary ballot, and the reclassification of property to reduce taxes.[33] This annoyed Olson's radical followers, but they comforted themselves by discounting it as campaign talk.

The campaign included the usual running exchange between candidates, although there were no dramatic personal encounters. At the outset Olson suggested a debate on agriculture, unemployment, conservation, and business chains. But Chase was too shrewd to appear on the same platform with such a master speaker. Except for a joint appearance before the League of Women Voters at Minneapolis, where both men delivered prepared addresses, Chase managed to move in a different orbit from his formidable antagonist.

The Republican campaign, too, was kept for the most part on innocuous subjects. Chase professed great concern over the seeming repudiation of socialist doctrine by the reformers. In his keynote address he lamented the fact that the Farmer Labor platform contained "not the slightest reference to the constructive principles for which, however wrong, its leaders within a decade vigorously fought."[34] He went on to pronounce the obituary: "The Farmer Labor party is dead. Its soul fled when its principles were abandoned." He concluded with an invitation to the rank and file to rejoin the G.O.P., claiming that the Farmer Labor leadership was a faction of disgruntled Minneapolis politicians and job hunters.

Olson's retort became famous. If the Farmer Laborites were a bandwagon of job hunters, he said, "it would just be another handful added to the hundreds of thousands walking the highways of the nation hunting jobs under a Republican administration."[35]

Chase did not come off much better in his charges that Olson was incompetent as a county attorney — lax in prosecution and adept at catching the small fish while the big ones got away. A highly critical statistical analysis of the Olson record was given widespread publicity, but the voters were more impressed by the spectacular conviction of the grafting Minneapolis aldermen.

Chase slowly fell back on the defensive, overwhelmed by charges that the Republican party had connived at securities swindles, mismanaged conservation, and done the bidding of the steel trust. Normally such indictments had little effect, but in 1930 they took root in public irritation. By early October it had become apparent that the sands of Republican supremacy in Minnesota were running out. The great corporations refused to contribute to the Republican war chest with the generosity of former years, while the smaller businessmen declared for Olson. The conservatives received a premonitory scare when the radical Philip La Follette captured the Republican primary in neighboring Wisconsin.

The last days of the Minnesota campaign were enlivened by Republican charges that the Farmer Labor senator, Henrik Shipstead, did not favor the election of Olson. The senator had neglected to mention the Farmer Labor state ticket before leaving for California in August, and as the weeks of the campaign slipped by without any endorsement from him, newspapers gave the matter increasing attention, partly to needle Olson and partly because the senator exercised a considerable influence on Minnesota politics.

Shipstead's striking personal appearance, ponderous Scandinavian dignity, and slow and majestic enunciation helped to nourish the myth that he was an elder statesman who decided every question on its merits. His carefully cultivated candor on small matters concealed a disposition to equivocate on large issues, which was all the more effective because it was done with an olympian disdain that the voters mistook for independence. This impression was heightened by his extraordinary victory in 1928, when he breasted the Hoover landslide with votes to spare. Insiders knew that Shipstead's success depended partly on his willingness to accept the role of errand boy and perform the most trivial services for his constituents, but his prestige stood so high in 1930 that even the Republican senatorial candidate, Tom Schall, pleaded for re-election on the ground that he had voted with Shipstead on major issues.

Although a Farmer Labor victory seemed certain without Shipstead's endorsement, Olson was determined to secure it whatever the cost. Perhaps the jeering of opponents got under his skin. Or he may have feared the defection of religious voters with whom Shipstead had great influence. In any case, Olson dispatched George Leonard to Los Angeles with a message for Shipstead. In substance the county attorney indicated that he would consider himself under deep obligation to the senator if the latter would give an endorsement.

When Leonard reached Los Angeles he found Shipstead in an uncooperative frame of mind. His stated reason for withholding the endorsement was Olson's alleged connection with the Minneapolis underworld, but in fact he probably balked at encouraging the rise of a rival in the reform movement.

Leonard and Shipstead fenced inconclusively for several days, although the senator professed himself satisfied about Olson's political morality when Fred Stinchfield, a Twin Cities lawyer of unquestioned integrity, presided at a testimonial dinner for the Hennepin County attorney on October 21. The battle of wills was transferred to the train as Shipstead and Leonard traveled back to Minnesota for the election. At last the senator reluctantly permitted Leonard to draw up an endorsement for his signature, and after rejecting several different drafts finally approved an extremely weak one. Leonard reasoned that any kind of an endorsement would touch off screaming headlines at such a late stage in the campaign and telegraphed it ahead from Omaha. Olson was content for the moment, but he took a subtle revenge four years later, when the tables were turned, by using the very same tepid phrases in endorsing Shipstead.[36]

If Shipstead's last-minute endorsement did anything for Olson, it simply made his majority larger. When the votes were counted, Olson received 473,154; Chase 289,528; and Indrehus 29,109. Never had a Republican candidate been so roundly defeated in Minnesota. Chase carried only five of the eighty-seven counties, being swamped in Nonpartisan League territory, in the German counties, and in the larger urban centers. He even lost the traditionally Republican counties along the Iowa border.

Undoubtedly Olson had received a great mandate from the people. But it was not clear what this mandate entitled him to do. During the campaign he had been all things to all men. He had spoken words of encouragement to radicals and conservatives alike. He had insisted that farmers, laborers, and independent businessmen possessed similar interests although economic realities gave little ground for such a contention. Those who voted for him did so primarily to express protest against depression rather than to endorse his doctrine of intergroup solidarity. The real test would come when Olson tried to drive his team of balky, ill-matched horses down the road together.

# Chapter IV   OLSON'S
# FIRST LEGISLATURE

No sooner were the ballots counted than an avalanche of problems tumbled into the lap of the governor-elect. He had to prepare an inaugural message, select an office staff, and lay plans for the organization of the new legislature – all against insistent pressure from job seekers who pursued him with unremitting vigor. Shortly after the election Olson fled to Colorado for rest and reflection, returning early in December to assume his new responsibilities.

One of the most pressing problems was the appointment of a secretary. The post required qualifications of a high order: a statewide acquaintance, adeptness in public relations, an ability to relieve the governor of irritating detail, and selfless personal loyalty. In addition, between Olson and his secretary there would have to be mutual confidence and respect. Without this relationship the governor would have to carry the staggering executive load alone.

Characteristically, Olson had given little attention to this important matter before the election and so found himself pressed for an immediate decision without anyone in mind. His first thought was to appoint Hjalmar Petersen, an obscure country editor who was just beginning his political career in the lower house of the state legislature. But Olson was tremendously impressed by the numerous recommendations for Vince A. Day, a Minneapolis lawyer who had taken part in the organization of the Nonpartisan League in Spokane, Washington, and helped

Townley draft the League's legislative program in North Dakota. Before settling down to private practice, Day had also served three years as legal counsel to the League, which brought him into personal contact with prominent left-wingers all over the Upper Midwest.

The drawback to the appointment was the fact that Olson had only a speaking acquaintance with Day. To take his measure, Olson asked him to a conference for advice regarding the choice of a secretary, and showed him a list from which Day's name had been conspicuously omitted. The latter made such straightforward, helpful suggestions that Olson was won over completely and offered him the job a few days later.[1]

The choice of Day proved to be fortunate in every way. Not only was he tactful, efficient, and loyal, but he cheerfully carried a heavy administrative burden that increased sharply in Olson's second term when ill health periodically incapacitated the governor. A quiet, reflective man who loved to close the office door and hold long intellectual discussions with a few cronies, Day was a sharp contrast to the aggressive, back-slapping politician. Small stature, unobtrusive manners, and a genuine desire to avoid the limelight partially concealed his fanatic devotion to Farmer Labor principles and his penetrating insight into party problems. As a clearinghouse of information for the governor, he exhibited good judgment, candor, and unselfishness.

In the weeks before his inauguration Olson devoted considerable attention to the drive for Farmer Labor control of the legislature, although he prudently left the actual skirmishing to others. Post-election political manipulation had become the rule in Minnesota as the result of a constitutional provision for the election of legislators without party designation. Intended to abate the influence of partisanship in state government, this clause merely transferred it from the polls to smoke-filled hotel rooms. Uncertainty as to the political affiliations of legislators opened the way for all sorts of political jobbery.

The evils of the system were not so apparent in the halcyon 1920s when a disciplined Republican majority disposed of or-

Cartoon from the Farmer Labor Leader, *December 17, 1930*

ganizational problems at a general legislative caucus. But the defeat of numerous incumbents in the 1930 election forced the Republican leaders to revise their tactics. Fearful that new members of doubtful affiliation would join the Farmer Laborites to organize the house, they called a caucus for late November and dangled choice committee assignments before them as bait. This maneuver placed the new members in a difficult spot. If the Republican caucus mustered a majority without them, desirable posts would be withheld. So their inclination was to see which side had the advantage and then jump on the bandwagon when the rush developed.

To counteract the Republican caucus, Olson considered some sort of appeal to the members-elect. Advised that direct intervention on his part would raise charges of dictatorship, he arranged for Frank Starkey, a legislator from St. Paul, to send out a circular letter urging the representatives to boycott any presession caucus that did not invite all members.[2] This gesture failed to block Republican plans. One hundred and seven out of 131 members, including a few Farmer Laborites who wanted good committee assignments, attended a St. Paul caucus on November 22. O. A. Swenson was endorsed for speaker of the house, and the so-called "conservative" slate was ratified without dissent.

The senate presented a different problem. The rules vested committee appointments in the hands of the lieutenant governor, who in this case was the Farmer Laborite Henry Arens. The Republicans were determined to win control, but they preferred to secure Arens' cooperation rather than rewrite the senate rules.

Negotiations started about three weeks before the opening of the legislature, with Arens demanding a five-to-four Farmer Laborite majority on the Rules Committee and the Republicans insisting on representation proportionate to their strength in the chamber. Neither side showed any disposition to break the deadlock. On December 28 the Republicans lost their patience and issued an ultimatum, threatening to appoint the Rules Committee by a resolution from the floor unless the lieutenant governor named a group satisfactory to them.

Olson countered with a public appeal, reminding senators that the people had voted for a new administration in November. But it was to no avail. When the senate met on January 7 the Republicans, by a vote of forty to twenty-seven, stripped the lieutenant governor of his appointing power and organized a conservative senate. Throughout these preliminary skirmishes the fiction of nonpartisanship was preserved, but it did not conceal the fact that the legislature had vested control in men hostile to Olson.

As the new administration prepared to take office there was widespread speculation regarding Olson's legislative program. The *Minneapolis Journal* felt sure the governor would recommend large-scale public works and a strengthening of the securities law.[3] Farmer Laborites secretly hoped he would throw off his campaign caution and launch a real left-wing program. But Olson said nothing to encourage them. In fact, his manner and behavior tended to reassure the conservatives. He made an excellent impression on all present at the traditional pre-inaugural reception given by the outgoing Governor Christianson. His courteous, friendly demeanor as he stood in the receiving line dispelled fears that Minnesota was entering a period of dangerous experimentation.

His inaugural address the next day came as close to offering all parties an olive branch as a political message can. After assuring the assembled legislators that he would cooperate with them in a nonpartisan spirit, Olson proceeded to outline his recommendations, which fell logically into three groups.

The first contained proposals that Olson had stressed in his campaign and deemed the least controversial: a unified conservation program, highway construction, and a more stringent law governing security sales. The second group included requests for action on several thorny problems: reclassification of property for taxation purposes, legislation to aid the independent merchant, and a statewide old age pension law. The final group included miscellaneous proposals for a uniform primary ballot, prohibition of injunctions in labor disputes, and establishment of minimum working conditions on state-financed jobs. These recommendations gave a mildly leftist tinge to the message, but Olson carefully refrained from references to the infirmities of the capitalist system.

Newspaper comment was almost as restrained as the message, though Henry Teigan found it necessary to apologize to the faithful for the lack of a major reform program. He conceded that none of Olson's proposals solved basic economic problems, but thought they were the "necessary initial steps leading toward further and more fundamental change."[4] Bluntly he warned the impatient against advocating impossible propositions that would make the movement ridiculous.

While the legislature was getting organized for the heavy work of the session, the governor wrestled with the vexing problem of patronage. Even before the inauguration, job seekers had stalked Olson relentlessly, crowding the entrances to the county attorney's office, roaming the corridors, and following him home. After he moved to the State Capitol, the main reception room became a glorified employment bureau with forty to sixty applicants waiting at all times.[5] During his first weeks in office Olson made a point of venturing into the crowd and chatting with those who had not secured a private interview, but he soon discovered they were all job seekers and discontinued the practice.

The unreasoning impatience of expectant Farmer Laborites severely tried the governor's good disposition. Two days after the inauguration one excited reformer complained that "Republicans still occupy key positions in the state," and before the end of the month Magnus Wefald was expressing fear that Olson would forget his father, Knud, who had been "through a baptism of fire for the party."[6] Lists of deserving Farmer Laborites who wanted posts flooded the executive offices in January. The St. Louis county chairman urgently recommended seven patriots who had carried the banner "in the face of ridicule," and Gaarenstrom of Fairmont sent in a geographically balanced list of candidates for game wardens and oil inspectors.[7]

The mountain of applications for a limited number of jobs made it impossible to take care of all bona fide Farmer Laborites, and the task of sifting them was too large for Olson to handle personally. He refused to delegate authority in any systematic way, however, partly because of his campaign pledge to retain efficient state employees and partly because he disliked the idea of zealous subordinates ousting jobholders for belonging to the wrong party.

Unable to reconcile magnanimity toward the enemy with the deafening wail for jobs, Olson resisted the establishment of any definite patronage policy during the first months of his administration. Although Henry Teigan, Vince Day, and others found places for the most deserving clients, several top state positions went to the governor's supporters outside the Farmer Labor party, and a few to men not affiliated in any way with the Olson campaign. Except for Knud Wefald, Henry Teigan, and George Griffith, there were no authentic radicals in the top layer of the administrative hierarchy during the early days. Olson even passed over the claims of Magnus Johnson in order to appoint R. A. Trovatten, a man without conspicuous political affiliations, as commissioner of agriculture.

This policy, which Olson adopted partly because the party lacked trained civil servants and partly because he wanted to broaden the base of his political support, was hazardous in that it aroused the antagonism of the old party wheel horses who were asked to step aside in the hour of victory.

The whole problem was further aggravated by the fact that the Republicans had made a clean sweep of the minor elective offices, thereby retaining control of important state departments. Even worse, some of the remaining departments nominally under the governor's jurisdiction were headed by holdover commissioners with two- to six-year terms. This arrangement reduced the number of jobs available for Farmer Labor applicants and placed the execution of party policies in hostile hands. Obviously Olson could do nothing about the elective officials, but he made careful plans to oust some of the appointive officials, despite the fact that the pertinent statutes forbade their removal at the governor's pleasure.

The two men on whom Olson concentrated his fire were N. J. Holmberg and F. A. Duxbury. Holmberg presided over the Department of Agriculture, which dealt directly with an economic group whose good will was essential to Farmer Labor success, and Duxbury sat on the quasi-judicial Industrial Commission, which handed down decisions in compensation cases affecting injured workmen. Both men were avowedly hostile to Olson and his policies. Holmberg had made it clear that he would not appoint Farmer Laborites to jobs in his department, and Duxbury had offended left-wing groups by frequently ruling against workmen.[8]

Since Governor Christianson had given these two commissioners recess appointments in 1929, Olson sought to block their confirmation by the senate. He was much too shrewd to state exactly what he wanted. Instead he took the unprecedented step of requesting the senate to return the entire list of one hundred and nineteen recess appointees so that he might pass on their fitness. This was asking for so much that the senate was maneuvered into a compromise. It saved face by refusing to return the appointments, but it dropped Holmberg from the list outright and denied Duxbury confirmation after an investigation of his record.

While Olson was investigating the nooks and crannies of state policy, he inadvertently found a hornet's nest in an innocuous-looking organization called the Great Lakes–St. Lawrence Tidewater Association, which received a biennial appropriation of $30,000 from the Minnesota legislature to push the St. Lawrence waterway project through congress. Olson considered the association useless, disliked A. O. Moreaux, the Republican editor on its executive committee, and hoped to force its liquidation by withholding fresh funds.[9]

Unfortunately an attack on the Tidewater Association carried the implication of hostility to the St. Lawrence waterway itself. And in Minnesota nobody could hope to remain in public life after opposing this project. The St. Lawrence waterway was represented as an economic cure-all which would turn Duluth into a great ocean port, replace expensive railroad transportation with cheaper water transportation, and retrieve for the Upper Midwest the processing and distributing functions lost after the construction of the Panama Canal.

Under the circumstances Olson would have been well advised to move slowly. But on January 29 he addressed letters to the governors of all the midwestern states that made appropriations to cover the lobbying activities of the Tidewater Association, calling their attention to the lack of progress in congress and suggesting that the personnel be changed or the association discontinued.[10] He asked the governors for their opinions and advised them that he favored discontinuing appropriations.

When the text of the letters leaked out, newspaper editors expressed bewildered indignation. Moreaux, leading the pack, solemnly accused Olson of trying to destroy a project that had "advanced from a dream to the threshold of realization," and from Duluth came the disconcerting information that thousands of citizens believed Olson was hostile to the waterway.[11] Such a spontaneous uproar frightened Olson into headlong retreat. He addressed an open letter to Shipstead, enthusiastically endorsing the St. Lawrence project and protesting that his investigation of the association was not prompted by hostility but by a desire to find out why its expenditures were so high.[12]

Gradually the agitation subsided, but it cured Olson completely of trying to interfere with the Tidewater Association. From that day forward he missed no opportunity to proclaim his allegiance to the Great Lakes–St. Lawrence waterway. The conversion may have been skin deep, but none of the faithful could fail to be impressed by the outward devotion of the penitent.

During his first days in office Olson also discovered the Rural Credit Bureau, another hornet's nest left for him by the previous tenant. This state corporation had been chartered by the 1923 legislature in response to the persistent demands of depressed farmers shut off from commercial sources of credit. It was expected to be self-liquidating, and the legislature placed restrictions on its loaning power to ensure proper business practices.

The bureau's solvency was jeopardized at the outset, however, because it served a class of clients unable to obtain loans elsewhere. It secured practically none of the business in prosperous southern Minnesota, where retired farmers and insurance companies underwrote loans at similar rates. Instead the bureau's files bulged with mortgages on marginal farms in northern Minnesota. Forty-three percent of the Hubbard County farms in the heart of the cutover region held bureau loans.[13] Frequently appraisers overvalued land for credit purposes and advanced money on inadequate security. They also made some loans on a political basis. A certain number of bad investments seemed inevitable if credit was to reach the hands of those who had agitated for the 1923 legislation, but when Olson took office, the Rural Credit Bureau had an indebtedness of $57,751,000 and only $43,000,000 in loans that were meeting interest.

The governor approached the problem cautiously, holding up a bureau request to issue $3,000,000 in bonds while his close friend, C. F. Gaarenstrom, conducted an investigation of loan procedures under the previous administration. This led to sensational charges of Republican mismanagement and prepared the public for a change of policy.*

While Olson was occupied with these problems, the legislature leisurely began hearings on bills embodying his recom-

* On March 4, 1931, it was disclosed that H. H. Flowers, former secretary of the Rural Credit Bureau, had received through his bank in Cleveland, Minnesota, $47,000 in commissions on insurance policies under the control of the bureau. Later findings showed that loans had been made to friends of the Republican administration on poor security.

mendations. Although the Republican majority exhibited considerable independence, the governor avoided the aggressive tactics for which he became famous in later years, confining himself to judicious lobbying for the enactment of his three key measures: a public works program, a unified conservation program, and a strengthening of the "blue-sky laws" for the regulation of securities.

A partial expansion of public works projects was easily secured by increasing appropriations for the construction and renovation of state institutions. But the heart of the Olson program was a $15,000,000 highway bond issue, and this ran into heavy opposition in both houses. The farmers feared the highway bond bill would raise rural taxes. The law required that all motor vehicle license fees be used for the payment of interest and principal on highway bonds before they could be diverted to other uses, and the administration considered this a sufficient guarantee against an increase of taxation.[14] But the farmers were not convinced. The intensity of their opposition varied directly with their distance from the trunk highways which were to be paved. Senator A. J. Rockne told his colleagues quite seriously that highway construction would "force" a boom and simply postpone labor problems.[15]

Highway Commissioner C. M. Babcock made the best case for the program by stressing its long-range financial aspects. He predicted that the proposed bond issue for eight hundred and twenty-five miles of paved road would be the last, justifying his contention on the ground that removal of such a large highway network from yearly maintenance was bound to release motor vehicle fees for bond retirement. With a barrage of facts and figures, Babcock attempted to convert Olson's relief project into a business proposition.

During the debate on the bond issue Olson embarked on one of the most controversial policies of his career. On February 26 he issued an order to the Highway Department amending contract specifications on state-financed jobs to include a minimum wage of forty-five cents an hour, a forty-eight-hour week, and overtime for extra hours. Had rural members of the legislature foreseen later reactions to this highway order, they would doubtless have killed the bond bill which implemented it. Fortunately for Olson, weather conditions postponed operation of the order until after adjournment. But when summer construction crews in rural areas quit work at 4:30 P.M. in full view of farmers laboring from sunrise to dusk, the reaction against the order was sharp.

For the moment, however, the fortunes of the bond bill did not suffer because of the highway order. It cleared the house seventy-three to fifty-seven and the senate thirty-seven to twenty-eight, and the governor signed it on April 1.

Olson then turned his attention to conservation legislation. His principal objective here was the creation of a unified department. To his dismay he found committees in both houses bogged down under a variety of proposals, most of which were "jokers" designed to maintain the status quo. An American Legion bill provided for a formal union of conservation activities which left divisional autonomy intact, while a Republican-sponsored bill vested the appointment of the conservation commissioner in the Executive Council in order to remove the new department from the governor's control.* The real opponents of a unified conservation department were officeholders in the state timber and land division, who were fearful of transfer from a Republican to a Farmer Labor department, and powerful business interests which maintained a close, working relationship with officials disposing of state resources.

Olson, knowing exactly which groups sought to sabotage conservation, kept in close touch with all developments. He talked personally with members of the house committee just before a bill was reported to the floor and succeeded in getting substantially what he wanted. The senate inserted a number of troublesome amendments, but the compromise measure that emerged

---

* The Executive Council was composed of the governor, the attorney general, the state treasurer, the state auditor, and the secretary of state. All but the governor were Republicans.

from the conference committee was a solid Olson victory. It provided for a union of all conservation activities under a five-man commission appointed by the governor, with a salaried director of conservation responsible to the commission. A companion bill set aside twelve areas of state land for new state forests.

Although the unification of conservation activities was only a first step, Olson considered it real progress. In fact, he later singled out the conservation law as the most important achievement of his first administration.[16]

Olson devoted almost equal attention to securities legislation. The existing statute exempted several important categories of stock from regulation and lacked adequate enforcement authority. Exposed criminals were beyond the reach of the commission if the appropriate county attorney refused to cooperate. The collapse of the Foshay empire dramatized these deficiencies.* Having lost thousands of dollars in that and similar swindles, voters were in an ugly mood and prepared to accept drastic regulations.

Olson, however, feared that comprehensive regulation of securities would discourage the investment of outside capital and provoke retaliation against Minnesota securities in other states.[17] As a consequence, the curative legislation proved to be very mild. It added a prosecution official to the securities commission, authorized the crime bureau to collect evidence in stock swindle cases, and made cooperation between county attorneys and control authorities mandatory.† But there was no attempt to extend the jurisdiction of the commission over securities from the New York, Chicago, and Boston exchanges, or from states supervising issues through a public commission. These shortcomings prevented the law from functioning effectively and illustrated the difficulties inherent in regulation at the

---

* Wilbur B. Foshay, promoter of the vast Foshay utilities organization, was convicted of using the mails to defraud and entered Leavenworth prison on a fifteen-year sentence April 17, 1934.

† Attorney General Henry N. Benson later declared this provision of the law to be invalid.

state level. Real protection of investors depended on national action. Even so, Olson's agitation helped to prepare the Minnesota public for the comprehensive Securities and Exchange Act of the New Deal.

The session ended on an angry note with the governor vetoing three major bills passed by the legislature. This negative action enhanced his prestige because in each case the conflict between special interests and the public was easy to expose. Also, two of the three bills concerned economic issues outside the area of party conflict.

The one measure that was clearly political was the act reapportioning congressional districts. The 1930 census deprived Minnesota of one seat, and failure to draw new congressional districts would force all nine representatives to run at large in 1932. Reapportionment is always a delicate and complex matter. Partisanship intervenes to prevent the equitable readjustment of boundaries, congressmen lobby to avoid disturbance of their districts, and rural interests resist changes which give increased representation to the ever-growing urban population.

These crosscurrents operated in the Minnesota legislature to produce a series of reapportionment proposals that all discriminated in one way or another against the big cities and the Farmer Labor party. The bill finally passed by the rural majority deprived Minneapolis of one of her two congressmen and dumped her heavily Farmer Laborite Third and Tenth wards into the Seventh District, which habitually elected third-party congressmen. This unblushing gerrymander made the Seventh District so large that it stretched from the Dakota border to the heart of Minneapolis.

Olson promptly vetoed this bill with a coldly logical message analyzing its glaring inequalities. He pointed out the extreme variation in the size of districts, which ranged from 228,596 inhabitants in the rural First to 344,955 in the urban Fifth.[18] He carefully made no mention of the gerrymander against the Farmer Labor party, but urged presentation of a more equitable plan before adjournment. The veto won unanimous approval in urban districts and even received some support in southern Minnesota, which stood to profit by the reapportionment.

The Republican leaders, contending that the reapportionment bill was valid without the governor's signature, purposely refrained from attempts to repass it over Olson's veto. The Minnesota courts sustained their contention, holding that the federal constitution conferred the power to draw up congressional districts solely on the legislature. But the United States Supreme Court reversed the decision early in 1932, forcing Republican congressmen to run at large when the political current was strongly against the party.

Olson's veto of the metropolitan sewage disposal bill offended powerful economic interests but had no obvious political overtones. Nobody could quarrel with the purpose of the legislation. Inhabitants of the river towns below Minneapolis and St. Paul had long objected to the dumping of sewage into the Mississippi and had joined forces with the Izaak Walton League in a systematic campaign for state action.

The first fruit of their agitation was the creation of a joint committee in 1925 to investigate the pollution of boundary waters between Minnesota and Wisconsin. After an exhaustive six-year study, the committee recommended legislation to create a metropolitan sanitary district and compel the immediate construction of a sewage disposal plant. It urged the inclusion of South St. Paul as well as St. Paul and Minneapolis in the proposed sanitary district since the river locks created a slow-moving pool of water which under certain conditions carried wastes from the packing houses north to the Twin Cities.

From an engineering standpoint the report was unassailable, but inclusion of the packing-house wastes from South St. Paul would increase sewage treatment costs and inevitably raised the question as to how they would be distributed. Minneapolis objected to the customary procedure of allocating costs on the basis of assessed property valuation, because she would be

71

forced to absorb most of the financial burden for South St. Paul, which had only two percent of the property but contributed thirteen percent of the sewage. Minneapolis suggested that the three cities divide the cost in accordance with the volume of waste material that each contributed.

The cost to St. Paul would be approximately the same under either method, but on the volume basis South St. Paul would pay $160,000 a year as compared to $30,000 on the assessed valuation basis. Since the schedule of payment was to extend over a thirty-year period and would involve nearly $4,000,000 in municipal revenue, negotiations were soon deadlocked, forcing the legislature to take up the explosive question of cost allocation.

Each side lobbied strenuously to secure the adoption of the plan it favored — St. Paul joining South St. Paul in contending that the benefit to the packers in the property valuation basis would also extend to Minneapolis creameries, paper mills, and gas plants.[19]

Some of the legislators would have preferred to take no action on the cost issue, but to create a metropolitan sanitary district without mandatory financial arrangements would only mean further postponement of the removal of river pollution, and the public was in no mood for further delays. So the legislature had to attack the problem frontally.

The decision lay with the rural members, who took little real interest in the question but jumped at the opportunity to vote on an expensive proposal that would not cost their constituents a penny.[20] Most of them succumbed to the blandishments of the South St. Paul packers, who operated a well-financed lobby[21] and piously promised that savings to their companies would be passed on to the farmers in some mysterious way — perhaps in the form of two-cent stamps, Olson scornfully suggested.[22] As a consequence the legislature, over the strenuous opposition of the Minneapolis representatives, passed a sewage disposal bill providing for the allocation of costs on the basis of property valuation.

Olson vetoed the measure as soon as it reached his desk, but his action was neither hasty nor ill-considered. He had sought professional advice regarding sanitary conditions in the Twin Cities and the river communities below them and had reached a decision only after assurances that a two-year delay in the installation of a sewage treatment plant would not constitute a health hazard.[23] His veto message compared cost distribution under the alternate methods and concluded that the legislature had allowed relief to private interests at the expense of the public: "The only beneficiaries through the allocation of the cost on an assessment basis rather than the volume basis are the private packing industries of South St. Paul, which would save $130,750 per year through this plan, which of course is paid by the taxpayers." [24]

The veto touched off outraged protests in St. Paul and South St. Paul, where newspapers charged the governor with playing politics at the expense of public health.[25] They made a concerted effort to stir up active feeling against Olson in the river communities below St. Paul, but even there the majority approved his effort to protect the public from the packers. The veto won him virtually unanimous applause in Minneapolis. Even his old enemy, the *Minneapolis Journal*, conceded that he had acted courageously.[26]

The governor showed his sincere interest in the sewage disposal problem by taking the initiative in reopening negotiations between Minneapolis and St. Paul. Harmony was eventually achieved by dropping South St. Paul from the sanitary district, so that when the legislature met in 1933 it had only to ratify a plan that had been accepted by both sides.

Olson used his veto for the third time against a bill purporting to regulate truck transportation but actually designed to deliver it into the hands of the railroads. The problem had come rapidly to a head because of the extraordinary postwar increase of automotive vehicles from 1,250,000 in 1920 to 30,-000,000 in 1930. This development was underwritten by a gigantic highway paving program that sharply reduced the operating costs of motorized equipment and created formidable competition for the railroads.

In 1925 the Minnesota legislature placed all commercial operators of motor transportation between fixed terminals and over a regular route under the jurisdiction of the state Railroad and Warehouse Commission. However, the rapid increase of "wildcat" freight trucks operating irregular routes generated widespread sentiment for further regulation. As a result a number of determined pressure groups converged on the 1931 legislature to help rewrite the transportation laws.

The public wanted to reduce highway hazards by putting specific limitations on the length, width, height, and load capacities of motor vehicles. The large trucking firms wanted legislation to curb wildcat operators engaged in cutthroat competition. The railroads professed to work for the reduction of truck competition and the recapture of less than carload business, although they were actually playing a deeper game. Organized labor was chiefly interested in regulation of the wages, hours, and working conditions of truck drivers, while railroad workers carefully checked all proposed transportation legislation to determine its possible effects on the security of their jobs.

The Railroad and Warehouse Commission called a conference of the interested parties to see if they could agree on a program to be presented to the legislature, but representatives of the railroads boycotted the conference and introduced their own bill, which the Transportation Committee of the house sent to the floor virtually unamended. It required all common carrier trucks to charge the same rates as railroads. Coupled with an application to the I.C.C. for an increase in railroad freight rates effective July 1, the bill seemed like a crude effort to legislate trucks out of business. However, its failure to redefine "common carrier" so that it would include 100,000 wildcat truckers indicated that the railroads were less concerned about the recapture of small freight shipments than with winning control of major automotive transportation systems and replacing high-cost spur-line trains with trucks.

Representative Frank T. Starkey of St. Paul, who understood this maneuver, tacked an amendment onto the house bill prohibiting railroad operation of trucks except to connect two lines.[27] But this amendment was eliminated by senators who had been worked into a proper frame of mind at the wide-open railroad lobby in the Minneapolis Athletic Club.[28]

When the bill reached Olson, there was extraordinary pressure on him to sign it. Alex Janes, the chief counsel of the Great Northern Railroad, was closeted with him for more than two hours, and State Senator Henry L. Morin went to him to plead the cause of the railroad employees, who saw greater job security in the elimination of common carrier trucks.[29]

Nonetheless Olson killed the bill with a pocket veto after the adjournment of the legislature. His accompanying message was one of his greatest state papers. After conceding the need for truck regulation and expressing his willingness to approve legislation that equalized competition, he launched into an analysis of the measure and bluntly declared that its purpose was "to force common carrier trucks out of business."

Anticipating criticism from the railroad workers, he argued that the bill offered them no real protection: "To attempt to insure continued employment of railroad employees by means of regulating two hundred and thirty-three trucks as opposed to over one hundred thousand unregulated trucks, is like attempting to stem the tide of the sea." He went on to chide the railroads for seeking protection from the consequences of the freight rate increase they had themselves demanded, and he concluded with his opinion that the bill would work a hardship on farmers and independent merchants.[30]

Of the three vetoes this was undoubtedly the most popular. The major truck companies were extravagant in their praise of the governor, consumers appreciated his decisive action to prevent a raid on their pocketbooks, and farmers expressed gratitude for the protection of wildcat truck operations.[31] Only among the railroad workers was there a disposition to criticize the veto, and this soon died out since their own leaders opposed the bill passed by the legislature.[32]

When an effort is made to appraise the accomplishments of Olson's first legislature, the negative character of the session stands out. The governor made no real attempt to mobilize state resources to withstand the depression. Highway construction and the erection of state buildings hardly scratched the surface of the unemployment problem. Even an innocuous bill to broaden the relief functions of the Executive Council remained bottled up in committee because Olson declined to make a public fight for it. He also evaded the problem of agricultural relief, refusing to take a stand even on such a minor palliative as the reduction of the farmer's tax burden.

His record on reform legislation was just as disappointing. He allowed bills embodying his inaugural recommendations on primary elections, chain stores, and old age pensions to shift for themselves, with the result that all of them died. All labor legislation was lost, except a bill regulating working conditions for state construction and maintenance employees. In fact, the only positive results of the Olson leadership appeared in the relatively noncontroversial fields of conservation, securities regulation, and highway building.

The contradiction between Olson's seeming lack of enthusiasm for social and economic legislation and his professed concern over the deepening troubles of farmers and workers subjected him to criticism from both right and left. Herbert Lefkovitz thought his policies amorphous and lacking in coherent social philosophy, and Congressman William Lemke, an old Nonpartisan Leaguer, complained that he had accomplished nothing of fundamental importance.[33] Both sides questioned publicly whether Olson believed in reform or merely paid it lip service like countless politicians before him.

Actually, good grounds existed for the governor's reluctance to push social and economic legislation in the spring of 1931.

Soundings of public opinion told him the voters would not support a sharp move to the left. His only public indication of this attitude was his statement to the Farmer Labor convention in 1930, but after the election he repeatedly told friends that premature advocacy of a radical program would discredit him and impair the usefulness of the reform movement. Wisely he postponed action until the incipient reform sentiment of early spring had crystallized into an overwhelming demand for change.

The instability of his political following also operated to chill Olson's crusading zeal. For twelve years the party had diligently cultivated the myth that there was a community of interests between all wealth producers. But the legislative session was not a month old before farmers and laborers were at loggerheads. Farm organizations lobbied actively to defeat the highway construction program, and rural representatives amended beyond recognition a bill fixing minimum working conditions on contract jobs financed by state funds. Even a perennial optimist like Henry Teigan conceded that the wealth producers were not cooperating.[34]

To these factors must be added the avowed hostility of the Republican legislature. As a political realist Olson knew there was little chance of getting controversial measures passed by his opponents. He preferred small victories on battlegrounds of his own choosing to futile assaults on impregnable fortifications — assaults that would only fritter away his prestige.

But this policy of political passivity annoyed the doctrinaire radicals who wanted the governor to tilt with windmills whatever the consequences. From the outset of its accession to power the reform movement was paralyzed by an inner contradiction — a theoretical program but a practical leader.

77

# Chapter V SLUMP AND RALLY

THE prestige of the Olson administration, which had stood so high at the close of the legislative session, ebbed steadily in the ensuing months, reaching a critically low point in October 1931. The deterioration of party fortunes was only in part due to the policies pursued by the governor. He worked against a background of deepening depression that provoked indiscriminate criticism.

Unemployment accelerated sharply in 1931, reaching 21.4 percent by the end of the year.[1] Farm prices buckled in the spring when the Farm Board discontinued the stabilization purchases that had held May wheat futures to nearly eighty cents a bushel. Wheat slumped to fifty cents on the Chicago exchange in July and skidded to an all-time low of forty-five cents on August 6.[2] The price of milk, butter, and cheese dropped correspondingly, reducing the income of dairy farmers twenty-five percent during the year.

This tightening of the economic vise intensified dissatisfaction and shortened tempers. People who had borne up well under two years of depression began to lose their patience, and there was a general disposition to make the state administration a scapegoat for all the irritations. Nor did the conservative press, which included an overwhelming majority of the state's newspapers, fail to stir up all the popular discontent it could.

Just as criticism of the administration was reaching a peak, Olson suffered a severe attack of stomach ulcers which incapacitated him most of the summer. Few reports on his condition leaked out because he remained in seclusion at Gull Lake, but for a time he was considered too ill to transact business.[3]

The problems that plagued the ailing Olson were the thorny issues he had evaded, postponed, or overlooked during the legislative session. The patronage question, which had bubbled angrily from the day he took office, boiled over in mid-June, embroiling him first with his own supporters and eventually with various other political groups.

The immediate cause of the controversy was the governor's announcement that henceforward department heads would be responsible for the hiring and firing of employees under their jurisdiction. Since Olson had given several top posts to Democrats and Republicans, this announcement made it clear to impatient Farmer Laborites that there would be no real house cleaning. This would have been hard to take in a period of prosperity; it was intolerable when depression made even the lowliest job valuable and when incumbent Republicans jeered at the faithful for their lack of influence in party councils.[4]

In the ensuing uproar all restraint disappeared. Senator Emil Regnier, one of the administration stalwarts, complained bitterly about the retention of a Republican game warden, notifying Olson that "we are thoroughly disgusted with some of these appointments and want you to know it."[5] Others, who did not address the governor directly, bombarded county chairmen with threats of political revolt. Olson was frightened into speeding up the dismissal of incumbents, especially of game wardens, whose easy work, tolerable pay, and leisure for political leg work made them universally envied.

Although only sixty-five game wardens were scheduled for replacement, the Izaak Walton League, which had a Republican board of directors, solemnly accused the governor of playing politics with the conservation of wild life.[6] Worst of all, one of the men dismissed was a veteran who promptly committed suicide. Whereupon the American Legion angrily accused Olson of violating the Veterans' Preference Act, and hostile resolutions at the Legion convention were sidetracked with difficulty.[7] The Republican press piously lamented the iniquities of the spoils system.

Olson lay flat on his back at Gull Lake during the worst of the controversy, but at his request the Fish and Game Department reinstated some of the Republican wardens.[8] This move stirred up the Farmer Laborites anew, and two months later Teigan was still trying to placate them with the remarkable assertion that no appointments could be considered final.[9]

The controversy over the Rural Credit Bureau also got completely out of hand during the summer. The governor persistently refused to take a clear-cut stand on the question of liquidating bureau holdings. Since more than one quarter of the loan installments were delinquent on May 1, immediate liquidation would doubtless have cut the burden of the taxpayer. But it would also have alienated poverty-stricken farmers in the cutover area who had supported Olson enthusiastically. For nearly six months he evaded the dilemma by quietly continuing operations, without definitely dashing the hopes of those who favored an early liquidation.

His equivocation might have succeeded but for a feud between two members of the Rural Credit Bureau which broke into print, re-opening the whole question. The origin of the dispute betwen C. F. Gaarenstrom and H. M. Johnshoy is not clear, but personal antagonism played a substantial part. Eventually it became necessary for Olson to remove one of the combatants, and he chose to part with Johnshoy rather than his personal friend Gaarenstrom.

The repercussions were resounding. Johnshoy issued a public statement condemning Gaarenstrom for incompetence and charging that farms were being dumped on the market wholesale. Then he departed on a speaking tour through rural Minnesota, amplifying his side of the story. The newspapers gave him a sympathetic hearing, although it developed that only three farms had been sold below market price — all on the recommendation of Johnshoy![10]

Whatever the merits of the controversy, conservative newspapers cited it as evidence that Olson was hostile to the farmer. In fact, the *St. Peter Herald* called him a labor governor who had kicked the last farm representative out of the bureau.[11] Ironically enough, most of the protests came from southern Minnesota, where few rural credit loans had been made. The farmers were seeking a scapegoat for falling prices.

Olson's highway code, which regulated working conditions on state-financed jobs, had elicited only passing comment in early spring, but it came under heavy fire when warmer weather permitted construction and maintenance crews to begin operations under its provisions: an eight-hour day at 45 cents an hour; a maximum of $1.00 a day for board and room; a limitation of charges for transportation to and from the job site to 3.6 cents a mile; and the outright prohibition of fees in connection with the hiring of highway workers.

These provisions went far to rectify substandard conditions in highway construction camps. Under the preceding administration men had often worked twelve to fourteen hours a day at thirty cents an hour. From this pittance employment agencies withheld fees as high as three dollars for securing jobs. The contractor took another large slice for board, lodging, and transportation, leaving a small residue that sometimes disappeared completely in gambling games. It had not been unusual for a laborer to leave the job at the end of the season without a penny to his name.

When Olson first considered setting up a code to outlaw such practices, he ran into the unyielding opposition of contractors who were still using horse-drawn equipment. When lumbering operations closed down in northern Minnesota, necessitating the maintenance of idle horses through the winter, most contractors had converted to motorized highway equipment, but a few held out and they saw ruin in the Olson proposal. The eight-hour work day meant running two shifts, which in turn required more housing space, camp equipment, cooks, and maintenance personnel. It also reduced the usefulness of horse teams; they could be worked effectively ten to twelve hours a day but could not stand up under two eight-hour shifts.

Olson held several conferences with disgruntled team contractors to explore possible avenues of compromise. They unanimously urged that teamster outfits be exempted from the highway code.[12] This solution would have created almost insuperable problems of classification and paved the way for easy violation of the code, so the governor rejected it along with a number of similar propositions. Throughout the discussions he maintained a conciliatory attitude but refused to budge from his original position. In the end the team contractors left emptyhanded, convinced that Olson intended to drive them out of business.

The highway code also added to the antagonism of the farmers. They listened readily to claims that motorized units cut down the use of horses, oats, and other farm products, decreased the number of rural laborers on highway projects, increased costs to the taxpayer, and forced farmers to pay higher salaries to retain their hired hands. A. H. Hendrickson, chairman of the Farmer Labor committee in the Sixth District, wrote Olson that there was no way he could explain the code to the satisfaction of the farmers.[13]

The steady increase of unemployment during the summer increased criticism of the highway code. It was plausibly argued that motorized contractors created technological unemployment. Rudolph Lee, publisher of the *Long Prairie Leader*, estimated that they required only one eighth the personnel used by team contractors and eliminated unskilled laborers altogether.[14] Sensing a good political issue, Republican editors and politicians upbraided Olson for improving the status of a few men at the price of increased unemployment.

As the argument grew more heated, Olson took the stump in June and made a series of speeches defending his code. He condemned the rumors of increased cost as groundless, pointing out that contractors made the same bids after the installation of the code as before. He told rural audiences that the forty-five-cent minimum wage increased the ability of the workers to buy farm products, and that the prosperity of both farmers and laborers depended upon their mutual cooperation.

The controversy smoldered for another month, marked especially by a strike of two hundred laborers near Cook, Minnesota. They charged that Winston Brothers, the contractors, had vitiated the minimum wage provision of the code by letting out subcontracts for most of the work under such arrangements that the workers received no more than two dollars for a fourteen-hour day.[15] After some two months of negotiations and some minor flare-ups of violence, the strike was settled in favor of the workers, but in the meantime the highway code had come in for additional criticism as a breeder of class war.

The whole problem burst spectacularly into the open on August 3 when the Frazer-Johnson Construction Company charged the governor with breaking a promise of April 7 to exclude teamster wages from the highway code. A few days later nine firms wrote Olson a letter protesting that their "horses, mules, harness, wagons, and tents, costing hundreds of thousands of dollars" had become nothing but a heap of worthless junk.[16] Coming more than four months after Olson's alleged promise and considerably after the awarding of contracts, the attack was timed to achieve the maximum political effect.

A participant at the April 7 conference categorically denied that the governor had made such a promise,[17] and Olson issued a point-by-point rebuttal, insisting that the highway code would be retained. The contractors retaliated by requesting an injunction to prevent the inclusion of the highway code in state contracts on the ground that it prohibited profits and the use of equipment. The district court issued a restraining order on September 4, and Olson faced the headache of legal as well as political battle when he finally ended his convalescence.

On September 14 State Senator Gerald T. Mullin confronted the harassed administration with a fresh dilemma by accusing the state Railroad and Warehouse Commission of connivance in irregular weighing and grading procedures at public elevator "M." He not only presented evidence of wrongdoing, but demanded that Olson conduct a formal investigation of the commission.

Behind this seemingly simple request lurked disconcerting dangers. The attack on grain grading in elevator M, ostensibly directed toward the Railroad and Warehouse Commission, in reality was aimed at the Farmers Union Grain Terminal Association, which had stored the grain under question. The association was a farm cooperative operating under the Agricultural Marketing Act of 1929, which had appropriated $500,000,-000 to help cooperatives in every phase of commodity marketing. Private grain dealers, who felt this legislation put them at a severe disadvantage, looked upon the Mullin investigation as an opportunity to discredit the Farmers Union.

Most of the questions raised by Senator Mullin involved the complexities of grain marketing, about which the general public had little knowledge and less concern. But the array of political interests touched by the controversy was formidable. A finding of gross negligence against the Railroad and Warehouse Commission would result in the removal of the three Republican commissioners, transferring control of the largest state department, with four hundred employees, to the Farmer Labor party. Unfortunately, it would also strike a blow at the Farmers Union, which contained many friends of the administration.

Court settlement of the elevator case might have diminished these political overtones, but the state constitution placed responsibility squarely on the governor, giving him power to oust elective officials for gross neglect of duties after conducting a hearing. Olson dared not dodge the issue by appointing a referee, lest the latter hand down a decision that would damage him politically. In the end he agreed to hear the case personally, although any verdict was bound to alienate important interests.

On top of all these irritants, A. C. Townley, who had spent the last eight years in the political wilderness, crossed the Red River from North Dakota to whip up criticism of Olson's half-hearted reform program. He began his tour of the western counties in May, speaking from a low-priced car with a public address system and passing the hat at the end of each meeting. His analysis of economic ills was the old refrain about Wall

Street, the profiteer, and the middleman siphoning off nine tenths of the farmer's income to pay parasitical bondholders. But the Townley solution was startlingly original: He proposed a five-year moratorium of interest payments on all debts, including mortgages,[18] and announced to gaping farmers that the Nonpartisan League would be revived in time for the 1932 election. His speeches were punctuated with sneers at the farmers for being such "damn fools" as to "rot on their farms" rather than unite for action.[19]

Hitherto Townley had always won the farmers by insulting them, but this time the needling technique could not create converts for his unorthodox economic program. Even his warm admirer, Henry Teigan, conceded that rural Minnesota had little faith in the moratorium proposal.[20] Nonetheless Townley continued to campaign throughout the summer, and in early September the lunatic fringe of the reform movement held a convention in Rochester and solemnly nominated him for president of the United States.[21]

Grotesque as this performance was, it created uneasiness at third-party headquarters. The proposal to rebuild the Nonpartisan League in the heart of Farmer Labor territory was an unfriendly gesture and stimulated centrifugal tendencies in the party. Furthermore, since Townley was considered the spiritual mentor and elder statesman of the reform movement, the voters tended to assume that the Farmer Labor organization endorsed his visionary recovery program. The confusion was deepened by Henry Teigan, who used his position as editor of the *Farmer Labor Leader* to comment favorably on Townley's activities.[22]

Many rank-and-file reformers objected to this semi-official encouragement and feared that Townley's nonpartisan approach to politics aimed at the disruption of the third party. Others distrusted his thirst for power. Old associates recalled that he had always pursued a rule-or-ruin policy, and Vince Day flatly warned Olson that he would try to dictate the policies of any enterprise in which he participated.[23] It was an open question whether Townley constituted a greater menace inside

or outside the party. Whatever the answer, his attempted come-
back injected fresh discord into the reform movement when it
needed to close its ranks against the enemy.

These were the multiple problems Olson faced when he returned to the capital in mid-September. Coupled with persistent rumors of the governor's ill health and impending retirement, they had reduced party morale to a low ebb.[24] Only an
aggressive battle against depression could revitalize the reform
movement, but even though the bellicose mood of the electorate seemed to augur well for a move to the left, Olson soon
discovered that a relief program broad enough to cover both
farmers and workers would generate as much ill feeling as it
removed. The two groups had nothing in common but their
dissatisfaction. Not yet miserable enough to consider cooperation, they proposed relief prescriptions which reflected their
conflicting economic objectives.

The farmer approached problems as a proprietor or petty
capitalist. Relief to him meant a mitigation of conditions that
interfered with successful farming. It involved such things as
tax reduction, easier access to credit, and a floor under farm
prices. His individualist psychology did not create scruples
against government aid, but he welcomed it only as long as it
improved agricultural conditions. When official paternalism
took the form of public works or the dole, he openly opposed it
because assistance on such terms forced him to abandon his
chosen profession, to submerge his individuality in the labor
crew, and to suffer the humiliation of the bread line. Besides, a
public works program required increased revenue, and since the
state relied heavily on the property tax, the cost of the program
seemed likely to fall primarily on him.

At the opposite end of the seesaw sat the city worker, who
sought relief from the hunger, exposure, and disease that
followed in the wake of unemployment. Dependent on an impersonal industrial machine, he had sloughed off the frontier
tradition of individualism for the more serviceable doctrine of

cooperation through trade unionism. Unlike the depressed farmer, the unemployed worker often had no property or economic stake to protect. He was largely immune to taxation and had nothing to lose by backing proposals to dilute property rights or redistribute the wealth. Driven by the primitive instinct to survive, the worker demanded financial relief measures from the state.

With organized labor clamoring for a special session of the legislature to appropriate funds for the unemployed, and farmers demanding that the cost of government be reduced, the Republican state auditor on October 1 set the property tax levy at 8.08 mills — an all-time high. Although the increase was due primarily to the shrinkage of revenue from other sources, rural newspapers blamed Olson for it, calling him a "city" governor and accusing him of loading the farmer with new burdens to create employment for the workers. Rudolph Lee solemnly predicted that the increased taxation would be the chief issue of the 1932 campaign, and others took up the cry.[25]

This outburst represented genuine rural irritation, but it was also part of a concerted campaign to scare Olson out of calling a special session. His patchwork coalition, which had made such a spectacular showing in the 1930 election, was dead in all but name.

In neighboring Wisconsin Governor Philip La Follette, facing the same dilemma, burned his bridges decisively by calling a special session of the legislature to enact a comprehensive relief program. La Follette prescribed strong medicine for the ailing economy: unemployment insurance, redistribution of the tax burden, community planning, stabilization controls for private business, and an extension of public ownership.[26] These measures were too drastic for a rural legislature to swallow, and La Follette frittered away his prestige in fruitless appeals for action. He alienated the farmers by his effort to help the workers and suffered a disastrous defeat in the 1932 election.

Despite intense pressure from labor leaders, Olson steadfastly resisted such a course. He sought to frame a fresh compromise which would satisfy the insistent demand for action without alienating either wing of his disintegrating party.

The formulation of a useful farm program presented the most difficulty because the basic problems of agriculture could not be solved by state action. The only popular measure of relief within the jurisdiction of the Minnesota legislature was a redistribution of the tax burden, and Olson enthusiastically took up the cry for tax reduction on homestead property. As an alternative source of revenue he proposed an income tax.

Since nothing further could be done at the state level, Olson sought to win support from the farmers by associating himself with national relief measures. In a burst of fanfare he convened an agricultural conference October 26, 1931, and submitted an elaborate program to farm leaders calling for: (1) government regulation of commodity prices to ensure farmers a fair return; (2) a federal loan of $37,000,000 to refinance Rural Credit Bureau loans at two percent interest; (3) national legislation along the lines of the McNary-Haugen Act; (4) a one-third reduction of the assessed valuation on farms and city homes for taxation purposes.[27]

Coming shortly after the announcement that he would be a candidate for re-election, the Olson farm conference was viewed with skepticism by Republican newspapers. The *Long Prairie Leader* thought it was "more for talking purposes than results." Cheney of the *Minneapolis Journal* called it the start of the 1932 campaign, but ruefully conceded that it was good politics to advocate tax reduction for the farmer and the small homeowner.[28]

To strengthen the impression that he was the "farmers' governor," Olson conferred on November 5 with nine Minnesota congressmen to formulate plans for the enactment of farm legislation when congress convened in December. Such a conference could not be expected to produce a meeting of minds. The Republican representatives were more conservative in outlook than the governor, and they resented his efforts to make political capital out of the occasion. Nevertheless he managed to extract a joint statement endorsing agricultural credit and a reduction of interest rates on mortgages.

Shortly thereafter Olson memorialized the President and congress in behalf of the Frazier Bill to refinance mortgages and sent C. F. Gaarenstrom to Washington as his personal representative to testify at hearings on the bill.[29] He supplemented these measures with a series of speeches in behalf of national price-fixing and farmer-labor cooperation.

Although rural Minnesota did not completely swallow the Olson program, it viewed the governor with new favor. Perhaps the rally of wheat from fifty cents a bushel on August 25 to sixty-five cents on November 20 accounted in part for the farmers' more tolerant attitude. However, John Hay, who as deputy commissioner of agriculture kept his ear close to the ground, gave the chief credit to Olson's hard-hitting autumn addresses. Invariably they seemed to strike the proper note of protest.[30]

The emergence of Olson in the role of an agrarian crusader was more than a political maneuver. It involved a complete reorientation of his social and economic outlook. From his earliest days he had been an urban radical, preoccupied with the problems of the city worker. He had taken the farmer for granted as a necessary but troublesome appendage of the radical movement. His Populist orations of 1924 flowed more from a sound instinct for political pyrotechnics than from any real understanding of the policies he advocated. Even as late as 1930 he was so badly informed on the farm problem that he made a campaign speech on wheat prices in a dairy region.[31]

It was the terrific impact of agrarian depression on Minnesota that changed Olson's perspective. He began to see that the farmer, as well as the city worker, was battling against a hostile economic system and for all his individualist psychology was a genuine member of the underprivileged class. This realization converted Olson from a professional agrarian to a sincere student of farm problems.

The governor's agricultural program did not soften rural

opposition to a special legislative session. Even the bait of immediate tax reduction failed to overcome the farmers' objection to unemployment relief as the opening wedge for an even larger financial burden. Political soundings of the overwhelmingly rural legislature indicated that it would probably sidetrack relief measures even if convened.

Nevertheless, Olson's urban following expected him to make the gesture. Official Farmer Labor doctrine had always prescribed large-scale government intervention to cure the ills of society, and left-wing newspapers kept up a steady drumming for a special session.[32] Besides, Olson himself felt a compelling inner obligation to champion the cause of the depressed classes. From his subsequent behavior it is clear that he favored state appropriations to relieve the unemployed. But the opposition of the farmers plus the loud clamor of his "all-party" middle class supporters for relief by subscription convinced him that a private drive would have to be tried and found wanting before government relief could command the necessary public support. So for the moment he decided to leave relief in private hands, as Herbert Hoover and Walter Gifford urged.

Olson tried to make the most of his momentary capitulation to the conservatives by extracting the maximum possible relief contributions from private donors; he threatened a special session of the legislature if the voluntary program failed.[33] After an Industrial Commission survey indicated that 137,000 family units would need winter relief, he set up a state committee of two hundred and seventy-five, headed by F. T. Heffelfinger, Minneapolis socialite, to collect money and clothes for distribution through existing relief agencies. On the whole, the job was done efficiently and unselfishly. But the resources made available through private subscription were pitifully inadequate to meet depression needs.

Olson was subjected to murderous criticism from the radical wing of the party because he refused to convene the legislature for relief appropriations. William Mahoney, pioneer Farmer Laborite, refused to serve on the relief committee, tartly observing that since it was a rich man's project, the personnel ought to be limited to the rich. The *Minnesota Union Advocate* could find no logical reason why the Farmer Labor administration refused to take the lead in meeting the problems of the state by official action, and warned that continued temporizing would imply "either incompetence or lack of courage." Even the *Farmer Labor Leader* sniped at the voluntary relief program, contending that "in the end it will be inadequately done." [34]

Despite all their grumbling, the urban radicals did not repudiate Olson's leadership. Some of them understood that once the failure of private charity had been clearly demonstrated, the governor would press for a state-financed unemployment relief program. Others stuck because they had no place else to go. At all events, it was clear by January 1932 that Olson had performed the political miracle of holding his heterogeneous following together.

Other storm clouds also blew over at the close of 1931. A. C. Townley was admitted to the organization and sent on a tour to secure subscriptions for the *Farmer Labor Leader*. Although he renounced his presidential aspirations, he continued his troublesome agitation for a moratorium on debt payments. Fortunately for Olson, he soon became so engrossed in the congressional campaign that he lost his urge to dictate party policy.

The governor managed to remove another potential source of trouble by handing down an exceedingly astute decision in the elevator M case. Since even the experts could not agree as to what constituted unfair practices in the grain trade, Olson happily adopted their ambiguity.[35] He absolved the Farmers Union from illegal activity, gave the Railroad and Warehouse Commission members a slap on the wrist without ousting them, commended Senator Mullin for bringing the charges in good faith, and pleased the farmers by condemning grain-grading laws as unfair.

The quarrels over the highway code and the Rural Credit Bureau also abated. The former died a natural death when winter suspended highway operations and the state supreme court vindicated the legality of the governor's order. The latter disappeared from the papers as the election approached, because the Republican party had no desire to rouse the farmers' ire by taking a definite stand on state loans.

As all these issues dissolved, the prospects for Olson's re-election improved. In fact, when the biennial meeting of the Farmer Labor Association convened in March, the only major source of discord was the vexatious patronage problem.

Olson's success in arresting the disintegration of the reform movement stands out as a great achievement in political logistics. The rapid growth of economic unrest in the summer of 1931 had threatened the termination of his political career and the absorption of warring Farmer Laborites by the rejuvenated Democratic party. All over the nation depression-conscious voters were preparing to turn incumbents out of office whatever their political creed. Olson survived by abandoning the pretense of compromise without giving up its substance. He convinced the dissatisfied that he was one of them without embarking upon ill-considered reforms, and he diverted public resentment from the state government to the hapless administration in Washington. Through it all, he never forgot the political axiom that people must be carefully prepared for an experiment in reform.

# Chapter VI    CAPITALISM ON TRIAL

THE fluidity in party alignments that had been a conspicuous feature of the 1930 Minnesota campaign seemed likely to persist in 1932. The depression acted as a powerful dissolvent of traditional political ties, leaving in its wake a floating protest vote to disturb the calculations of professional party managers.

This development was most dangerous to the Republicans, since many of the malcontents had deserted their ranks and further defections threatened. In an effort to revitalize the party a statewide young Republican organization was created December 20, 1931. It began to hold pep rallies, debate party policies, and issue ringing challenges to the old guard leadership. Such manifestations of youthful vitality were intended to assure the new generation of voters that the G.O.P. offered a real haven to thoughtful and progressive Americans.

To enhance party solidarity Republican strategists imitated the Farmer Labor practice of holding an endorsement convention, but the anticipated advantages did not materialize. Bleak election prospects and the withdrawal of the three leading candidates — Earle Brown, Stafford King, and John Haugen — from the gubernatorial race dampened enthusiasm even before the convention met.

Only intense pressure from the Republican hierarchy induced Earle Brown to retract his withdrawal and accept the endorsement. This last-minute capitulation helped to thaw the atmosphere since Brown headed the State Highway Patrol and was

93

genuinely popular with the rank and file, but it did not disguise the fact that his party loyalty had triumphed over his political realism.

The Republican platform pointedly ignored worker grievances but took sufficient notice of rural unrest to recommend an income tax with a replacement provision, national aid for agriculture, and state legislation to stabilize banking. These vague promises represented the maximum concession Republicans would make to radical sentiment.

The Farmer Labor Association held its biennial convention at St. Paul nine days after the Republican adjournment. The problems confronting it were those of influx rather than exodus. It had to assimilate voters of divergent outlooks shaken from their political moorings by the economic crisis, and the governor faced the unpleasant task of drafting a program wide enough to include every shade of radical thought. The transactions of the county conventions provided a foretaste of intraparty conflict. Ottertail County Farmer Laborites adopted a resolution censoring Olson for partiality to big business and urban interests, while the radicals of Hennepin County called for a comprehensive public ownership program. Complicating the economic cleavage was the feud between regulars and "all-party" Olson supporters, which found expression in proposals to expel anyone backing a candidate not endorsed by the convention or the executive committee.

As in 1930, the Farmer Labor convention was strictly a one-man show. Olson gave the keynote address, guided the deliberations, and drew up the platform. Although not a single roll call marred the tranquility of the proceedings, the governor again dominated wholly by persuasion. He carefully avoided an open display of power, appearing only once on the floor of the convention.

His keynote address was the high point of the two-day meeting. He necessarily devoted considerable time to an account of his stewardship and an exposition of new policies that were to find their way into the platform. He skated quickly over the thin ice of patronage. Conceding that he had been forced to disappoint many of the faithful who sought state jobs, he defended his stand with the argument that the party was committed to the improvement of public service rather than to the creation of a political machine. With a touch of irony he observed that his strong devotion to public duty had meant the retention of Earle Brown in the Highway Department: "My friend has great police ability. I think that after November 8th, when he has been disillusioned, I will recommend that he be taken back again." [1]

On this neatly turned phrase Olson coasted away from patronage to a general denunciation of the Republican party. He indicted its platform as just so many "weasel words" and its candidates as tools of big business. He also condemned President Hoover for aiding the few at the top of the economic ladder while ignoring the masses at the bottom. The only defensive note in the speech was an indignant denial of charges against his moral character which enemies had been clandestinely circulating in the spring of 1932. [2]

In framing the party platform, Olson's strategy called for a gradual shift to the left. Encroachments upon the free enterprise system were to be exploratory and piecemeal. Remembering the damage done by the radical 1924 platform, he strove to avoid truculent language that would alienate the cautious voter or discredit the party. The preamble was permitted to announce that capitalism was "on trial for its life," but the statement burned no bridges; it merely served notice that henceforth the Farmer Labor party would scrutinize the system carefully rather than accept it uncritically. [3]

The main planks of the platform followed the same cautious line, appearing completely innocuous when measured against the socialistic constitution of the Farmer Labor Association. It was only by setting them beside comparable planks in the 1930 platform that their mild leftward orientation could be detected. Whereas the earlier document advocated only a state-owned printing press, the 1932 platform proposed state ownership of water and electric power. The most uncompromising planks called for unemployment insurance, a statewide old age pension, an income tax, and a license tax on chain stores. They were followed by a series of miscellaneous planks in favor of the St. Lawrence waterway, the veterans' bonus, the Frazier Bill to refinance mortgages at cheaper rates, and state taxation of margarine, which catered to sectional economic interests and cost the Farmer Laborites nothing.

Before adjourning, the convention adopted a resolution empowering a twelve-man committee to investigate the feasibility of a Farmer Labor presidential ticket. Although this meant the final decision would be left to Olson, party philosophy circumscribed his freedom of action. A literal interpretation of Farmer Labor principles would have obligated him to a national third party, because enactment of a real socialist program depended on control of the federal government. The very fact that the Farmer Laborites stood for a different organization of society than the older parties prohibited neutrality or cooperation with them.

Many Farmer Laborites took their articles of faith seriously and favored a national third party whatever the political consequence.[4] The group that pressed most actively to unify radicals was the League for Independent Political Action organized in 1930 by eastern socialists. The league made little impression on the midterm elections in Minnesota, but H. Y. Williams, its leading organizer, appeared in Minneapolis the following summer to discuss plans for a national third party. Simultaneously, R. M. Harrup, Farmer Labor leader in Iowa, asked Olson to call a conference of progressive leaders.

All these pressures made Olson uncomfortable. As a political realist he knew there were no third-party units outside Minnesota capable of waging a state campaign, to say nothing of a national campaign. He particularly resented the radical leaders who wanted to use the Minnesota Farmer Labor party as a base for their national ambitions. Remembering the complications created by the La Follette presidential campaign in 1924, Olson was quite cold to plans for a national third party in 1932. He always paid the proposal lip service, but contended that a presidential ticket could not win until healthy organizations were built up in neighboring states. He flatly refused to sponsor the call for a national meeting until third-party advocates met this condition, and he pointedly ignored H. Y. Williams when he came to Minneapolis. The *Farmer Labor Leader* was accurately expressing the Olson viewpoint when it observed that a practical leader could do nothing effective with several million progressives as long as they remained "an unorganized mass of discontent and diversity of opinion." [5]

The governor relented momentarily in December 1931 and issued a statement predicting a national third party unless one of the major parties nominated a progressive candidate, but the elation with which radicals greeted this pronouncement proved to be premature. Olson gave the project no further support and refused to attend the national convention of progressives at Omaha on April 26, 1932.[6] Convinced that a national third-party movement would be abortive in 1932, he tried to evolve a plan whereby Minnesota reformers would support a progressive presidential candidate in return for major party support of the Farmer Labor state ticket.

The most promising collaborator was the Democratic governor of New York, Franklin D. Roosevelt. He had gained the attention of Minnesota left-wingers because of his enthusiasm for public power projects. As early as May 1931 A. C. Welch, chairman of the Farmer Labor executive committee, talked about instructing presidential electors for Roosevelt, and about the same time Henry Teigan was telling friends that he did not favor a third-party ticket if Roosevelt received the Democratic nomination.[7] Olson probably shared their views, but dared not give public expression to such heretical doctrine as cooperation with a "capitalist" party.

The decisive event in the genesis of Farmer Labor-Democratic cooperation was Olson's chance meeting with Roosevelt at French Lick Springs, Indiana, where the annual governors' conference was held from May 31 to June 3, 1931. Between the formal sessions Olson and Roosevelt had an opportunity to exchange views and were pleasantly surprised by the similarity of their approach to economic problems. Some years later Olson recalled that he had been won to the Roosevelt candidacy at the Indiana conference by a striking speech the New York governor made in behalf of conservation and land utilization.[8]

The following spring when Roosevelt came to Minnesota for the Jefferson Day rally on April 18, he began his address in the St. Paul auditorium with a reference to "my colleague and friend, Governor Olson."[9] Later the two men had a private conference in the State Capitol. Undoubtedly politics came up for discussion, but the nomination of Roosevelt was still too uncertain for them to reach a definite understanding.

Olson's friendly reception of the New York governor, following so closely upon his convention speech attacking Hoover, strengthened the belief that he contemplated some kind of a tie-up with the Democrats. Many veteran Farmer Laborites objected to the idea. State Senator Victor Lawson recalled that the Democrats had swallowed up the Populists and predicted a similar fate for Farmer Laborites if they flirted with the enemy.[10] Old Knud Wefald, another of the party "nestors," also opposed an understanding with the Democrats.

Olson saw that he could not deliver the party vote unconditionally to Roosevelt. Nevertheless, he occupied an excellent bargaining position because his Farmer Laborites held the balance of power in Minnesota. Judicious application of pressure might push the Democratic party into a more radical position nationally and force concessions to his state ticket. If these tactics failed, he could return to his 1928 position, asking his followers to remain neutral in the presidential contest.

The prospects of cooperation with the Democrats depended partly on the outcome of their intraparty struggle in Minnesota. Since 1924 the lethargic state organization had been under the control of National Committeeman Joseph Wolf. Unlike most professional politicians, Wolf possessed a genuine social conscience, and though his progressivism was of an older and milder vintage than Olson's, he gave covert support to the newly organized Farmer Labor movement when his party went into its long postwar eclipse. In 1930 he delivered the Democratic vote to Olson, and when the latter found himself unable to reciprocate with Farmer Laborite support for Hoidale, Wolf generously attributed the failure to inability rather than bad faith and prudently left the door ajar for future cooperation.

Normally the Democratic party had such an insignificant following in Minnesota that nobody bothered to challenge Wolf's leadership. But as depression gradually undermined Republican incumbents, the prospect of a Democratic administration in Washington with countless political plums to distribute touched off a party struggle in Minnesota. Wolf's effort to swing the organization behind Roosevelt aroused the opposition of the top-heavy Irish majority. Aware of rumors regarding Al Smith's possible candidacy, they demanded at least an uninstructed delegation.

After the first of the year this movement gained momentum so rapidly that Wolf doubted his ability to control the regular convention scheduled for April. So he called a snap convention six weeks early which instructed delegates for Roosevelt and endorsed Dr. A. A. Van Dyke for governor.

These tactics split the party wide open. The Smith faction promptly called a rump convention which selected a set of Smith-instructed delegates and nominated John E. Regan of Mankato to run against Van Dyke in the Democratic primary. On the assumption that a clean-cut primary victory would assure recognition of their delegation at the national convention, the rumpers launched such an intensive campaign against Wolf and the regulars that the two factions became irreconcilable. Their feud cast fresh uncertainty on the question of Democratic-Farmer Labor cooperation.

Since Olson faced no opposition in his own party, he conducted only the most superficial preprimary campaign. Attendance at the annual governors' conference kept him out of

Minnesota the last ten days of April, and even after he returned, he made no swing around the state. He delivered a few formal addresses in late May and early June, but saved his heavy guns for the main campaign.

Interest in the Farmer Labor primary was sustained by the scramble for congressional nominations. Thirty-five candidates had filed for the nine seats to be filled at large. Almost all Farmer Laborites who had served the public in some capacity participated, but in spite of keen rivalry between the contestants, there was little mud-slinging or personal abuse.

The other parties did not escape so fortunately. The Republicans were confronted with a candidate who unexpectedly emerged to contest the nomination of Earle Brown. Shortly after the Republican state convention Tom Davis, perennial reformer and Farmer Labor candidate, solemnly proclaimed his identification with the G.O.P. and his determination to save the party by purifying it. He called on the rank and file to repudiate Earle Brown, whom he termed the candidate of reactionary business leaders. Calling a second convention at the West Hotel in Minneapolis on May 6, 1932, he presided as chairman, wrote the platform, and presented the new savior of the Republican party, F. F. Ellsworth, a former Nonpartisan Leaguer. The bewildered Ellsworth made a few ineffectual speeches, but Tom Davis put on a real show, embarking on a statewide tour and distributing thousands of pamphlets that charged Brown with tax dodging, membership in the Ku Klux Klan, and subservience to big business.

Nobody mistook this one-man rampage for a groundswell of discontent against the leadership of the Republican party. The *Minneapolis Journal* dryly observed that Davis was a good friend of the governor and hoped to soften up Brown for the Farmer Laborites by attacking him under Republican auspices.[11] Senator Regnier expressed the same opinion,[12] and Olson removed all doubt when he consulted Davis before substituting K. K. Solberg for Henry Arens, who declined a second nomination as lieutenant governor in order to seek a seat in congress.

The Ellsworth candidacy did not have the remotest chance of success, but it forced Brown to spend most of his time refuting the Davis charges. The episode amused everybody but the Republicans.

The preprimary campaign of the Democrats set new records for vituperation. The speeches of both regulars and rumpers deteriorated into pure mud-slinging. Regan accused his opponent of hiding in a butcher shop to avoid a debate, and Van Dyke's manager hotly retorted that the Mankato lawyer was an "unmitigated liar more to be pitied than scorned." [13]

The primary election vindicated the aggressive rumper tactics. Regan piled up a two-to-one victory over Van Dyke, thereby winning control of the state organization and improving the prospects of rumper recognition at the national convention.

The other party primaries ran truer to form. The Republican organization ground out a huge majority for Earle Brown, and the convention-endorsed Farmer Labor slate won easily.

Eight days after the primary the Democratic national convention partially reversed the rumpers' victory. Controlled by the Roosevelt forces, it refused to seat the pro-Smith delegation, recognizing instead the regulars, who promptly re-elected Wolf as national committeeman. This decision, coupled with the nomination of Roosevelt, cleared the way for Democratic-Farmer Labor cooperation.

The alliance fell far short of fusion. It called for the national Democratic leadership to keep hands off the state campaign and for Olson to deliver to Roosevelt as many Farmer Labor votes as possible. [14] Neither side could risk the public arrangements necessary to achieve more thorough collaboration. Simon-pure Farmer Laborites abhorred even informal arrangements with middle class parties, while the regular Democrats dared not show open friendliness for Olson lest they drive the rumpers to vote for Hoover.

These hard political facts drove cooperation underground. It operated in the ward and precinct clubs rather than from the hustings. The public statements of party leaders were monotonously orthodox. Joseph Wolf endorsed the Democratic ticket "all the way," while Olson carefully avoided outright endorsement of Roosevelt, although he predicted in July that "his public statements as presidential candidate will be direct and entirely progressive."[15] The alliance created a remarkable dispensation under which politicians refrained from telling the public how to vote.

Cooperation also suffered at the hands of firebrands in both parties who defied all efforts to control them. Regan flatly refused to lie down for Olson as Indrehus had done two years earlier, and on the other side Townley, H. Y. Williams, and others attacked Democrats as often as Republicans.

Nonetheless, the principals on both sides cooperated in good faith. After an interview with Roosevelt at Albany, Wolf announced that the national Democratic campaign would be distinct from the state campaign, and James A. Farley confirmed this arrangement.[16] Still more pointed was the deliberate omission of Democratic state leaders from regional party conferences. Beyond his slashing attacks on Hoover, Olson gave few public indications of solidarity with the Democrats. He actually had to repudiate the fusion committee organized for a joint Olson-Roosevelt campaign, but his preferences were not concealed from insiders who ran the local Farmer Labor clubs.[17]

Meanwhile, the deepening depression was tearing apart political alignments faster than they could be built. In February 1932 an ominous tone appeared in reports from rural Minnesota. Insurance and mortgage companies began to cut off all agricultural credit, including even the routine short-term loans for livestock feed. Minnesota farmers who had contracted mortgages at the height of the postwar land boom and renewed them at five-year intervals faced foreclosure and eviction. A steady drop in agricultural prices and income had made them poor risks. To aggravate their plight a swarm of grasshoppers descended on the northwestern counties in late spring. The Executive Council voted $50,000 to combat this scourge, but the fields were badly ravaged before help arrived.

These accumulating misfortunes created a general spirit of desperation in rural areas. Whether from inherent defects, fluctuations of the business cycle, or the machinations of Wall Street, the capitalistic system no longer provided the farmer a living. Reluctant to abandon his independence for collective action, he had waited more or less patiently for two years for a change in the economic weather. But the evaporation of credit and the imminence of mortgage foreclosures drove him to adopt some of the tactics of trade unions.

The organization created to solidify rural militance was an offshoot of the Farmers Union called the Farm Holiday Association. It proposed to raise the prices of nonperishable agricultural commodities by withholding them from the market. Such a scheme required a high degree of cooperation among farmers from the grain-growing states.

Precedent did not offer much encouragement. A gigantic farm strike arranged by the American Society of Equity in 1906 fell apart because those who abstained took over the markets of those who participated.[18] The Farm Holiday program ran this same risk, plus the additional risk that a strike in the United States would have little effect on commodity prices set in the world market. However, Holiday leaders counted upon farmer militance to overcome all obstacles. John Bosch, the organizer for Minnesota, believed a ten-day shutdown of marketing would exhaust the supply of basic commodities in storage and enable the farmer to fix retail prices like any other entrepreneur.

The strategy of the Holiday Association was to organize the sixteen bread-basket states before calling a strike. In Minnesota local units began to spring up all over the central counties during late August. Their spontaneous appearance was something of an illusion, because the association recruited most of its officers and personnel directly from the Farmers Union, which did not care to become legally involved in the strike.

The new organization failed to achieve rural solidarity. The conservative Farm Bureau, which was composed of the more prosperous farmers, denounced the strike proposal in unsparing terms. The large dairy cooperatives were even more hostile because they had nothing to gain by withholding perishable commodities from the market and feared that a strike would interfere with the delivery of feed crops. Nevertheless there was a large bloc of desperate farmers in western Minnesota ready to give any program a trial.

The effect of the Farm Holiday Association on the political campaign could not be easily calculated. Olson's radical supporters urged him to endorse the program on the ground that he would achieve national stature as a farm leader, but others urged caution because many farmers and businessmen opposed a strike.[19] His own sympathies undoubtedly lay with the Holiday Association. He had always believed that collective action was the only method by which the depressed classes could force a redress of grievances, and the strike proposal seemed to be a step in that direction. But if Olson allowed himself to be maneuvered into the position of condoning violence and lawlessness, he would lose his more conservative followers.

Habitual discretion triumphed, and the governor's statements contained equivocation without destroying hope. In a speech at Princeton on August 26 he defended the right of farmers to organize and suggested a statewide cooperative federation of forty-six hundred local units to ensure the success of the Farm Holiday program.[20] The advice was both sound and harmless, since a federation that included everything from livestock shipping associations to filling stations could never agree on a policy.

Later statements reflected the same specious militance. Olson forthrightly defended the constitutional right of farmers to strike[21] but balanced this concession to radical sentiment by denouncing the use of violence. In fact, he became so alarmed by the violent encounters between Holiday pickets and truck drivers in Iowa, where irate farmers had started a wildcat strike, that he began to explore avenues of compromise. Partly on his initiative, a meeting of midwestern governors was convened at Sioux City, Iowa, on September 9.

Although little could be done for agriculture on a state or regional basis, the conference provided an excellent safety valve for rural discontent. The Iowa Holiday Association suspended its strike for twenty-four hours out of respect for the governors, and twelve thousand farmers clad in overalls and work shirts greeted them with a gigantic parade. The rest of the day farmers lounged in hotel lobbies and milled around in the streets, while the governors listened patiently to the proposals of their spokesmen. From noon until midnight there was a steady stream of petitioners. Even the cranks managed to secure a hearing. One of them advocated the growing of sunflowers to solve the agricultural crisis,[22] and another gesticulated so wildly in explaining his pet plan that a bottle of whisky flew out of his overcoat pocket, breaking at Olson's feet and drenching his shoes.

On the second day of the conference Holiday leaders confronted the governors with their official program: (1) a floor under agricultural prices which would ensure farmers return of the cost of production, (2) a moratorium on all mortgages and chattels until prices increased to that cost-return level, and (3) enactment of the Frazier Bill to refinance farm loans at lower rates of interest.

Inasmuch as most of these proposals required congressional action, the Holiday Association demanded stopgap action in the form of mortgage moratoriums and embargoes on the export of farm commodities. Holiday leaders threatened to call a nationwide strike on September 20 unless the governors complied with this demand. Not one of the state executives was willing to make an unconstitutional proclamation, so the Sioux City negotiations broke down completely.

Thereafter Olson worked to extract a pledge from Minnesota

Holiday leaders outlawing violence, and he finally succeeded on the eve of the strike. But John Bosch proved unable to control his own following. Two days before the September 20 deadline, local enthusiasts in Nobles County called a sympathy strike to support their Iowa brethren and sent out three hundred pickets to turn back produce trucks on the ten state roads leading into Worthington.

Discipline improved during the first week of the national strike, but when it became apparent that unsympathetic farmers were shipping great quantities of nonperishable commodities to market, sentiment for active picketing and road blocks revived rapidly. In western Minnesota, farmers blocked off nine areas on September 29, using force to stop truck drivers. Two weeks later they made a concerted effort to tighten the noose around the Twin Cities. Pickets sealed off the main approaches by placing nail-studded planks across the highway and turning back produce trucks.

Olson winked at these practices, but the county authorities were not so tolerant. The sheriff of Anoka County recruited forty special deputies on October 18, armed them with ax handles, and drove one hundred and fifty pickets off the main highway. The State Highway Patrol completed the job by raiding the remaining picket camps the next day and smashing their nail-studded planks.

The destruction of the siege lines around the Twin Cities foreshadowed the end of the strike. It was a symptom of failure rather than a cause. The basic weakness lay in the inability of the Holiday Association to mobilize rural opinion solidly behind its program. The resort to blockade and violent picketing was an open admission that farmers had not cooperated in withholding commodities at the source. Moreover, the strike had little effect on market conditions. Continued low prices led to defections. This resulted in a larger flow of goods to market, which in turn produced further defections, breaking the back of the farm strike at the end of October.

The strike subsided rather than ended in Minnesota. Organized activity was quietly suspended before the election, partly to save face and partly to avoid embarrassing the governor.[23] The Farm Holiday Association blamed local authorities for the removal of road blocks, and even the intervention of the State Highway Patrol did not impair Olson's standing in the strikers' camp. Fortunately, the agitation subsided in time to spare him the choice between calling troops to clear the roads and condoning lawlessness.

The economic conditions that produced a farm strike also made for desperation in the big cities. Unemployment advanced like a creeping paralysis until it had struck down nearly one third of the labor force. On the Iron Range conditions had become so depressed by October 1932 that seventy percent of the workers were either totally unemployed or working a maximum of six days a month.[24] According to prevalent economic practice, responsibility for relieving destitution devolved on the county governments. Unfortunately, most of them lacked sufficient resources to shoulder the burden. The rising curve of tax delinquency made it difficult for the counties to provide routine services, much less relief. Cook County had to open its jails because it lacked funds to feed the prisoners.

Perhaps the state government ought to have assumed part of the burden, but Olson had been under fire steadily since the summer of 1931 for the high cost of state government and he knew his opponents intended to wage the fall campaign on this issue. A special session would simply give them another forum from which to assail him for extravagance. Also, they controlled enough votes to block relief appropriations. The probable outcome of a special session hardly justified the risk.

The federal government was left as the sole source of relief. There seemed little chance, however, that its resources would be made available on a large scale as long as Hoover remained president. He preferred to stimulate recovery by expanding credit facilities for sound business ventures rather than by appropriating funds for the direct relief of needy individuals.

Eventually the pressure on Hoover became so strong that he signed a compromise bill releasing limited funds to the states. Olson, who had bombarded the President off and on with requests for various relief projects, took advantage of this legislation to secure grants of $657,506 and $696,467 for Minnesota. The money was distributed in accordance with the regulations of the State Board of Control, reaching in most cases the neediest families. But like the private relief expenditures of the preceding winter, it proved entirely inadequate to prevent destitution.

The suffering of the unemployed did not lead to a conspicuous protest like the farm strike, but it intensified urban radicalism. Toward the close of 1932 even moderates were demanding that the government take over the services which capitalism could not or would not provide.

The radical drift of popular sentiment was most congenial to Olson. Wanting to extend the functions of government for the benefit of the underprivileged, he edged slowly leftward during the year. Many of his political speeches were educational in tone, designed to accustom people to the idea of government intervention. In a notable address at Red Wing he developed his argument clearly: "The old pioneer idea of government as confined to police power has passed off the stage. We have now reached the socialized state. Just how far it shall extend its functions and services is no longer a matter of theory but a problem of practice and expediency. The present economic system has shown its inability to provide employment and even food or shelter for millions of Americans. Only government can cope with the situation." [25]

Olson frequently spoke about the curative function of government, laying special emphasis on the taxation power. Properly applied, he said, it could redress the haphazard distribution of wealth under the capitalistic system and provide social services for the underprivileged. He conceded that this was strong medicine but presented it as the only alternative to complete socialization of wealth. Characteristically, he took a position on middle ground, attacking capitalism as a system "steeped in the most dismal stupidity"[26] but rejecting socialism except as a last resort. His plea for expanded governmental functions soon received practical expression in New Deal legislation. But while Roosevelt talked about a balanced budget and tariff reduction, Olson described the shape of things to come. He set out for a promised land halfway between Populism and socialism.

The frenzied campaign oratory and the indignant charges and countercharges of party leaders partially concealed the fact that depression was the decisive factor in 1932. Throughout the nation, it loaded the ballot boxes against incumbents except where they moved clearly and decisively to the left. Olson escaped the general fate because he assessed the popular mood correctly and because he joined forces with the Democratic presidential candidate.

He also benefited from the fact that neither of his opponents could match him as a campaigner. Earle Brown was a genial standpatter of the McKinley vintage, orthodox and regular in every way. He appealed to the Republican leadership principally because of his wide personal contacts. As head of the Minnesota Highway Patrol he had met political and business leaders all over the state who were attracted by his friendly, easygoing manner. But the folksy, middle-aged businessman simply could not be built up as an attractive political leader.

Brown was intensely uncomfortable whenever he mounted the platform and betrayed his inward agitation even before he began a speech. To prevent the contrast from being painful, he refused to appear on the same platform with Olson. He flatly turned down all offers of debate, making careful arrangements to be in southern Minnesota when the League of Women Voters held a joint meeting for candidates in Minneapolis. He even allowed his running mate, T. O. Streissguth, and the state auditor, Stafford King, to substitute for him in several major addresses.

Another handicap for Brown, especially in a depression year,

Cartoon from the Farmer Labor Leader, *August 15, 1932*

was his well-publicized wealth. Farmer Laborites indignantly denounced him as an irresponsible plutocrat and imaginatively described his sinister connection with big business. They also charged him with tax dodging, insisting that he had secured an assessment of $2044 on thirty-eight prize Belgian horses in 1928, after these had been valued at $125,000 by livestock experts.[27] Republican headquarters issued a convincing denial, but the damage was already done. Possession of prize horses in such troubled times aroused disgust rather than envy. Third-party orators repeatedly referred to the "gentleman" farmer and his "thoroughbred Belgians," and radical publications carried cartoons about "the famous 38."

Brown was also vulnerable because he had been an outspoken nationalist during the war era. Whether or not he belonged to the Ku Klux Klan and other antiforeign organizations as his opponents contended, the accusation made real trouble for him in Minnesota, where many voters were first- or second-generation Americans.

With depression cutting deeply into their strength, the Republicans could hardly have chosen a candidate more poorly equipped than Brown to restore public confidence in the party.

The Democratic candidate for governor, John E. Regan, did not offer Olson much more competition than Earle Brown. His chief asset was his party label, and even that became valueless as a result of the informal cooperation between Roosevelt and Olson. The bitter quarrel between rumpers and regulars for control of the party left its mark on Regan, and the public lost sight of his generous, Celtic disposition as the factional fight goaded him into ever more intemperate statements.

He became the angry man of the campaign, venting his spleen on all within range. He attacked the regular Democrats for supporting fusion, Olson for trying to ride Roosevelt's coattails, the Republicans for getting the country into a mess. Only the most elementary political necessities prevented him from denouncing Roosevelt, whom he heartily disliked for beating Smith and cooperating with the Farmer Laborites. Regan's campaign managers suffered through every address he made because they could never be sure what he would say. Even when the text had been prepared in advance, Regan sometimes got so worked up emotionally that he launched into an extemporaneous discussion of issues.

Another troublesome matter was Regan's record in the state legislature. Conservative in his approach to economic questions, he had voted consistently with the Republicans during the 1931 session. Consequently, when he tried to don the toga of a reformer in 1932, he was vulnerable to Olson's attack. In a speech at Mankato the governor pointed out that "Regan fulminates against extravagance, but sat on a legislative investigating committee which failed to file a report, complains about superfluous bureaus, but urged the creation of a state board of embalmers, proposes farm relief, but championed a license tax on hogs." [28] Such jibes made a joke of the Regan candidacy.

The weakness of his two opponents encouraged Olson to shift the emphasis of the Farmer Labor campaign to national issues. This was a drastic departure from his 1924 position, when he had indignantly denied that national issues had anything to do with a state election. Along with countless other candidates, he found it profitable to run against Hoover in 1932 and managed to reverse himself without visible embarrassment.

Olson set the pace in his keynote address on October 3, castigating the President for idleness during the crisis and failure to do his duty by humanity. He jabbed still harder at Hoover in later speeches, charging him with indifference to the plight of the farmers and unemployed. Taking their cue from the governor, third-party orators reworked this theme with minor variations at every crossroads in Minnesota.

Under ordinary circumstances such unrestrained abuse would have resulted in a reaction for the victim, but 1932 was not an ordinary year. To the great mass of bankrupt farmers and jobless workers, defeat of the national administration had become a necessity. They would cheer attacks on Hoover when they would cheer at nothing else.[29] Farmer Laborites capitalized on this mood by picturing the G.O.P. state organization as a miniature replica of the Republican party and Earle Brown as the local agent of the President.

Despite its seeming strength, the Farmer Labor party was seriously afflicted with internal disturbances. The addition of nine congressional nominees to the regular list of statewide candidates created a babel of voices and blurred the tone of the campaign. Townley advocated the most extreme and irresponsible schemes; Teigan hit at Democrats as well as Republicans; H. H. Peterson, candidate for attorney general, talked telephone rates in rural areas; K. K. Solberg lambasted everything; and F. H. Shoemaker, who was running for a congressional seat, interlarded his attacks on Hoover with all manner of fantastic promises.

Also, the old feud between the simon-pure radicals and the all-party supporters of Olson flared up intermittently. A number of prominent Farmer Laborites boycotted the Olson keynote address because they were not asked to sit on the platform by the all-party group that arranged the rally. Hard feelings also developed between regular candidates and those who wore the Farmer Labor label but flirted with the all-party group. J. P. Kvale and C. F. Gaarenstrom were especially resented because they conducted their congressional campaigns without reference to over-all Farmer Labor strategy.

Much to the disgust of party regulars, Senator Shipstead maintained his customary independence during the campaign. In reply to a direct request from the Farmer Labor executive committee for help, the senator stated that he would make his own speaking dates and campaign for progressive candidates without regard to party. This attitude did not reflect hostility toward Olson. In fact, the senator went far beyond his grudging endorsement of 1930, telling a Labor Day audience that the governor's record "has taken him out of the category of politicians, and made him an outstanding statesman." [30]

But Shipstead refused to mention the Farmer Labor party by name or to endorse any of its congressional candidates except his colleague, Representative J. P. Kvale. To make matters worse, he urged the re-election of Republican Congressman Victor Christgau, who was running as an independent. This cavalier disregard of party ties intensified the factional quarrels in 1932 and prepared the way for the bitter fight against Shipstead's renomination two years later.

When all these disruptive tendencies are taken into account it is remarkable that the Farmer Labor party withstood destruction. The key to its survival seems to lie in the easy tolerance of the leaders toward breaches in discipline, Olson's ability to reconcile opposites, and the alluring prospects of victory. Such cohesive factors outweighed the demoralizing effect of party warfare.

Farmer Labor quarrels gave little comfort to Republicans, who faced the discouraging task of reversing a national trend. As early as February they had concluded that the campaign could be won only by minimizing the connection between Minnesota Republicans and the Hoover administration. After a feverish search for suitable local issues, they decided to emphasize the increased tax rate as an example of Farmer Labor extravagance and a cause of the depression. Accordingly, they based their entire campaign on the contention that Olson's unsound fiscal policies had produced the economic crisis.[31]

The governor answered this charge in several ways. He argued that the reduction of revenue from iron ore and railroad taxes had raised the burden on land, and blamed his budget increase on his predecessor's policy of deferring essential maintenance and construction. He also insisted that the total appropriations would be lower for 1931 than for 1929 if certificates of indebtedness were added in. These explanations did not do Olson much good. Discussions of fiscal policy bored the voters, and no amount of reasoning, specious or otherwise, could explain away the fact that taxes had increased.

Recognizing that the constant emphasis on government economy had slowed down the Farmer Labor offensive, Brown followed up in mid-September with a clever but irresponsible pledge to cut the budget by $5,000,000 and still maintain all essential services.

Olson denounced the Brown pledge as a fake, saying he could "teach a parrot to sit up and talk about reducing taxes $5,000,000." [32] He challenged the Republicans to specify where the cut could be made. "Do they expect to take it from education? Do they expect to take it from the state's children, from the needy, from the physically and mentally defective?"

The sharpness of his speech betrayed Olson's irritation at being forced onto the defensive. He was sure the Republican pledge could not be kept, but he sensed its dangerous appeal and the necessity for presenting a counterproposal of his own. Consequently, on October 7 he promised to have a state budget embodying substantial reductions prepared before the election.

This was nothing more than a grandstand play to outdo the Republicans. Olson knew that a valid breakdown of budget estimates could not be produced in a month. He also knew the political risk of releasing detailed figures during a campaign. So nobody was surprised when the governor presented an apology instead of a budget, with the bland assurance that estimates indicated a minimum cut of $3,187,000.

The agitation over economy proved to be a teapot tempest, but the amount of time Olson devoted to the issue in October suggests that it bothered him considerably. All other Republican efforts to put the governor on the defensive failed, although his subordinates frequently expressed concern over the whispering campaign about his private life that was carried on behind his back.[33]

As usual, Olson put on a strenuous campaign, speaking in every part of the state and shaking hands with thousands of voters. He appeared at most of the county fairs and Farmer Labor picnics in the late summer and started his major swing around the circuit after the keynote address on October 3. He spent three weeks among the economy-minded farmers of southern Minnesota, paused in the central counties for a few days, and wound up the tour with a heavy week of campaigning on the Iron Range. The final days were reserved for a series of radio addresses and personal appearances in the populous Twin Cities.

After mid-September there could be no doubt as to the trend of public sentiment. Voters listened grimly to indictments of the national administration and cheered wildly at all predictions of impending change. In every part of the state the postwar aversion to radicalism was collapsing.

On election day the voters went to the polls determined to wreak vengeance on the Republicans. Olson won an outright majority over his two opponents, the final count showing: Olson 522,438; Brown 334,081; Regan 169,851. Franklin D. Roosevelt gained an equally impressive victory over Hoover.

Olson could take pride in his achievement. He piled up heavy majorities in the big cities and the Red River Valley, winning every county north of the Minnesota River except Stearns. Only in the south did he recede from his margin in the preceding election. In 1930 the prosperous farmers of the southern counties had cast a spite vote against the Republican party, but in 1932 many of them returned to their traditional allegiance or voted Democratic. Olson's political philosophy held no attraction for them, while his advanced position on government spending and his flirtations with the radical Farm Holiday Association aroused their active hostility.

The defection of the south foreshadowed the end of the honeymoon period for Olson. Despite his exceptional skill in welding together diverse groups, he could not be all things to all men in a time of crisis. As the political revolution of 1932 sought to express itself in far-reaching economic changes, Olson's position as mediator between the two wings of the Farmer Labor party became increasingly untenable. His second term opened with an ambitious attempt to lead the revolution while reassuring men of property. It closed with Olson branded as a dangerous radical and fighting for his political life.

# Chapter VII THE EMERGENCE OF A RADICAL

W<small>ITH</small> the election over, politicians of all parties turned their attention to the problem of organizing the new legislature. The Farmer Laborites had improved their prospects by devoting considerable effort to winning local elections. Although Olson had not indulged in a systematic purge campaign, many of his speeches contained denunciations of opponents in the legislature. And his efforts were ably seconded by the railroad brotherhoods, who sent questionnaires to nominees asking whether they would attend a liberal or a conservative caucus if elected.[1]

This kind of pressure aroused the resentment of candidates who wanted to run with both hares and hounds, but it also stimulated a healthy popular interest in the presession maneuvering which redounded to the benefit of the Farmer Laborites. Even so, they were confronted with numerous obstacles. Nothing could be done about the senate because the entire membership had been elected for a four-year term in 1930. And the nonpartisan election system had prevented Farmer Laborites from securing an outright majority in the house. They controlled about one third of the membership and the Republicans approximately the same number, leaving the decision in the hands of about forty doubtful representatives. Both sides bid feverishly for their support.

Olson, who departed for a vacation shortly after the election, left the administration campaign in the hands of Representatives

Hjalmar Petersen and Dewey Johnson.[2] To attract the waverers, they proposed a nonpartisan progressive coalition and selected Charlie Munn, a radical Republican, for speaker. They also called a caucus for November 26 and sent a letter to new members warning them against "lining up with W. I. Norton, R. W. Hitchcock, J. R. Sweitzer, and other utility-minded members." Vince Day supplemented this effort with telegrams endorsing Munn as the administration candidate and urging progressives to attend the caucus.[3]

The conservatives in retaliation called their own caucus a week earlier and to create bandwagon sentiment predicted an attendance of ninety. Only fifty-five legislators showed up and several of these tried to back out after they discovered that the conservatives were eleven short of a majority.

When the progressives assembled on November 26, Olson appeared in person to lead the fight for Munn. He justified this unprecedented open participation in the organization of the legislature by saying, "I am here in behalf of the people with a clear mandate for the program I have sponsored."[4] He denounced the leaders of the conservative caucus as representatives of the chain banks and pledged himself to work for a liberal organization in the senate as well as the house.

Sixty-five legislators declared themselves for Munn. The addition of four proxies gave the progressives a majority of three.* Olson tried to consolidate this precarious margin by a series of personal interviews with the more doubtful legislators, while Munn passed out patronage plums to the new recruits so rapidly that all positions at his disposal were filled by the first of December.[5]

The conservatives did their best to keep Olson on the anxious seat. Andrew Finstuen, their candidate for speaker, sent out letters to all representatives but avowed Farmer Laborites, asking that they specify their committee preferences. Through

---

* Charles B. Cheney claimed that the proxy of an absent member was voted without authorization, and this made the necessary sixty-six and caused three waverers to climb on the bandwagon. (*Minneapolis Journal*, January 3, 1933.)

the columns of his newspaper, the *Kenyon Leader,* Finstuen argued that the Munn coalition was a clique of urban representatives who sought to wrest authority from the farmers.[6] He also insinuated that Olson had intervened in the organization of the legislature so that pending investigations of the administration would be in friendly hands.

These efforts to undermine the progressive majority proved futile, and when the house convened in January it elected Munn speaker by a vote of seventy-four to fifty-six.

The victory of the administration was more apparent than real. The house did not pass into the control of zealous Farmer Laborites but of cautious reformers in the major parties. To win at all, Olson had been forced to sign away the key committee chairmanships as well as the speakership. At best, he would have to fight for the adoption of Farmer Labor measures.

Despite the fact that Olson was saddled with an avowedly hostile senate and a lukewarm house, events played into his hands. The wave of mortgage foreclosures and bank failures that broke on the nation during the early months of 1933 induced widespread panic. Sullen resentment yielded to an unreasoning fear from which no group was immune. Even the middle class succumbed as evaporating savings accounts crumbled its confidence. Farmers, laborers, and businessmen, so long at each other's throats, cried in unison for strong leadership. Momentarily at least, a common desire for resolute action submerged their antagonisms.

The incoming Democratic president was the major beneficiary of this new spirit of cooperation, but Governor Olson shared the happy effects of it in Minnesota. Outspoken criticism of the existing system had set him apart from the political and business leaders who resisted change, and when events thoroughly discredited the obstructionists, people instinctively turned to the governor for guidance.

The enhanced stature of Olson as a tribune of the people was soon reflected in his relations with the legislature. The uncertain veering and shifting so characteristic of his first administration ceased abruptly. He goaded and whipped the legislature into action, appealing to the people whenever it proved recalcitrant. Four times he lashed his opponents mercilessly from the steps of the State Capitol, where impoverished farmers and workers gathered to protest the postponement of relief legislation. Each week he made a radio report of his stewardship to the people. Sensing that the general feeling of calamity gave him an opportunity to shift the axis of society leftward, he worked for the enactment of the Farmer Labor program with grim determination.

In the role of militant crusader Olson's prestige reached its zenith. He became the public conscience of the state and the alter ego of the masses. His personal activities made it clear that his concern for destitute citizens flowed from genuine humanitarian instincts rather than from cynical political motives. When spokesmen for the unemployed made a demonstration for social legislation, he invited them to lunch at the Capitol cafeteria and paid the bill. He sometimes passed out as much as fifty dollars a day to suppliants, although he had no income besides his salary.

But he never forgot that people had pride and feelings. Invariably he softened objections to charity by saying, "That's all right, I'm just loaning it to you. You can pay me back someday when you get a job again."[7] Much of his time was spent in trying to secure work for the unfortunates who thronged his office. And when jobs completely disappeared, he gave money for all sorts of self-help projects, on one occasion contributing five hundred dollars to establish an opportunity shop for destitute women.[8]

He accepted without protest the most outrageous demands on his time. An endless stream of suppliants flowed through his home on Sundays, and his unlisted telephone rang incessantly. Frequently Mrs. Olson would have to intervene so the governor could get a hot meal. He hated to turn down petitioners who had waited all day in the outer office for an interview and sometimes invited them to drive back to Minneapolis with him so they could present their problems on the way.[9]

No individual was too insignificant to warrant his attention. During August 1933 he interrupted work he was doing in Washington to visit a Negro sentenced to death there for murder.[10] As county attorney Olson had convicted the man of robbery, then had freed him when careful study indicated a miscarriage of justice. He had told the man to call on him at any time for help. Now, years later, the Negro, hearing that Olson was in Washington, asked to see him, and the governor made the trip to the death cell as a self-imposed penance for a wrong done many years earlier.

Olson always took a special interest in the welfare of young people. His experience as county attorney had convinced him that youth would go straight if given a decent environment and trustworthy guidance. He conducted virtually a one-man campaign to secure federal relief funds for the education of unemployed youth,[11] and he always took pains to give young people honest advice. Some of his most straightforward interviews were given to high school newspapers.[12] When talking to groups of teen-agers, Olson dropped the equivocation that so frequently characterized his political pronouncements. Guy Stanton Ford of the University of Minnesota rated him a favorite with the students because of the "frankness with which he shot back answers and the fairness with which he treated the questioner."[13] He firmly believed that the salvation of the country depended upon the education of youth, and strongly urged college graduates to forsake the business world for unselfish careers in government service. He tried to bring promising young men into the state administration, although his efforts were persistently hampered by niggardly pay scales.

Olson never professed formal allegiance to the Christian religion, but his daily life was suffused with its spirit. The recollection of early hardships, instead of breeding the complacent, scornful pride of the self-made man, stirred his sympathy for the lowly.

Olson rarely spoke of his inner life, but on one occasion he told Leif Gilstad, political writer for the *Minneapolis Journal,* how the memory of his humble origins both sobered and heartened him. "I find now and then when I get smug with position and perhaps inclining to forget — or if my spirits are low — I go down into the Gateway * and bum around a bit. It brings me back on my feet, and puts new fight in me." [14] Behind the flintlike facade of the political realist was the warm heart of a sentimentalist who fought in his own faltering and sometimes unethical way for the day when the meek would inherit the earth. It was this spirit of Christian brotherhood that gave a fleeting touch of greatness to the Olson administration.

Olson's second inaugural address gave Minnesota a foretaste of things to come. Alluding to the poverty and distress of the time, he expressed fear that "rampant lawlessness and possible revolution" would develop unless the legislature adopted strong remedial measures.[15] Then he launched into a long series of recommendations to combat the depression. For the relief of agriculture he urged a state income tax and amendments to the legal regulations on mortgages that would encourage adjustment rather than eviction. To implement the latter proposal, he requested (1) the extension of the period between delinquency and foreclosure to two years, and (2) the creation of machinery for the negotiation of reduced rentals after foreclosure so that mortgagors could remain on their farms.

A companion group of measures to relieve industrial workers called for (1) unemployment insurance financed exclusively by employers, (2) extension of the relief powers of the state Executive Council to include those suffering from economic distress,† and (3) the prohibition of injunctions in labor disputes.

These were followed by proposals to increase taxes on cor-

* A downtown district in Minneapolis in which, during the depression of the 1930s, many of the unemployed tended to congregate.

† The Executive Council already possessed authority to relieve calamity distress (i.e., flood, fire, and drought).

porations and extend public ownership. Specifically, Olson demanded a graduated tax on chain stores, an increase in the gross earnings tax of public utilities and railroads, and a constitutional amendment to permit state development of power resources. However, he indicated that in lieu of a pure state ownership program he would accept legislation enabling municipally owned power plants to extend their operations beyond the city limits.

Conservatives received the Olson program with anger and dismay. His proposals for unemployment insurance, public relief, and the readjustment of mortgage burdens at the creditor's expense carried the inescapable implication that prosperous citizens were to be taxed to support their less fortunate brethren. The calamity atmosphere prevented open obstruction of remedial measures, but defenders of the old order quietly prepared a depth defense in the Minnesota legislature.

The conflict between Olson and the conservatives was postponed by the specter of agrarian revolt and the paralysis of the banking system.

Alarming rumors of lawlessness were drifting out of western Minnesota. The year for the redemption of farms engulfed by the foreclosure wave in the spring of 1932 was rapidly drawing to a close, and since the intervening months had brought no relief, the curve of evictions and sheriff's sales mounted ominously. Driven to desperation by the prospect of utter ruin, farmers prepared to resist foreclosure sales with force. They rebelled against a legal process that deprived them of property representing a lifetime of sweat and toil.

Their extralegal activities were organized and systematized by the Farm Holiday Association. Its officers investigated the circumstances in each foreclosure sale in the western counties and drew up plans for obstruction when the worthiness of the victim was beyond question. In the case of chattel mortgages, teams of farmers carrying shotguns passed through the crowd during the sale, intimidating all prospective bidders so the items, bought for three or four cents apiece, could be returned to the original owner.

Where a farm was to be auctioned at a sheriff's sale, agents notified all farmers in the township when the sale would take place. About fifteen minutes before the appointed hour, grim, silent men would filter into the county courthouse, filling it so full that the sheriff was unable to get through the crowd to post his sale. Each time he tried to work his way out, the ranks would draw more tightly together. Finally a Farm Holiday spokesman would urge the sheriff to phone the governor for permission to call off the sale. Since the sheriff could not initiate a postponement without violating his oath of office or forfeiting his bond, he usually acted on this advice and found that Olson would grant the necessary permission to avert violence. In this manner the mortgagor gained a short breathing spell while the sheriff went through the process over again of advertising the sale of the farm.

Extremists hoped the agitation in western Minnesota would get sufficiently out of hand to permit a general debt repudiation. A. C. Townley, believing a revolutionary situation had been created by mid-February, urged a march of one hundred thousand farmers on the State Capitol to demand debt legislation. Anticipating obstruction from the conservatives, he proposed that the farmers forcibly take over both houses and pass the law themselves.[16]

John Bosch, whose Holiday Association had stimulated the revolutionary ferment, insisted that he sought only a statutory remedy.[17] But his behavior put him in the equivocal position of advocating unlawful action to created sentiment for a legal solution. Perhaps violence was required to call public attention to the farmer's plight.

The governor was deeply concerned about developments in the western counties. He felt genuine sympathy for the farmers but disapproved of their recourse to extralegal methods. For all his incendiary oratory and aggressive political tactics, Olson believed the democratic process was adequate to cope with all problems. At the height of the agitation he rebuked the farmers for tarnishing a just cause by resorting to force.[18]

Unfortunately, Olson faced an almost impossible task in devising valid legal remedies. The federal courts had always interpreted the constitutional prohibition against the impairment of contracts so strictly that he considered it useless to attempt statutory relief or to proclaim a mortgage moratorium.[19] Nevertheless there was widespread sentiment for summary action, whether it was constitutional or not. Delegations of farm officials and state legislators urged Olson to issue an executive order suspending mortgage payments, and the judiciary committees of both houses received more than thirty bills providing for some kind of relief from mortgage foreclosure.

Senator Sherman Child, chairman of the senate Judiciary Committee, felt that any kind of relief would be unconstitutional and refused to report out any of the bills. Representative John A. Weeks, head of the corresponding committee in the house, was somewhat less defeatist. He appointed a subcommittee to consider various bills and made a thorough personal study of debt legislation. He and the subcommittee together gradually worked up a bill which left the mortgage principal and rate of interest intact but slowed up the foreclosure procedure.

Meanwhile the rising tide of mortgage foreclosures was causing fresh violence and increased interference with mortgage sales. Legal procedures threatened to break down completely in western Minnesota. The governor dared not wait for national action — or for the legislature either.

On February 23 Olson issued a proclamation halting all mortgage sales until May 1. He justified this extraordinary step on the ground that violence threatened the state: "I am doing that which I could do under martial law without declaring martial law to halt impending riots and insurrection. It is my duty as governor to preserve law and order in the state. The duty is imposed by the state constitution and carries with it implied power to perform it. The express power under the

Cartoon by John Baer, from the Farmer Labor Leader,
January 30, 1934

constitution would be to call out the militia to preserve law and order, and the alternative would be to remove the cause of such disturbance." [20]

The moratorium proclamation created confusion all over Minnesota. Some sheriffs postponed sales in accordance with Olson's instructions, while others, fearful of forfeiting their bonds, defied the governor. Lawyers tirelessly debated the constitutionality of the proclamation. The uproar subsided partially on March 2, when the legislature rushed through a temporary measure legalizing the postponement of foreclosures by Olson and relieving sheriffs of the usual publication requirements. Seven days later the Ramsey County court upheld the law as a valid exercise of legislative power, but it pointedly refrained from passing on the legality of the governor's proclamation.

We can only guess at Olson's motives in suspending mortgage payments by executive proclamation. He knew he lacked the authority to take such a step.[21] Apparently the threat of bloodshed in western Minnesota convinced him that only a dramatic gesture would save the situation. Or he may have thought an extreme step would focus public opinion on the mortgage problem and thereby force quick action by the legislature.

Recognizing the legislature's stopgap act for what it was, Representative Weeks whipped his mortgage moratorium bill into final shape. As passed by the house, it gave to the holder of land on a mortgage past due an extension of the redemption period until May 1, 1935. The district court, which granted applications for extension, was also to fix tax and rental payments during the period.

Senator Child fought a stubborn rear-guard action against the Weeks Bill, but Olson's proclamation had generated such strong sentiment for action that the senator was overborne by his colleagues, and the state supreme court upheld the law.[22] The mortgage moratorium legislation did not solve the problem of farm debts, but it did provide a measure of relief until the federal government could institute a large-scale program for agriculture.

As the rebellion against mortgage foreclosures was reaching its climax, the banking structure of the nation threatened to collapse completely. The financial panic that toppled great urban financial citadels in January and February simply dramatized a trend that had begun much earlier in rural areas where many of the smaller institutions held farm mortgages whose value dropped along with land prices. The mortality rate for banks was so high in Minnesota that the total number decreased from 1536 to 704 during the twelve years after 1921.[23] As a result, the fresh rash of bank failures in early 1933 looked less like a crisis than a worsening of an already chronic malady.

Long before acute paralysis was reached in March 1933, the state administration took steps to prop up the flimsy banking structure of Minnesota under the direction of Banking Commissioner John N. Peyton, a conservative financier whom Olson had appointed to the dismay of the currency cranks. When Peyton took office he sought to establish confidence in state banks by permitting closed banks to reopen only when they met a standard of fifty percent liquidity.[24] This stringent requirement created enemies for the administration among depositors in rural communities, who resented outside supervision and optimistically assumed that securities would appreciate if a bank reopened.[25]

Peyton, however, wanted to go farther and set up definitive standards for banks still open. With this end in view, he guided a bill through the legislature which granted the commissioner emergency powers to close banks and to specify the conditions under which they could operate. Olson signed the bill, assuring the public that it removed the necessity for a bank holiday. But as soon as Olson had boarded an eastbound train to attend Roosevelt's inauguration, Twin City bankers, who feared ruinous runs the next Saturday morning, prevailed on Acting Governor K. K. Solberg to proclaim a holiday.

When Olson received word that his solemn assurances had been set at naught, he was furious. Already partially incapacitated by a severe attack of appendicitis, he decided to return home at once. But before leaving Chicago, he conducted such a heated inquisition of state officials over the telephone that John P. Devaney, one of his political advisers, wired his train in alarm, pleading with him not to make any premature statements for publication.[26]

By the time he reached Minneapolis, the governor had calmed down sufficiently to tell reporters that Solberg had acted in good faith, but he announced, with ill-concealed irritation, his intention of finding out "at whose demand the holiday originated." [27]

Roosevelt's proclamation of a national bank holiday, however, distracted his attention from the culprits in Minnesota. Olson had opposed a state bank holiday because of fear that further contractions in currency circulation would reduce business activity and deepen unemployment. He disliked the Roosevelt proclamation for the same reason, and opened a determined drive to exempt state banks from its provisions. At his direction, Peyton worked up a plan which would enable them to reopen without endangering their liquidity. He proposed to prohibit withdrawals but allow banks to form clearinghouse associations and issue certificates of indebtedness at the rate of $100 for $120 of bank assets. The certificates would circulate freely for thirty days in place of legal tender currency, providing a medium of exchange for business operations during the emergency.

An acquiescent legislature quickly approved the Peyton plan on March 6 and Olson drew up a proclamation to end the bank holiday, pending authorization from Washington. When the federal government did not respond rapidly enough to suit him, he began to bombard the Treasury Department with wires and phone calls. His efforts were fruitless until congress passed emergency banking legislation on March 9. The same night he got a satisfactory response from the Treasury Department,[28] and the next day Roosevelt issued an executive order permitting banks to reopen.

The federal legislation obviated the necessity of the Minnesota clearinghouse plan, but Peyton refused to permit the reopening of state banks until they had complied with conditions which in effect required one hundred percent solvency. This aroused fresh protests in rural communities since national banks had been reopened on a more lenient basis. Vince Day felt that the administration of state banks generated more bitterness at this period than anything except mortgage burdens.[29] Resentment was allayed only when the forthright Peyton resigned to accept the chairmanship of the Fifth Federal Reserve District.

Had Olson been able to force a vote on his entire program in the critical days of February and early March, much of it would probably have been adopted. Even the most hardened conservatives dared not obstruct the governor during a period of such widespread panic. But as the banks reopened and the threat of agrarian revolution receded, the conservatives abandoned their unaccustomed role of cooperation.

This did not make so much difference in the house, where the moderate coalition controlled the legislative machinery, but it was decisive in the senate. There, behind the bewildered, dispirited Republican majority, stood a little clique of determined and resourceful leaders who had ruled the upper house for more than a decade. Clinging jealously to power, this group perpetuated itself by co-option whenever death or an electoral mishap intervened.

When Olson became governor the clique was a compact quadrumvirate composed of George H. Sullivan, Charles N. Orr, Claude H. MacKenzie, and A. J. Rockne. Rockne was their titular head and spokesman. He had risen to the top through seniority, persistence, and hard work rather than any special ability. More than any other member of the upper house, he symbolized the unyielding opposition of rugged individualism to the encroachments of government.

Of Norwegian ancestry, a well-to-do-farmer, and a newspaper publisher from Zumbrota, Rockne reflected the inborn distrust of rural Minnesota toward the masses with their newfangled socialistic schemes. His horizon was limited to his native Good-

hue County, which had been relatively free of starving workmen and wild-eyed farmers. He dismissed the agitation for
relief and unemployment insurance as the work of chronic
idlers who sought to be maintained at the expense of their more
industrious brethren. The possibility that depression could
strike down energetic and lazy alike never occurred to him. He
saw his first bread line during the fight over relief appropriations in 1935, when an insistent colleague literally dragged him
through the slum area of Minneapolis. On that occasion Rockne
expressed surprise at the extreme misery of the unemployed, but
he never really comprehended the magnitude of the economic
crisis. From first to last he judged all proposals by upright but
narrow provincial standards.

A head-on collision between Rockne and Olson was inevitable. During the 1931 legislative session, the governor steered
such a dexterous course between right and left that he momentarily averted the duel, but his 1933 proposals for public
relief, unemployment insurance, and state-operated power
plants cut at the very heart of Rockne's social and economic
philosophy. The senator's first reactions were muffled in the uproar over farm debts and closed banks, but once the immediate
crisis had passed, it became clear that he intended to mobilize
the senate for an all-out battle against the governor's program.

Never was a personal contest more unequal. Rockne lacked
the adaptability, the finesse, and the magnetism of the younger
man. Where Olson led by a combination of subtle pressure,
cajolery, and dramatic arguments, Rockne lunged clumsily at
his objective, seeking to overpower it by brute force. The governor scrupulously avoided any appearance of dictation, while
the senator ran the upper house arbitrarily — sometimes in open
defiance of parliamentary rules.

In public debate the difference was even more clearly
marked. Rockne had neither the instinct nor the inclination to
play for the gallery. His blunt candor in public controversy was
a commendable personal trait but hardly a political virtue. He
alienated potential supporters by his crabbed and uninspired

manner, lacking the adroitness to conceal his motives behind a series of polished platitudes. Rockne would have been at a disadvantage against an average opponent; against an accomplished orator and phrase-maker like Olson he appeared painfully inept.

The first issue on which the two crossed lances was unemployment relief. Olson opened the encounter with a special message to the legislature on January 18 requesting increased state aid for the jobless and expanded authority to dispense relief. In addition to direct appropriations, he asked for (1) expansion of the borrowing powers of cities beyond the debt limit, (2) extension of the calamity powers of the Executive Council to include direct relief, and (3) enlargement of the governor's authority to negotiate with federal agencies for relief.

As an improvisation to deal with the emergency, the Olson program was modest enough, but conservatives doubted its temporary character and feared such measures would set a dangerous precedent.

When Olson appeared before the senate Finance Committee to explain his program, Rockne asked him on whose authority relief money had been borrowed from the federal government and received the hot rejoinder that "starving people are not interested in legal quibbles." [30] But the senator saw no reason for haste and kept relief legislation bottled up in committee.

The day Roosevelt was inaugurated the governor dispatched a public message advising him that "if the so-called depression deepens, the government ought to take and operate the key industries of the country," [31] not hesitating "to conscript public wealth" should such a step be necessary to relieve suffering. Then, serving notice that he thought this advice applicable to Minnesota, Olson issued state conservatives a separate ultimatum, threatening to call out the militia as a last resort to see that the needy were fed, clothed, and sheltered. Ominously he concluded, "The state will proceed to take what it needs and pay for it with script." [32]

Rockne took no notice of these statements. The shaft that

finally got under his skin was a March 15 editorial in the *Farmer Labor Leader*. Entitled "Commander-in-Chief of the Hunger Brigade," it charged that Rockne had prevented the distribution of Reconstruction Finance Corporation funds in Minnesota by his deliberate refusal to report out relief bills. This adverse publicity hit Rockne where it hurt. After extracting a face-saving promise from Henry Teigan, chairman of the Farmer Labor newspaper board,* to repudiate the obnoxious paragraph, he reported out the bill broadening the governor's powers to deal with relief and condescended to defend his conduct on the floor of the senate. Even the *Minneapolis Journal* felt it necessary to explain apologetically that relief had been sidetracked only to expedite banking legislation.[33]

After Rockne's dramatic retreat in late March, the relief bills began to clear the legislature slowly. Nevertheless the senator tried to snarl up the measures for $2,000,000 in direct relief and the removal of municipal debt limitation so they would be lost in the last-minute rush before adjournment. Whereupon Olson threatened to take direct action unless the legislature passed the bills: "I shall declare martial law. A lot of people who are now fighting the measures because they happen to possess considerable wealth will be brought in by the provost guard. They will be obliged to give up more than they are giving up now. As long as I sit in the governor's chair there is not going to be any misery in the state if I can humanly prevent it."[34]

The fact that this revolutionary pronouncement went almost unchallenged indicated the changes which the economic crisis of early March had wrought in public opinion. At any other time Olson would have been denounced as a dangerous demagogue who sought to overthrow democratic institutions. But now the conservative press dismissed the speech as a grandstand play "which pleased the bonus marchers and capitalized the emotions of the proletariat."[35]

* Teigan was also a state senator at this time, having been elected from the Twenty-ninth District in Minneapolis to fill a vacancy created by the death of Senator Lewis Duemke.

Rockne lamely defended his inactivity by saying that Olson already had an unused $500,000 in the calamity fund and that he discriminated against rural counties in the distribution of relief. As an afterthought he added that the house rather than the senate had held up the bill. His counterattack was the prelude to another retreat, and in the end Olson secured the adoption of his relief program practically intact. It was his greatest single victory over the conservative legislature. He had mobilized public opinion so effectively behind relief expenditures that no individual or group dared to block them.

With the other controversial planks of his reform program the governor came out less well. He was definitely worsted over the Rural Credit Bureau. Olson had made the bureau a campaign issue and had called upon the legislature to continue its operations, although the annual deficit had reached the alarming figure of $400,000 in 1932. He might have secured authorization of unlimited deficit spending to keep the bureau afloat if the sectional issue had not split the rural bloc in the legislature. Almost all bureau loans had been made to bankrupt farmers of northern Minnesota, and their prosperous southern brethren strenuously objected to being taxed for such a program.

Conservative senators paved the way for elimination of the bureau by creating a committee to investigate its affairs. H. M. Johnshoy obligingly repeated his indictments of 1931, and H. M. Feroe, the ousted Republican attorney of the bureau, lambasted Gaarenstrom for dumping farms on the market at a loss and for turning the bureau into a patronage machine.

When the committee settled down to a review of bureau operations, it found little evidence of corruption or mismanagement that did not antedate the Olson period, but it easily made a case for discontinuing bureau loans because the steady decline of land values threatened ever larger deficits. Senator Rockne, who directed the investigation from behind the scenes, came forward with a proposal to halt further loans and to liquidate state holdings slowly with the least possible loss. Olson made a show of resisting Rockne, but economy sentiment was so strong that he had to give in and accept legislation providing for a conservator to wind up bureau affairs and authorizing a long-term issue of tax certificates to distribute the burden over an extended period. Olson justified his unavoidable retreat by expressing confidence that the federal government with its larger resources would take up the burden of refinancing farm debts.

Harder for Olson to take was the legislature's rejection of unemployment insurance, because he believed this legislation would protect urban unemployed from the worst effects of depression. Although the public was in an experimental mood, the very novelty of the proposal worked against it. Several European countries had set up unemployment insurance systems before World War I, but in the United States only Wisconsin had ventured into this uncharted sea.

At the outset the governor made a tactical mistake by departing from the recommendations of the Employment Stabilization Research Institute, to which he had applied for advice. The University of Minnesota professors who conducted the Institute study proposed a payroll tax with employers and employees each contributing two percent, but the governor decided on a four percent levy paid solely by employers. He also brushed aside the suggestion that compensation payments be delayed until 1935, insisting instead on provision for immediate payments.

Olson would have faced determined opposition in any event, but the stringent provisions of his bill gave the conservatives an additional lever. They promptly began telling the public that passage of the bill would cause a wholesale exodus of industry from the state and increase unemployment.[36] According to their dire prophecies, even the hardy corporations that remained behind would have to discharge employees and raise prices to meet the added levy.

A stream of witnesses paraded before the legislative committee considering the bill to echo and re-echo this argument. J. S. Clapper, chairman of the Minneapolis Manufacturers Committee, solemnly insisted that employers had already taken severe salary cuts themselves rather than discharge employees and simply could not absorb this additional burden. Others, concealing their self-interest more adroitly, contended that unemployment insurance was admirable in every way but ought to be postponed until normal times, when reserves would accumulate more rapidly.[37]

Olson appeared in person before the house committee to defend his bill. He likened the arguments for delay to the reasoning of an incompetent physician who would not vaccinate the healthy during a plague. He conceded that there might be weaknesses in the bill, but urged correction rather than rejection. As a parting shot, the governor reminded the legislators that he was on their side, attempting "to patch up the social system and continue it as such to prevent socialization of industry." [38]

His arguments had little effect. Although the bill was amended to split the contributions equally between employers and employees and to postpone initial payments until January 15, 1935, concessions could not save unemployment insurance. The progressive house itself killed the bill by a vote of sixty-eight to fifty-four.

Undaunted, Olson appealed to the people for support and applied the most unremitting pressure on recalcitrant legislators. Speaking over the radio, he assailed industry for trying to load the cost of depression on private charity, workers, and farmers.[39] From the steps of the State Capitol he told an audience of unemployed that if state authorities did not act resolutely to prevent the recurrence of present misery he hoped "the present system of local government would go right down to hell." [40]

His perseverance forced the house to revive and pass the Unemployment Insurance Bill, but only after the addition of a crippling amendment postponing operation in Minnesota until six of nine midwestern states had enacted similar unemployment insurance laws. Even this illusive victory evaporated as conservative senators with malevolent cunning restored the bill's original provisions and left it to die in the last-minute jam.

The legislature dealt just as roughly with the proposed constitutional amendment for state development of water power and distribution of electricity. The best the governor could salvage was a law permitting municipally owned power plants to extend their lines and service twenty-five miles beyond the city limits.

Overshadowed by these dramatic encounters between Olson and the legislature was the running battle over the budget. All parties had made solemn campaign pledges to cut expenditures in response to the overwhelming public demand for tax relief. Even a confirmed public spender like Henry Teigan admitted the political necessity of supporting such a program.[41] But the legislature and the governor soon found themselves at loggerheads over the size of reductions. Conservatives generally favored flat percentage cuts in all appropriations, although such a procedure would involve wholesale salary reductions for state and municipal officials. The governor feared that such sweeping retrenchments would aggravate the deflationary spiral and cripple essential services.

There was a strong hint of Olson's attitude in his reply to the petition for a twenty-five percent tax cut presented by the "Root Hog or Die Club," an organization of prosperous farmers and businessmen from southern Minnesota. Spotting some bankers among the petitioners, he asked why they did not cut interest rates on mortgages when they asked for a twenty-five percent tax reduction.[42] He then pledged his cooperation in cutting expenditures but made it clear that he would not approve wholesale reductions.

Although Olson trimmed the budget below forty million dollars for the first time since 1921, A. B. Pfaender, chairman of the house Appropriations Committee, teamed up with Rockne to make further reductions in the appropriations for education, state institutions, and various departments to a point where heavy salary slashes were inevitable.

Legislative procedure required five separate appropriation

bills rather than a single omnibus measure, so by threatening vetoes the governor forced his opponents to back down on the more indefensible cuts. He was particularly successful in routing Rockne on the educational appropriation and received heartfelt thanks therefor from the university's president, Lotus D. Coffman.[43]

But Olson's fight to block salary reductions in state departments failed miserably. The only concession he could wring from the legislature was a clause permitting department heads to grant a payless vacation to employees earning over $1200 instead of a twenty percent cut spread over the year. His annoyance at this defeat found expression in a veto message killing a separate bill for a blanket twenty percent wage slash for all state and county employees. He denounced the action of the legislature as "on a par with the performance of the so-called captains of industry who have been slashing wages and destroying buying power, and who seem to expect that by some species of magic their business will improve despite the destruction of buying power in the people."[44]

During the final week of the session the report issued by the special senate committee investigating the Highway Department widened the rift between Olson and the conservatives. The committee had listened only to critics of the administration, such as former Commissioner Babcock and the disgruntled contractors. It had written into the records charges admittedly hearsay to create an impression that the Highway Department was run by corrupt and irresponsible individuals. Consequently, the report compiled from this evidence condemned the governor and his highway code in a most direct and personal way.

With withering sarcasm Olson characterized the committee's conclusions as "the report of elder statesmen of the Republican party" which would be interesting "to the taxpayers of the state as a party document if the cost was substantially less than the $4,000 which will be expended therefor."[45] He observed that the denunciation of the highway code put him in the "anomalous position of being lined up with Mr. Herbert Hoover, the former president of the United States, who advocated and approved a federal law directing an eight-hour day" and expressed regret "that the Great Engineer and the elder statesmen were at variance."

With these jibes ringing in its ears, Olson's second nonpartisan legislature adjourned.

The heated wrangling between the governor and the legislature tended to obscure the fact that a surprising number of less controversial bills were written into law. The three measures Olson had vetoed at the close of the session two years earlier passed in just about the form he wanted. The elimination of South St. Paul from the metropolitan drainage district made clear sailing for the Sewage Disposal Bill. The Republicans disliked the Farmer Labor version of congressional reapportionment but accepted it rather than face another election of representatives at large. Truck transportation brought a swarm of lobbyists down on the legislature, but Olson's firmness triumphed over the cupidity of special interests and the bill that was enacted regulated trucks without forcing them to charge the same rates as railroads.

The legislature also took a tentative step toward equalizing the tax burden by passing the controversial income tax bill. As originally drafted, it had provided that income tax collections would go into the state revenue fund, decreasing the general property levy by that amount. This would have made the income tax a strict replacement tax instead of an additional burden as the conservatives had feared. But before passage, the bill was amended to earmark tax receipts for the public schools. Because many school districts were hovering on the edge of bankruptcy, Olson dared not object to the transparent political trick of reducing local taxes rather than the high state taxes for which Republicans blamed the administration.

The 1933 legislature also approved a cluster of labor bills which prohibited yellow-dog contracts, limited women on industrial jobs to a fifty-four-hour week, and outlawed the use of injunctions in labor disputes. These new safeguards did not revolutionize the status of workers in Minnesota, but the fact that they passed at all indicated a more sympathetic public attitude toward organized labor.

Some of the most constructive work of the session was done in the relatively unspectacular field of conservation. The particular problem here that came to a head in the spring of 1933 concerned the disposition of state lands in the beautiful border lakes region between Minnesota and Canada. On the surface it appeared to be a trivial matter, but it was actually the final phase of a protracted struggle between private interests and conservationists over the management of the area.

The conflict had begun in 1925, when the federal government referred to the International Joint Commission the question of developing the Rainy Lake watershed. On that occasion E. W. Backus of the Minnesota and Ontario Paper Company produced a general plan for water power development requiring the construction of seven dams. Since his project would have raised the water level from five to eighty feet in various lakes,[46] it provoked the determined opposition of conservationists, who objected to the inundation of forest lands, the creation of fire hazards, and the disturbance of fish and wild life. The Izaak Walton League set up a special organization, the Quetico-Superior Council, to fight for the maintenance of the border lakes in their natural state. The lobbying of this council eventually bore fruit in the federal Shipstead-Nolan Act of 1930, prohibiting the lease of lands in the Superior National Forest for private use.

Unfortunately this legislation did not afford complete protection. If the International Joint Commission, which was still studying the Backus proposal, approved water power development in the Rainy Lake watershed, the United States and Canada would probably implement its recommendation with a treaty extinguishing the benefits of the Shipstead-Nolan Act. Even worse, the Minnesota Light and Power Company had already flooded the Gabbro Lake area owned by the state and was attempting to legalize its trespass.

Recognizing that they could do nothing to control the decision of the International Joint Commission, the conservationists converged on the Minnesota legislature to demand a little Shipstead-Nolan Act outlawing private exploitation of state lands.

Their first attempt in 1931 failed miserably. The governor, who could have given valuable help, was inactive for fear of jeopardizing his bill to create a unified Conservation Department, while Senator Morin, the chairman of the Public Domain Committee, was believed to be cooperating with power interests in St. Louis County to delay action.[47]

Two years later Olson joined the conservationists, and their combined efforts produced legislation outlawing further power development or logging operations on state lands within the Shipstead-Nolan area. The Minnesota Light and Power Company was allowed to retain its holdings in the Gabbro Lake region at the price of an annual rental fee and triple damages for the timber destroyed. Six months after the Minnesota legislature acted, the International Joint Commission declared against further exploitation of the Shipstead-Nolan area, thereby removing the threat to conservation of the border lakes.

The 1933 legislature also created thirteen state forests from tax-delinquent lands in northern Minnesota, climaxing Olson's long campaign for intelligent utilization of land in the cutover area. The governor had prepared the ground by appointing a nine-man committee to make a nonpartisan study of the problem. Directed by Lotus D. Coffman, president of the University of Minnesota, the committee, after a six-months study, issued a report proposing a modest rehabilitation program on tax-delinquent lands. This Olson used as the basis for a special message to the legislature.

Unfortunately the state forests were the only tangible result of the committee's recommendations. Sectional jealousy and legal obstacles killed Olson's dream of a scientific conservation program. The southern counties were afraid they would pay the bill for any improvements made in cutover regions. Residents of the affected area suspected that if the state stepped in, it would pay very low land taxes to the county governments. Even the Conservation Department viewed the project askance because under existing law the state could not gain title to tax-delinquent land for five years or prevent the removal of timber by trespassers during the interim.[48]

Besides conservation, labor, and tax legislation, the 1933 session saw a strengthening of the securities law and a beginning of statewide old age pensions. The considerable body of hitherto controversial measures written into the statute books suggests that the entire axis of public opinion had been tilted to the left and a new equilibrium set up.

So changed was the public temper that Olson's open aggressiveness during the session actually increased his prestige. The *Princeton Union*, after criticizing the governor's stand on salary reduction and other matters, concluded dolefully, "Floyd B. Olson is the idol of the hour. He can do no wrong." [49]

# Chapter VIII TOWARD
## NATIONAL LEADERSHIP

O<small>LSON'S</small> prodigal expenditure of energy during the 1933 legislative session exhausted his physical reserves and seriously weakened his health. At first his condition was concealed by his good humor and stubborn refusal to curtail a strenuous daily program. But the pretense of physical robustness could not be indefinitely maintained.

The tragedy of Olson's illness was that his temperament and chosen profession conspired to prevent a cure. A victim of stomach ulcers, he could not tolerate for long periods the kind of environment that promised relief. Rest and a rigid diet were the minimum requisites for recovery, but Olson was incapable of real relaxation. The frenzied activity of politics with its endless round of interviews, speeches, and hair-trigger decisions was like a fever in his blood. The constant atmosphere of crisis and tension acted as a stimulus to volcanic discharges of energy. He appeared at his best when the going was toughest, living for the moments when he could focus all his vitality and sagacity to confound an opponent. The bustle and confusion of public office was as necessary for him as food and drink for others. He seldom allowed his mind complete repose, keeping paper and pencil handy to jot down ideas between naps.[1] To enforce relaxation upon such an intense, mercurial personality was impossible.

It was equally futile to impose dietary limitations on Olson. He lived in a whirl of picnics, banquets, and receptions, forcing

143

an endless variety of foods and beverages into his outraged stomach. He obligingly ate whatever was served him to avoid displeasing an anxious host. Maurice Rose, his chauffeur and handyman, recalled that during the 1930 campaign Olson downed four meals in one night.[2]

Nothing short of retirement from politics could have saved Olson's health. But this was a price he was unwilling to pay. It would have involved parting with something dearer to him than life itself.

For a few months after his serious seizure in the summer of 1931, Olson's health had improved. But he drove himself recklessly through the campaign of 1932 and the ensuing legislative session with all its irritations of rural violence, bank closures, and patronage squabbles. An iron man would have staggered under the load, yet Olson uttered hardly a word of complaint.

In late February the sharp pain of an inflamed appendix was added to the nagging ache of ulcers. He ignored the danger signals, ramming his emergency bank bills through the legislature and then departing for the presidential inauguration. On the train he suffered a severe attack of appendicitis. This, plus the unwelcome news of the bank holiday proclaimed in Minnesota, forced him reluctantly to turn back, but the inflammation subsided sufficiently for him to plunge into the thick of state business when he stepped off the train.

He managed to keep going through the remainder of the session and the strenuous days that continued after the legislators went home, but a long business trip to Washington proved to be the final straw. Olson suffered an acute attack the day after his return, and an emergency operation was performed on May 12.

He rallied quickly from the appendectomy, but a postoperational flare-up of his ulcers kept him bedridden for nearly a month.[3] A two-weeks vacation at Gull Lake did not restore him completely, and although he returned to the office on June 15, his health remained precarious. The ulcer attacks appeared with greater frequency and the periods of relief grew shorter.

Olson made few concessions to his malady. Physical suffering would force him momentarily into idleness and a diet, but he always lapsed into his old routine at the first sign of recovery. Eventually he came to rely on sheer will power to carry him through. Occasionally members of his office staff, seeing Olson double up with pain before an interview, would gaze open-mouthed as he straightened up without a trace of discomfort on his face to greet an incoming delegation. Political enemies might have behaved more considerately if they had been aware of his condition. But he managed to conceal nervous tension and physical pain behind a façade of unruffled confidence.

Olson's chronic ill health had far-reaching effects on the Farmer Labor party and the state administration. As his absences from the office became more frequent, many details were necessarily shifted to other shoulders. He never lost control of policy formulation, but his grip on the party machinery gradually relaxed.

During the early days of his administration Olson had been virtually omnipresent, animating every phase of state and party business with his master touch; whereas after 1933 whole segments fell into the hands of subordinates whose work was infrequently reviewed. Some state departments suffered from this process, but the greatest damage was done in the Farmer Labor party, where the more unscrupulous elements gradually gained control of the machinery and manipulated patronage to entrench themselves.

Also, as Olson's health deteriorated the job of harmonizing and placating the diverse wings of the reform movement became less endurable. It required eternal vigilance to keep Farmer Laborites from the throats of the all-party men and to mediate the doctrinal disputes of his motley following. And for all his outward insouciance, Olson bore this burden with increasing reluctance.

While Olson was struggling to regain his health in 1933 he instituted a new patronage policy that ultimately transformed the Farmer Labor party from a band of devout crusaders into a professional political machine. Republicans were unceremoniously evicted from their positions in state departments and replaced by politically conscious Farmer Laborites.

This long-postponed house cleaning came as a result of increased unrest within the reform movement after the overwhelming victory of 1932. A post-election editorial in the *Minnesota Union Advocate* pointed out that the Olson victory was a party accomplishment rather than a personal affair of volunteer committees as in 1930.[4] Irate Farmer Laborites filled the governor's office for months after the election, lodging specific complaints against Republican officeholders.[5]

The ugly mood of party leaders was revealed when a substantial number of Farmer Labor senators refused to vote for the confirmation of Harry E. Boyle, a Republican appointed by Olson to the Tax Commission. Even the docile A. C. Welch, chairman of the Farmer Labor executive committee, threatened to convoke his group for a patronage discussion because the mail was so full of complaints "against Republican holdovers and bandwagon Farmer Laborites." [6]

Vince Day, who siphoned most of the discontented into his office, was so alarmed by the fierceness of their protests that he took a quiet trip around the state to secure a firsthand impression of conditions. His confidential report to Olson sounded an urgent note of warning:

"There is great dissatisfaction among the party members. I found this to be widespread throughout the range. The Highway Department, the Forestry Department, and the Conservation Department do not recognize the importance of rewarding members of the party. The feeling against these departments is bitter and is being used by Republican agents to stir up dissension for political purposes. These agents are meeting with some success and unless their agitation is checked patronage may become the issue in the next campaign. . . . They point to the Republicans who are holding public jobs and ridicule local Farmer Laborites for being unable to remove them.

It is not merely a matter of employment, but injures the pride of members of our party and humiliates them. This propaganda is taking place in every community in the state where Republicans are employed in any of the above departments. The party cannot continue to win elections unless this condition is remedied. It affords your opponents an opportunity to enter a disgruntled member of the party as a candidate in the primary against you. If this condition is corrected in time such action will not be serious, but unless corrected might place the party in the same condition that the Democratic rumpers placed that party. The emergency is such that it warrants the removal of those department heads that neglect or refuse to cooperate in distributing patronage to members of the party." [7]

With such conclusive evidence of disaffection it would have been folly for Olson to resist a house cleaning. And in any case, events had gradually transformed the governor into the same kind of partisan as rank-and-file Farmer Laborites. The vicious whispering campaign against his character conducted by the Republicans in 1932 and the avowedly personal basis of the attack on his highway program by the senate investigating committee stung Olson beyond endurance. Moreover, experience with Republican Highway Commissioner C. M. Babcock, who refused to name a single Farmer Laborite to an important post in the department,[8] diminished the governor's appetite for bipartisan cooperation. He was in the mood for a change in patronage policy, although he wanted to move slowly so as to avoid the unfavorable publicity that would accompany wholesale discharges.[9]

The first step was the replacement of Babcock by N. W. Elsberg, city engineer of Minneapolis and a personal friend of Olson's from county attorney days. The situation in the Highway Department did not immediately improve, however. Elsberg was strictly an engineer without the slightest interest in politics, and as a matter of convenience he retained Walter Pilcher, Babcock's private secretary, and other key men of the former administration in their posts.

Nothing was done during Olson's illness, but after his recovery Vince Day prevailed upon him to appoint Joe Poirier, an efficient spoilsman, personnel manager in the Highway Department. Within a matter of weeks Poirier converted the department into a happy hunting ground for Farmer Laborites.

The appointment of I. C. Strout as budget commissioner in May 1933 inaugurated the third-party drive on the remaining departments under the jurisdiction of the governor. Strout operated like a professional politician of the Tammany school. His declared goal was the creation of a party machine based on a solid nucleus of loyal state jobholders. As a member of the Finance Commission, which had wide authority to classify state employees and set up scales of compensation, he was able to exert leverage on political appointments regardless of the attitude of department heads.

Strout's efforts soon produced a quiet purge of undesirables in the Conservation and Agriculture departments. Simultaneously he levied a three percent contribution on state employees to sustain the *Farmer Labor Leader*. Since the paper had never been self-supporting, a wider distribution of the deficit seemed desirable. Strout stressed the voluntary nature of the contribution, but it often proved awkward in practice for jobholders to refuse this little token of gratitude to the party.

The Farmer Labor party was following a traditional pattern in building a machine once it secured power and responsibility. Olson played an active role in this shift of policy, presiding over the purge of Republican officeholders and heading the list of three percent contributors to the newspaper fund. Unwittingly he acquiesced in the creation of a Frankenstein which in the end he could not control.

The fall of 1933 saw the emergence of Olson as a national political figure. The public approval that greeted the first phase of the New Deal also guaranteed a sympathetic hearing for reformers of every stripe. The distrusted innovators of the Coolidge era suddenly became heroes in the war against depression. Almost overnight it became good form to be a left-winger.

In this climate of opinion, Olson attracted notice by his able exposition of advanced radicalism. His dramatic threat to invoke martial law to relieve destitution caught the public's imagination. He assumed the role of supporter and constructive critic of the New Deal recovery program, enthusiastically commending the administration for taking "a lot of things that used to be called socialism" and dressing them up "in the scheme of readjustment by which they are trying to make conditions fair to all."

At the same time he did not hesitate to chide the New Deal for failing to move far enough. In a notable address at the Eagles' National Convention in Cleveland, August 4, 1933, he said: "I am willing and zealous that the national recovery program shall succeed, but I do not believe that there can be any economic security for the common man and woman in this country until and unless the key industries of the United States are taken over by the government." [10]

These forays into national politics attracted widespread attention, but it was Olson's militant crusade for farm relief that increased his stature as a public figure.

The general confidence which the Roosevelt administration inspired did not extend to the more desperate farmers of the Midwest. They felt little inclination to wait patiently for the New Deal farm program to unfold. The farm strike had been called off after the presidential election, but the leadership of the Holiday Association made it clear that Roosevelt's period of grace was to be brief. Unless his new congress granted substantial relief immediately, the strike would be renewed.

Roosevelt's pledges to agriculture had been specific and categorical. Before and after his election he had endorsed the domestic allotment plan, which proposed benefit payments to farmers for restricting production.[11] There was naturally some disagreement as to the wisdom of the President's plan, but it offered so much more than anything previously proposed by a responsible leader that most of the national farm organizations hopefully waited for its enactment by the special session of congress.

Not so the Farm Holiday Association. It demanded relief far beyond that contemplated by the domestic allotment plan. As its minimum program, the association demanded (1) prices guaranteeing the cost of production plus a reasonable profit, (2) a moratorium on farm foreclosures until prices increased, and (3) passage of the Frazier Bill to refinance mortgages at cheaper rates of interest. If these terms were not met by May 3, it threatened to tie up the bread-basket states with another farm strike.

There was doubtless an element of bluff in this ultimatum to the new congress which met March 9, so that when the strike deadline approached without any farm legislation completed, the association found itself in an awkward position. Agricultural prices were rising and congressional passage of the domestic allotment plan seemed assured. Milo Reno, the national president, and the conservative wing of the association viewed a strike with reluctance, but the radicals led by John Bosch still favored it.[12] The best Reno could secure was a week's postponement. On May 9 the Minnesota chapter voted for a strike on the thirteenth, calling on the chapters in neighboring states for cooperative action.

At this stage Olson intervened. He had gone to Washington to discuss unemployment and farm relief with Roosevelt. Apparently Milo Reno hoped the conversations would bring concrete assurances permitting a further postponement of the strike, because he phoned the governor repeatedly from Des Moines on May 11.[13] Unable to reach Olson, he headed for St. Paul the following day, only to receive the dismaying information that an emergency operation had been performed on the governor at 4 A.M.

Talking with Vince Day about the sincerity of the administration in its farm program, Reno hinted that the slightest indication of Olson's opinion would be decisive at the strike meeting

The young Floyd B. Olson, as county attorney

Olson receiving "with pleasure" the $5,000,000 relief bill, ready for his signature, from his secretary, Vince Day, 1934

With Senator Henrik Shipstead, a man of "Olympian disdain," around 1931

The governor's electric speaking style, 1932

Chief Justice John P.
Devaney, swearing Olson in
for his third term, 1935

Patricia and Ada Olson
leaving home to attend the
governor's third
inauguration, 1935

Representative Leonard Eriksson and attorney George C. Stiles
with Olson at the signing of the Mortgage Relief Bill, 1935

Olson at work, February
1936

Minnesota Secretary of State
Mike Holm watching Olson
file as the Farmer-Labor
candidate for United States
Senate, 1936

Farmers stormed the State Capitol in March 1933 to demand
relief. Thousands gathered in the rotunda to hear Olson (top left)
speak and then marched to downtown St. Paul after the rally.

Striking Hormel Company workers gathered outside the Austin plant in November 1933.

Olson conferring with leaders of the Hormel strike in Austin, 1933

Pickets battle Minneapolis police during the 1934 truck drivers' strike

Procession, more than a mile long, for the funeral of Henry B. Ness, the first trucker killed by police during the 1934 strike

Strikers outside the Strutwear plant, Minneapolis, 1935

Endorsing the annual Veterans of Foreign
Wars fund-raising campaign

Joining in the celebration of Kolacky Day in Montgomery, 1931

Olson delivering a nationally broadcast radio address at the dedication of the Christopher Columbus statue on the State Capitol grounds, 1931

Iowa governor Clyde L. Herring delivering Floyd of Rosedale at
the State Capitol, 1935

A portion of the huge crowd that flocked to the Minneapolis Auditorium for Olson's funeral service, August 26, 1936. The building seated 14,000; an estimated 40,000 more clustered outside and heard Wisconsin governor Philip La Follette's oration over loudspeakers.

Pallbearers at Lakewood Cemetery (left to right): Elmer A. Benson, Maurice Rose, Gerald P. Nye, Robert La Follette, Jr., Henrik Shipstead, and Charles Ward

the following day. This left the matter squarely up to Olson, who dictated a letter from his sick bed expressing confidence that Roosevelt would do something for the farmer and asking that the strike be postponed until the administration's program had been given a fair test.[14]

This statement tipped the vote against the strike, and Reno was able to announce over the radio "that in conformity with the request of Governor Olson the association agreed to call off the strike for ninety days." [15]

Conditions grew worse during the respite. Farm prices, which had risen spectacularly during the three months after Roosevelt's inauguration, lost their momentum in midsummer. Wheat reached a high of $1.18 on July 17 and broke sharply the following day, dragging other commodities down with it. The political ferment revived quickly and received fresh impetus when hot winds unrelieved by rain scorched the western counties of Minnesota and the Dakotas, endangering forest crops and livestock. In Minnesota the Executive Council voted $60,000 for relief and authorized the cutting and distribution of hay from tax-delinquent lands. Even so, the drought wrought terrific damage, especially in the very area that had given birth to the Farm Holiday Association.

Unfortunately, New Deal legislation did not bring immediate help. The act establishing the Agricultural Adjustment Administration had been passed on May 12, but most of the summer months were consumed in setting up the gigantic administrative machinery to supervise production and distribute the all-important allotment checks. Impatient farmers interpreted the delays as evidence of the utter inadequacy of the domestic allotment plan.

During the summer Olson gradually moved over to the camp of the critics, partly in the hope of moderating their counsels but also because he had honest doubts about the adequacy of the New Deal program. He distrusted the voluntary features of the A.A.A. and feared there would not be enough curtailment of acreage to raise prices. In common with other left-wingers, he disliked the concept of a scarcity economy inherent in the program. The restriction of crops when thousands verged on starvation seemed to him retrogressive. More and more he came to believe that the solution was a flat price-fixing program that would give the farmer a decent standard of living. He proposed to abandon crop restriction in favor of a specific limitation on the quantity of a commodity to be marketed.

The rise in industrial prices which coincided with the adoption of National Recovery Administration codes reinforced his conviction that the same system should be extended to agriculture. Fearing the collapse of the entire recovery program unless the purchasing power of the farmer was placed on a parity with industry, he became increasingly outspoken in his advocacy of price fixing.

If Olson hoped to weaken the hand of extremists by his plan of farm relief, he was disappointed. The Farm Holiday Association enthusiastically endorsed price fixing but continued preparations for a great strike during the harvest period. On September 26, John Bosch called on Minnesota farmers to "sell nothing, buy nothing, and pay nothing" until a code for agriculture and the Frazier Bill were adopted,[16] and the following day a Farm Holiday committee appealed to President Roosevelt for the insertion of a clause guaranteeing the cost of production on all codes affecting agriculture. When their petition was rejected, the national Holiday Association called a strike for October 21, urging farmers to withhold all produce from the market until their grievances were redressed.

The strike started tamely enough, but it carried potential dynamite. Success depended on a high degree of cooperation by farmers, or barring that, the forcible prevention of produce moving on the highway. Resort to the latter alternative was almost inevitable, and this in turn seemed certain to bring violence and bloodshed. Sooner or later governors in threatened states would have to choose between the striking farmers and the irritated public.

Strike leaders resisted counsels of moderation on the ground that their demonstration at least focused attention on the farm problem. Seemingly the only way to end the strike without alienating the radical farm leaders was to persuade the national administration to offer additional measures of relief. This necessity dovetailed with the views of the Minnesota governor, who feared the spread of violence and wanted more resolute action from President Roosevelt.

Olson arranged for a meeting of five midwestern governors at Des Moines on October 29 to consider farm problems. Although the formal invitations were issued by Governor Clyde L. Herring of Iowa, Olson dominated the proceedings and secured an endorsement of his price-fixing program.

The governors adopted a series of resolutions that envisaged a comprehensive regulation of agriculture. Specifically, they proposed (1) special codes licensing sellers and processors of basic food commodities, (2) price fixing at rates to ensure primary producers a reasonable profit, (3) periodic determination of amounts to be sold on the domestic market, (4) a national embargo on the importation of fats, oils, canned meats, and starches, and (5) immediate establishment of price floors, pending the formulation of codes.[17]

The conference took on a wider significance when the five governors resolved to present their program personally to Roosevelt. This decision was reached after Olson had got in touch with the President and secured what he believed to be a positive commitment on price fixing. The governors arrived in Washington November 1, and with Olson as their spokesman presented the Des Moines resolutions to the President. Roosevelt told them to work out the details with the Department of Agriculture and return when the job was completed. He gave the price-fixing program such a cordial reception that the governors announced after the conference that Roosevelt favored it.

But Henry A. Wallace, the secretary of agriculture, from the outset considered the scheme unworkable and was determined to torpedo it. While his experts wore down the governors' patience by raising all sorts of administrative problems, Wallace went to the White House and stated his objections to price fixing so positively that Roosevelt beat a hasty retreat and two days later permitted word to leak out that price fixing was dead.

The governors, irritated by the fruitless conferences at the Department of Agriculture, were in no mood to accept defeat. They stormed the White House for a final appeal to Roosevelt. Olson, who had a marked predilection for front-step speeches, made a short address from the steps of the White House. Telling his audience of newspapermen that the governors were in Washington to secure for agriculture the same benefits that had been accorded industry, he pointed out that the farmers had suffered a twelve-year depression, whereas industry had been in the doldrums only three years. He concluded with a stirring appeal for justice to the farmer: "All we are asking is parity price for him, a return to him of his purchasing power so he can buy the goods of the factory. If you give him this he will buy all the paint you can make, all the leather goods you produce, and many other products, and then the depression will end." [18]

Immediately after the speech the governors went inside for their last-ditch debate with Roosevelt. The President was gracious but unyielding. He said the administrative objections to price fixing were for the moment insuperable, but held out the hope of action along lines recommended by the governors at a more propitious time.

Roosevelt's rejection of price fixing elicited varying responses. Governor William Langer of North Dakota was the most bellicose, telling his colleagues that "we just voted one son-of-a-bitch out of office and can do it again." [19] Olson, keenly disappointed, issued a statement declaring that the governors would stick to their program and move in on the next congress. But the sharp disagreement over farm relief did not interrupt the political collaboration of Roosevelt and Olson.

As a political rallying cry, Olson's proposal for farm relief possessed an undoubted appeal. The idea of increasing rural income by price fixing was simple and direct. It could be understood by the most unsophisticated mind, and it offered almost instantaneous relief. These features commended the plan to depressed farmers and focused popular attention on its author.

Nevertheless, behind its seeming simplicity the Olson program involved many complex problems. Effective price control would require the licensing of all processors of basic commodities and of millions of affected farmers. It would also require considerable enforcement machinery to prevent the producer from selling commodities in excess of his quota on a black market.

Secondly, the plan was based frankly on regimentation, and the voters' reaction to regimentation was well known. Although the calamity atmosphere had induced a generous spirit of co-operation, the native tradition of individualism remained deeply rooted. The price-fixing scheme contained elements of compulsion far beyond that contemplated by the A.A.A., and these might well stir up all the latent antagonism to centralized authority. Roosevelt saw the danger and instinctively shied away from it. Had Olson been responsible for executing the program, his enthusiasm for it probably would have been a good deal diminished.

A third and politically troublesome objection to the price-fixing program was its sectional character. The governors considered only cattle, hogs, corn, wheat, milk, and butterfat to be basic commodities. The omission of sugar, cotton, and tobacco from price-fixing benefits would have generated a political storm of major proportions. In fact, Olson thought it was the sectional issue that jettisoned his program; he told the press, "The administration is more fearful of unfavorable reactions in the east and south than it is fearful of the practicability of the program." [20]

Olson approached national problems from a strictly sectional viewpoint. He evaluated each phase of the recovery program in terms of what it would do for Minnesota and was indifferent to other regional interests. On one occasion he advised Governor Langer not to attend a farm conference at Oklahoma City because nothing would be discussed but "oil, sheep, and peanuts." [21] The six basic commodities for his price-fixing program were chosen specifically to advance the economic interests of Minnesota and the surrounding states. Olson was an unblushing partisan of his constituents. But whereas he could afford to pursue a strictly sectional policy, the President had to formulate a farm program acceptable to a variety of economic interests.

A final uncertainty in the Olson program was the cost of financing it. One observer estimated that parity for agriculture would raise farm prices approximately seventy percent.[22] Cost was never the dominant consideration in New Deal relief policies, but Roosevelt must have thought it safer in this instance to stick by his more modest program.

As long as the farm crisis remained acute, the administration was roundly condemned by leftists for its timidity and lack of imagination. For the moment Olson replaced Roosevelt as the supreme deity for agrarian radicals. Although his program was rejected, the Minnesota governor achieved a national stature accorded to few state executives.

The Farm Holiday Association, which had suspended the strike during the Des Moines and Washington conferences, promptly renewed it after the breakdown of negotiations over price fixing. In Minnesota sporadic violence broke out in the southern and western counties when extremists tried to close down creameries and dairies. Occasionally churns were broken and kerosene was dumped into cream in an effort to halt the marketing of perishables as well as nonperishables.[23]

The damage done was isolated and negligible, but the newspapers alarmed the public with screaming headlines. And the rural population got the impression that the Farmer Labor party endorsed the strike. Solberg, Gaarenstrom, and Congressman F. H. Shoemaker made sympathetic speeches in the affected areas, and although Holiday officials were guarded in their statements, they often implied that the governor approved of their entire program.

Olson was working feverishly behind the scenes to end the

strike before events forced him to take a public stand. And the ineffectiveness of the strike gradually worked the Holiday leaders into a more conciliatory frame of mind. To save the faces of all parties concerned, Olson wrote a letter to Bosch on November 20, stating that the strike had already accomplished its purpose of focusing public attention on the plight of agriculture and requesting that it be suspended to prevent enemies from dividing the farm movement.[24] Bosch responded by formally calling off the strike until congress had another opportunity to act.

The whole episode lasted little more than two weeks, but it undoubtedly weakened the standing of Olson in southern Minnesota, where the more conservative farmers believed him to be an accomplice of the Holiday Association.

The strike in Minnesota coincided with the worst phase of the farm crisis. A gradual price rise, beginning at the end of the year and gaining momentum in 1934, took the edge off rural militancy. Simultaneously, the cumbersome machinery of the A.A.A. began to grind out payments for acreage reduction. The first checks under the wheat program were mailed out October 31, and the bulk of the first installments had reached the farmers by March 1, 1934, when farm taxes fell due. The agitation for a price-fixing program subsided.

Olson struggled against the trend. All winter he drummed up sentiment for a big farm conference to formulate fresh demands on congress. It met at Des Moines in March 1934 and approved the program of the preceding year. Olson promptly wrote Roosevelt that there was "almost unanimous" sentiment for price fixing, but the President responded evasively.[25] Time had vindicated his caution and placed the game in his hands. The vacillation of the administration gave way to confidence, once rising prices and A.A.A. checks began to fill the empty pockets of the farmers.

Olson took up the matter again in August when Roosevelt visited Minnesota,[26] but nothing could conceal the fact that the governor's grandiose plan for farm relief was politically dead.

Had the condition of agriculture grown worse rather than better in the spring of 1934, Olson could conceivably have snatched the leadership of midwestern farmers from the President. As it was, dollar wheat and A.A.A. payments, more than anything else, militated against Olson's prospects of leading a national third-party rebellion in 1936.

Olson made further headlines during the second half of the year because of his conspicuous association with the N.R.A., the controversial New Deal agency set up to prevent cutthroat competition and to stabilize industry by a system of codes defining fair trade practices and conditions of work.

Of all phases of the New Deal program, the N.R.A. appealed to Olson most; he characterized it as "the only plan" that would end depression. His extravagant praise was underwritten by the tacit hope that the code system would pave the way for a co-operative commonwealth which would harness the productive capacity of industry for the welfare of society rather than of individuals. He expressed special pleasure at Section 7a of the National Industrial Recovery Act, which gave labor the right to organize and bargain collectively.

Olson's outspoken enthusiasm for the regulation of industry led General Hugh S. Johnson, the N.R.A. administrator, to appoint him special code enforcement officer in Minnesota. He was pleased, and when asked by reporters if there was a title to the job, he said "Huey Long calls himself the kingfish, but I am going to be the codefish of Minnesota." [27] He promised to set up machinery which would make it "a moral crime to cheat on the codes."

The duties of "the codefish" turned out to be considerably less consequential than he had expected. The routine enforcement work soon devolved on the nine-man N.R.A. state board appointed by the President. All complaints were initially referred to this board, which functioned by districts and attempted to enforce the codes mainly by moral suasion.

Despite the nebulous lines of authority, Olson labored diligently to set up effective compliance machinery. He designated the state Industrial Commission to handle complaints that could not be settled by the district boards, and personally took up the cases of persistent violators.[28] He was so interested in the protection of labor's right to organize that he systematically gathered evidence on violations of Section 7a, turning it over to the federal district attorney for prosecution.

As Olson grappled with the problem of code enforcement, he became increasingly critical of the voluntary features of the N.R.A. and called repeatedly upon the President to invoke his licensing powers and compel cooperation. In a speech at Powderhorn Park in Minneapolis he questioned the professions of cooperation by the "overlords" of industry and asserted that history contained no record of a ruling class voluntarily "giving up privileges it already had." [29]

Much to the relief of harassed code violators, Olson resigned his position as "codefish" in late October at the request of the national authorities, who sought to institute a nationwide system of compliance boards. Apparently this was the sole reason for Olson's withdrawal,[30] but critics of the N.R.A. like Senator Schall gleefully credited the action to disillusionment with the recovery program.

Olson promptly denied these insinuations, but rumors continued to circulate because many of the governor's followers criticized the N.R.A. John Bosch condemned it as a "distinct and long step in the direction of military dictatorship of fascism as in Italy or Germany," [31] and Lieutenant Governor K. K. Solberg, on a statewide speaking tour, assured his auditors that Olson did not believe in the New Deal's industrial program.

Meanwhile, the N.I.R.A.'s Section 7a was upsetting the old equilibrium between labor and management. Under the stimulus of its collective bargaining provisions, a nationwide rash of industrial disputes broke out during the closing months of 1933. In Minnesota the employees of the Hormel meat packing plant at Austin struck with such determination that Olson had to intervene to avert possible violence and effect a settlement.

Apparently the strike grew out of the refusal of the company to grant a substantial wage increase, although more general demands for seniority and modification of working conditions were also involved. It started without specific warning at 10:00 P.M. Friday, November 10, when squads of workers came to the plant and ordered the night crew to suspend operations. Foremen were permitted to finish picking sheep, but other work stopped immediately.[32] As soon as the night shift left, the intruders set up picket lines.

The following day the strikers took a further and more questionable step when they occupied the plant and cut off the refrigeration system, subjecting large quantities of meat to possible spoilage. This led to a brief encounter between local law enforcement officers and the strikers, and although only three men were slightly injured, Sheriff Syck considered the situation serious enough to telegraph Olson for troops. The governor refused to act precipitately, but mobilized three hundred guardsmen at Owatonna. He dispatched Frank Starkey of the Industrial Commission to arbitrate the strike and promised his personal intervention if negotiations broke down.

During all this the company management played a curiously passive role. Jay C. Hormel, president of the firm, conceded the right of the workers to strike and actually considered going off on a vacation.[33] His moderation and good sense prevented a forcible effort to dislodge the pickets. Fortunately, just at this time Congressman F. H. Shoemaker, one of the more radical Farmer Labor leaders, drifted into Austin and with extraordinary tact and judgment induced the strikers to turn the refrigeration system back on before the hundreds of thousands of dollars' worth of meat had spoiled. His timely intervention prevented the workers from burning their bridges irretrievably and created a more friendly atmosphere for discussion.

Deciding that his direct participation in negotiations was necessary to break the deadlock, Governor Olson drove down to Austin Sunday afternoon and began a series of conferences with both parties. He took a stiff line with the union leaders, telling them bluntly that a sitdown strike gave labor a black eye. His effort to make the management see reason was realistically seconded by R. C. Lilly, personal friend of Olson and president of the First National Bank of St. Paul. Lilly was in a position to force an early settlement because the Hormel company owed money to his St. Paul bank.[34]

The simultaneous application of pressure at all points gradually closed the gap between the principals, and after a long night of negotiations a settlement was reached at 4:45 Monday morning. The key point of the agreement pledged both sides to accept arbitration by the Industrial Commission. Pending its action, the strikers agreed to evacuate the plant and return to work at the old wage.

The settlement of the strike, following so closely on the heels of his dramatic intervention, was considered a great personal victory for Olson. It enhanced his prestige with all classes. The sole note of discord was sounded in the newspapers. The *Chicago Tribune* had become so exercised about the strikers' violation of property rights that it sent reporters and photographers to cover the dispute. The Twin City dailies also dispatched full staffs to the scene and directed a tirade of criticism against the governor for his failure to break the strike with troops.[35]

Blazing with indignation, Olson purchased radio time to present his case. Persuasively he argued "that there were only two alternatives — first to peacefully persuade the employees to leave the plant, or second to eject them forcibly with the use of troops." He went on to state his faith in peaceful persuasion and to point out that the strike had been settled by that means. Recalling his personal experience with strikebreakers on the Seattle docks, he commented sarcastically on the editorials demanding troops: "Apparently the mistake made by me — in the light of these writings — was that I did not turn the machine guns of the state on some 2700 citizens and create some widows and orphans."[36]

This forceful defense of his conduct impressed the people

and a heavy mail endorsed his stand.[37] Once again enemy strategy had backfired, leaving Olson unquestionably the victor.

The curtain rang down on a strenuous year for Olson with
a special session of the legislature. The repeal of the Eighteenth
Amendment necessitated the rewriting of Minnesota's liquor
laws, and the exhaustion of state relief funds obliged the legislature to vote fresh money or face the curtailment of federal
aid. Olson called the lawmakers together on December 5. By
starting the session so close to the Christmas holidays he sought
to encourage rapid passage of the requisite bills and to protect
himself against the introduction of extraneous issues or other
dilatory tactics.

His strategy did not reckon with the recalcitrance of the
legislators. Liquor control immediately touched off a controversy. The prohibitionists and the beer interests for different
reasons hoped to block by a filibuster any legislation permitting
the sale of hard liquor. The wets had a clear majority but split
badly over procedure, some favoring a state dispensary system
and others backing a variety of plans to permit the purchase of
liquor at private stores, hotels, and restaurants. There were so
many interests involved that party lines splintered completely,
making it difficult to report out any kind of bill.

Olson prudently refrained from taking a definite stand on the
issue. He had appointed a composite group of sixty-six legislators, ministers, lawyers, and educators to work out a liquor
control plan, insisting only that the right of local option be
respected and that safeguards he inserted to prevent the return
of the saloon. And when the special session convened, he in-
corporated the committee's recommendations in his message,
with a reminder that the people had already expressed their
will on prohibition. He cultivated the impression that his function was to implement the repeal of the Eighteenth Amendment
without regard to his personal opinion.

This olympian detachment almost killed liquor legislation.
The drys watched gleefully while the wets knifed each other's
bills. This went on for more than two weeks, and the legislature

prepared to adjourn without having accomplished anything. Then Olson threatened to recall the lawmakers immediately unless they substituted a holiday recess for the adjournment resolution, and once it became clear that the session would be continued until a liquor control bill reached the governor, the legislature buckled down to work. It rejected the state dispensary plan, which had unofficial Farmer Labor support,[38] but shortly after the new year it passed a patchwork measure which Olson called "a good compromise" and signed.

The squabble over liquor legislation was a nonpartisan affair, but the request for relief appropriations revived the Olson-Rockne vendetta in acute form. The governor was determined to secure adequate appropriations for relief of the needy. He had traveled to Washington four times during the year to secure federal aid and expedite the flow of funds, but despite the substantial quantity of federal money pumped into Minnesota toward the end of 1933, certain categories of unfortunates such as drought sufferers were ineligible to receive relief under the current rules.

Accordingly Olson requested the legislature to appropriate an additional five million dollars for distribution by the Executive Council. Anticipating strenuous objections to an increase of state debt, he recommended that the cost be met by levying a heavy excise tax on liquor and boosting the gasoline tax one cent a gallon.

Rockne's declaration of war came in the form of a counterproposal that five hundred thousand dollars be made available for relief as loans from state to county and from county to individuals. With unexpected adroitness, he dodged the social and economic issue at the outset, basing his opposition to relief on constitutional scruples.

Although the legislature had already broadened the powers of the Executive Council to include relief from economic distress as well as from natural calamities, Rockne argued that state contributions to federal projects for conservation and flood control violated the constitutional provision prohibiting appropriations for internal improvements. The attorney general disputed this interpretation of the state constitution,[39] but if the legislature supported Rockne, the relief bill was dead because it earmarked part of the money for conservation projects.

Olson had no intention of allowing the discussion to bog down in legal technicalities. On December 15 he appeared before the senate Finance Committee and twitted Rockne for his feigned concern about the constitution, pointing out that the senator had responded quickly enough in 1919 when a Republican governor requested relief. Coolly he offered to retire from public life if the supreme court ruled his bill unconstitutional.

A week later he carried the fight to the people over the radio. He told them Rockne was employing a cheap subterfuge to obscure the real issue, and branded him as the "leader and symbol of a dying social, economic order which brought about this catastrophe in American life, which we call a depression." [40] He summarized the senator's viewpoint as that of the selfish provincial who says in substance, "I can take care of myself, let others fend as best they can."

This searing attack goaded Rockne into dropping the mask of a constitutional lawyer and attempting to defend his social philosophy, out of favor as it was at the moment. Replying over the radio, he condemned relief as an intolerable burden on farmers and small homeowners. With inconceivable ineptitude, he alienated the drought-stricken counties by declaring, "I'll not vote $5,000,000 for a half-baked flood control program in a waterless county." [41]

Once again Olson had outmaneuvered his antagonist. In a second radio address on December 27 he countered Rockne's contentions point by point. By insinuation, humor, and sharp ridicule, he made the senator appear a devil incarnate. It was one of Olson's greatest efforts, and the public deluged him with congratulatory telegrams. One supporter thought the speech so interesting that he stopped his bridge game to listen! [42]

When the legislature reassembled after the holidays, it was clear that St. George had slain the dragon. The senate quickly passed the relief bill in the form Olson had requested.

# Chapter IX  A TROUBLESOME PLATFORM

THE sensational victory over Rockne at the special session marked the height of Olson's prestige and popularity. The people had been deeply moved by his assertion of public responsibility for the care of destitute citizens, and when the legislature finally passed the $5,000,000 relief appropriation, expressions of approval poured in from every part of the state. One voter voiced the general satisfaction when he wrote: "You have never been so strong politically with the average man in Minnesota." [1]

Lionized by the tolerant businessmen and idolized by the masses, Olson seemed invincible. Even Farmer Laborites, who quarreled about almost everything else, were virtually unanimous in their admiration for the governor. They regarded him as indispensable to the success of the party and groaned audibly when rumor hinted at his appointment as the first United States ambassador to Soviet Russia. [2]

None but the most prejudiced observers doubted Olson's reelection in the fall, and during the opening days of 1934 opposition editors vied with each other in conceding an Olson victory. Charles Cheney even made the suggestion that the Farmer Labor sweep might extend to the traditionally Republican legislature. [3] Never had the opposition been so demoralized. The Democrats bickered incessantly among themselves over the distribution of federal patronage, while the twice-drubbed Republicans lined up wearily for the coming campaign like a football team constantly fighting in the shadow of its own goal posts.

Yet the outlook changed with such suddenness and completeness that midsummer found Olson fighting for his political life and the whole reform movement in danger of irretrievable disaster.

In the midst even of the rosy prospects of January, inauspicious portents were easily discernible. The unstable alliance of farmers and industrial workers, which had functioned so effectively during the crisis, was showing signs of dissolution. Publication of a seemingly innocuous analysis of legislative voting records by the Farmer Labor educational bureau provoked an ill-tempered controversy, with rural editors contending that only labor measures were used as criteria of party regularity.[4]

Equally disconcerting was the determined effort of a small clique headed by George Griffith and I. C. Strout to turn the reform movement into a professional machine composed exclusively of subservient jobholders. Aided by the constitution of the Farmer Labor Association, which explicitly vested authority in the hands of dues-paying members, they gained control of several county delegations to the 1934 convention and circulated a list of "official" candidates. Vince Day denounced these tactics, complaining that "jealous, ambitious, and greedy spoilsmen had organized local clubs and denied membership to the best friends of the movement."[5] The machine politicians were prudent enough to remain in the background during the convention, but the episode provided a foretaste of things to come if they were allowed to consolidate their grip on the Farmer Labor party.

Even before this the spoilsmen had very nearly split the party by a synthetic campaign to deny Henrik Shipstead a third nomination for United States senator. No genuine anti-Shipstead movement could have been generated because he enjoyed wide support among rank-and-file Farmer Laborites, to say nothing of his standing with Germans, Scandinavians, and churchgoers in the old parties. However, his haughty aloofness from organization politics, his elder statesman complex, and above all his refusal to work for the party ticket in 1932 offended Farmer Labor professionals.

During the fall of 1933 Shipstead had aroused the ire of the truculent and erratic congressman, F. H. Shoemaker, who toured southern Minnesota lambasting the senator for his frequent absences from roll calls and for neglect of his constituents. Shoemaker compared Shipstead to Judas Iscariot and accused him of stinginess and ingratitude to the party which had done so much for him.[6]

Shoemaker was preparing to enter the senatorial contest, but party professionals knew they could not use the excitable, intemperate congressman, who brawled with capital taxi drivers and policemen, to spearhead the anti-Shipstead drive. In fact, the only Farmer Laborite who could possibly unseat the senator was Olson himself. Fearing the governor would not voluntarily enter a contest against Shipstead, the machine politicians decided to generate an Olson boom for senator without asking his consent.

The scheme was particularly irresponsible because it ignored the threat of a Shipstead candidacy on an independent ticket, and because it made no provision to fill the vacuum that would be created in the state leadership if Olson switched from governor to senator.

Ignoring these problems, Griffith, Strout, and Carl R. Erickson, the state purchasing commissioner, who were the chief conspirators, launched the Olson senatorial boom on February 12. Henry Teigan, who had been recruited because his Farmer Labor Press Service was used in a large number of rural papers, led off with an article proclaiming that Shipstead's failure to cooperate with the party had "proven offensive to the rank and file."[7] The same day C. D. Johnston, political reporter for the *St. Paul Pioneer Press*, wrote a front-page article predicting that important Farmer Labor leaders would meet during the week to organize a draft movement for Olson.[8] Other Twin City newspapers obligingly played the game. The *Minneapolis Journal* wrote with enthusiasm about the great Olson boom and the letters of advice flooding his office.[9] Cheney, enchanted by visions of a ruinous schism in the reform movement, observed hopefully that the governor had not positively forbidden the use of his name.

The synthetic quality of this journalistic outburst was emphasized by the complete silence of the *Farmer Labor Leader*. Also, a number of Farmer Labor papers promptly came to the defense of Shipstead.[10] Even Robley D. Cramer, editor of the *Minneapolis Labor Review* and close friend of Olson, strongly defended the senator, scornfully observing that Shipstead was not Paul Bunyan and could not single-handedly establish "the cooperative commonwealth on a national scale."[11]

Although a senate seat would give Olson relief from the interminable quarrels of his Farmer Labor following and an opportunity to push his reform program at the national level, he remained cold to the plans of the spoilsmen. He undoubtedly understood the motives of newspapers which had heretofore handled him roughly, but the controlling factor was probably his private pledge of support to Shipstead in 1930 when the latter gave him a last-minute endorsement.

Olson had made his position explicit at a press conference on August 26, 1933: "I expect to be a candidate for re-election. I have no intention of running for the senate."[12] Finding this categorical statement undermined by the incipient boom, he made a second statement on February 13. After complaining that he couldn't find anyone who knew anything about the movement to draft him for senator, Olson concluded, "My first story stands. I am not a candidate for senator."[13]

When this terse announcement failed to end the speculation, Olson took the unprecedented step of filing for governor on February 24, although the endorsement convention did not meet for another month. In words reminiscent of 1930, when Shipstead was the arbiter of Farmer Labor politics and vouched for Olson's good behavior, the governor said, "Some time ago Senator Shipstead informed me he would campaign with and for other candidates of the Farmer Labor party for state and national office. I will not therefore become a candidate by reason of being drafted or otherwise." [14]

Griffith, Strout, and Erickson countered with the demand that Shipstead put in writing for the state executive committee the categorical pledge of cooperation which he allegedly had given Olson.[15] Vince Day, speaking for the governor, made a strong plea for moderation, urging that Shipstead be invited to address the Farmer Labor convention.[16] The executive committee overruled this cautious counsel and designated Erickson to extract an explicit pledge of support from Shipstead. At the last minute, however, Frank Starkey prevailed upon the firebrands to be satisfied with a moderate telegram followed up by a phone call.

Shipstead's return wire was a masterpiece of equivocation. He pledged loyalty to the Farmer Labor cause and party candidates provided they "have records that will win us the confidence of our people and reflect credit on the party and the state."[17] This put Olson in a difficult position, but he managed to isolate the Shipstead opponents in the ensuing week and was able to wire the senator on the eve of the convention that "clouds are rapidly clearing away and prospects for fine weather next Tuesday and Wednesday are definite."[18] Despite some intemperate attacks that were made on Shipstead from the convention floor, in the end the delegates gave the senator their endorsement for re-election.

Olson had averted a split in the party, but there was little reason for complacence. The episode exposed the disruptive forces at work in the reform movement. Energy, sublimated as crusading fervor during the long years in the political wilderness, was being squandered on an internal struggle for power now that the party had won control of the state. Success at the polls intensified rather than diminished quarrels because the stakes were higher. The fledgling political machine had not hesitated to cross Olson or flout majority sentiment. All in all, conditions within the party were not reassuring on the eve of another campaign.

The disaster that overtook Olson in the spring of 1934 was in part his own fault. People close to him, particularly those outside the party, detected a new note of carelessness in his attitude just before the convention. From his remarks it was clear that the strain of perpetually mediating party quarrels was begining to tell on him. He could hardly avoid an unpleasant comparison between his heavy responsibilities and the dignified indolence of Shipstead. While Olson was working feverishly to keep the Farmer Labor organization from splintering into a dozen fragments, the senator sat calmly in Washington waiting for the inevitable call to duty.

Although a causal relationship cannot be documented, the situation seems to have pushed Olson into an experimental mood. Whether he consciously renounced his role of mediator or allowed it to lapse by default through exhaustion or ill health, Olson abruptly changed his tactics at the 1934 convention. In preceding years he had carefully organized the agenda, passed on the nominees, and participated in the formulation of a platform, but this time he planned a trip to Washington immediately after the keynote address. The restraint of exuberant delegates and the contraction of socialistic principles to innocuous political slogans were to be left to others. When a close friend urged him to stay until the platform was written, he responded with a sigh of disgust, "They'll have to learn to do something for themselves eventually. They may as well start now." [19]

The most painful consequences of this new policy might have been avoided if Olson had not been swept by his own oratory into a dangerous statement. A careful reading of his convention speech does not indicate that he favored a further leftward movement by the party in 1934. It contained the usual admonition against precipitous change. The transition to the new order was to proceed gradually and methodically rather than by "jerks, or jumps, or spurts."

But these words of caution were drowned out by his call to action. Candidly he outlined the goal of the party as "a cooperative commonwealth wherein the government will stifle as much as possible the greed and avarice of the private profit system and will bring more equitable distribution of the wealth produced by the hands and minds of the people." As he developed this theme in ringing prose, the convention applauded frantically. And Olson, sensing the need for a climactic statement, departed from his prepared text to proclaim dramatically, "I am frank to say I am what I want to be. I am a radical." [20]

The response was deafening, but the glittering phrases touched off a chain of unexpected events. The extremists of the Farmer Labor party hailed the governor's convention speech as a declaration of total war against capitalism and prepared to implement it with a forthright party platform. The frenzied elation of the delegates played into their hands by diminishing the influence of moderates and political realists. Olson, who had contributed so much to the crusading fervor, might have recalled the crowd to a sense of reality, but he blithely departed for Washington, leaving the convention in the control of the zealots.

The platform committee reported to the floor the most extreme document ever drawn up by an American party actually holding political power. The preamble opened with the grim observation that millions were poverty-stricken in the midst of great material resources. It predicted that "palliative measures will continue to fail" and expressed the conviction that "only a complete reorganization of the social structure into a cooperative commonwealth will bring economic security and prevent a prolonged period of further suffering." [21]

Worse was to follow in the main body of the platform. Among the standard Farmer Labor planks for agricultural relief, increased taxation of unearned wealth, and conservation appeared a sweeping public ownership clause. Not only mines, public utilities, and transportation, but banks and factories, too, were listed for operation by the state.

When those responsible for rounding up votes saw this public ownership plank, they were petrified. Surely the farmer and the small merchant, who had been wooed so diligently over the years, would be irretrievably lost to the party if the convention approved this provision. Frank Starkey and Senator Emil Regnier, who had managed the 1932 campaign, raised vigorous objections, but the firebrands would not listen. The critics managed to send the platform back to committee, but it reappeared shortly thereafter with only one change: the exemption from public ownership of "bona fide cooperatively owned and operated enterprises." [22]

Oblivious to danger, the convention adopted the platform and adjourned at 2 A.M. on March 29, pleased with the evening's work.

This extraordinary attempt at political suicide grew partly out of a collective insanity. Such a revolutionary spirit had been generated by flaming speeches and manifestoes that the delegates lost the power to reason clearly. Vince Day believed that nothing could have blocked the convention action.[23] All distinctions between moderates and radicals had momentarily disappeared in a fit of wild crusading ardor. Except for a few practical men like Regnier and Starkey, the convention exhibited an unbelievable unanimity. The majority on the platform committee was a composite group of seven farmers and four representatives of organized labor.[24] The small minority was similarly constituted and objected to the platform not so much because of opposition to its principles as out of fear that the people lacked preparation for such a bold step. But they, too, succumbed to the contagious enthusiasm. The convention simply stampeded itself into adopting the platform.

Nonetheless, Olson cannot be absolved for his part in the debacle. H. Y. Williams, chairman of the platform committee, thought the governor's speech paved the way for the triumph of left-wing principles.[25] The judgment may be too severe, but Olson certainly set the pattern for succeeding denunciations of capitalism which worked so powerfully on the emotions of the delegates. At the same time, he fatally weakened the moderates. They could have little effect when left-wingers were able to quote the governor to buttress arguments for an advanced program of social reform. The rank-and-file delegates were sure they were doing what Olson wanted.

The initial reaction to the Farmer Labor platform was stunned silence, but within twenty-four hours the opposition had recovered its breath and begun a propaganda barrage that continued unabated until November.

The *Minneapolis Journal* pronounced the platform "more enlightening than pages of comments or hours of campaign speeches" and predicted, "It may well be reprinted by Democrats or Republicans." Vin Weber, state senator from Slayton and an implacable foe of Olson, rejoiced that "for the first time . . . the Farmer Labor party goes before the voters stripped of camouflage and expediency, revealed as the menace it is, supporting principles of government un-American and unwise to experiment with." Representative R. W. Hitchcock denounced the platform as an attempt to "substitute the Russian for the American system." Not to be outdone, Senator Schall accused Olson of drawing up a communistic program at the behest of the New Deal brain trust. Even the judicious *New York Times* thought it probable that right-wing Farmer Laborites would henceforth be classed as Tories.[26]

Farmer Laborites themselves began to suffer misgivings about their handiwork. Realistic politicians considered the platform a blunder of the first magnitude. George Leonard thought it had "resuscitated the Republican corpse."[27] State Senator Charles A. Hausler credited the public ownership plank with large-scale defections in rural areas. Vince Day reported that the platform had shaken public confidence in the Farmer Labor cause and frightened small merchants, bankers, and manufacturers. Bluntly he characterized the blanket proposal for state operation of factories as "sheer nonsense."[28]

Even the party firebrands realized that election prospects had deteriorated. One of them actually wrote Olson a letter of congratulation for jeopardizing his political future by defending "an unpopular principle and frankly avowing himself a radi-

Cartoon by John Baer, *from the* Farmer Labor Leader,
*April 15, 1934*

cal." [29] Only Griffith and Strout had the temerity to predict that the platform would increase the party vote.[30] Realistic observers agreed that the precipitate action of the convention had blown up a squall capable of capsizing the Farmer Labor party.

News of the platform and of the uproar about it, reaching Olson in Washington, left him sober and chastened — aware that however he felt, he dared not again abdicate his responsibility for the wayward children of reform. He issued a statement from Washington glossing over the platform's more dangerous implications and spent the last leg of the return journey to Minnesota listening attentively to an opponent lambast the public ownership plank over the railroad radio.

It was evident that the revival of party prospects required more than Olson's determination and fighting spirit. Somehow the unfavorable impression created by the socialistic planks had to be counteracted. The platform could not be changed without a fatal admission of error, yet elementary political strategy dictated some sort of modification. What eventually emerged from strategy deliberations was not so much a settled policy as a series of improvisations designed to repudiate the most radical planks in the platform without appearing to do so.

These tactics jelled slowly, but Olson pressed instinctively toward them at the outset. His first statement on the platform from Washington was an accurate preview of the party line: "I interpret the public ownership plank as approving federal and state ownership of public utilities and key industries. It does not contemplate any general ownership and operation of business beyond that." [31]

This motif was repeated for reporters when Olson arrived in Minnesota. He categorically stated that there would be no hedging on the party program, and then cheerfully contradicted himself by observing that "the platform of the Farmer Labor Association with reasonable interpretation can be made consistent with my statement as the candidate for governor of the Farmer Labor party." [32]

Apparently the prophet intended to alter holy writ on his

return from Sinai. Omniscience, that is to say, reposed in the candidate rather than the convention. This doctrine was hardly new to American politics, but it had seldom received such frank expression.

Then Olson glided on to a castigation of the entrenched interests who attacked the platform: "These forces are up to the same old tricks. They are endeavoring to frighten the people of Minnesota so that the people will regard them as saviors, and they will again have the opportunity to loot the state in the name of salvation."

The governor's uncompromising language raised the drooping spirits of Farmer Laborites, but it did little to counteract attacks on the public ownership plank, which were making serious inroads into party strength. As early as April 4, Vince Day urged Olson to meet this issue squarely and give the public explicit assurances that the party did not favor state competition with small business ventures.[33] He also suggested that the governor deliver his message over the radio to reach the widest possible audience. A week of sounding public opinion convinced Olson that both these steps were necessary. So on April 12 he took his case to the people over a statewide hook-up.

The speech was for the most part devoted to a further interpretation of the Farmer Labor platform. Olson ingeniously insisted that public ownership of factories referred only to idle factories which would manufacture goods for the needy, and he denied that this proposal was a communistic project, reminding his auditors that such patriotic organizations as the Red Cross had run self-help programs for years.[34]

Continuing in the same vein, he minimized the novelty of Farmer Labor proposals for federal ownership of key industries. With more enthusiasm than accuracy, he argued that the government already possessed power to take over key industries under the N.I.R.A. He even cited President Roosevelt as an advocate of public ownership of water power. He quoted from such diverse sources as the social welfare program of the Presbyterian church and an encyclical of Pope Pius XI to prove that the Farmer Labor party merely aimed at the implementation of Christianity. He protested that the party goal was not public ownership, "but a cooperative commonwealth in which enterprises will be carried out cooperatively by organizations of producers and consumers." That, he insisted, "is essentially a championing of private business, but of business carried on for mutual aid and not avaricious profit." [35]

The speech was a masterpiece of political dialectic. It presented Farmer Labor objectives in such a plausible light that only outspoken critics could remain either fearful or antagonistic. Skillfully it shifted the emphasis from socialistic planning to voluntary cooperation.

Olson's textual criticism stripped the platform of planks dear to the hearts of left-wingers. In fact, if the third Olson interpretation was authoritative, Farmer Laborites were hardly more radical than Republicans who occasionally showed a lukewarm interest in cooperatives. This impression received confirmation in a front-page editorial of the *Farmer Labor Leader* issued immediately after the speech. It accepted the Olson version of the platform, admitting tacitly if not explicitly that the party stood for sane bourgeois principles. And it dwelt almost cheerfully upon the numerous constitutional obstructions to a public ownership program in Minnesota.*

But the conservative hounds had picked up the scent and refused to be distracted. They bayed about the communist menace with such monotonous regularity that Robley Cramer called it the most vicious propaganda campaign since the days of the Public Safety Commission.[36]

The Farmer Laborites were in no condition to fight back energetically. Each mail brought news of fresh defections in rural Minnesota. H. W. Bless of Wells wrote Olson that he could not be elected senator on the Farmer Labor platform, adding that the party has "lost thousands of votes here in southern Min-

* (1) Action by a majority of the state legislature, (2) a referendum vote in Minnesota, (3) review by the Minnesota supreme court, (4) final decision by the U.S. Supreme Court. (*Farmer Labor Leader*, April 15, 1934.)

nesota, and if the platform is not amended, I would not know how to get them back."[37] O. J. Rustad found much adverse sentiment even in the Ninth District, traditional hotbed of agrarian radicalism and cradle of the Minnesota Nonpartisan League.[38]

The flow of disheartening information to Farmer Labor headquarters created a condition bordering on panic. Vince Day noticed that the leaders were inclined to condemn everyone who did not actively oppose the platform and feared the spread of this dangerous spirit to the rank and file.[39] Several county organizations threatened a revolt unless the platform was amended, while some legislative and congressional candidates ignored it entirely. The situation became so critical during the first two weeks of May that the survival of the party seemed in retrospect to be nothing less than miraculous. Olson later said that he would probably have lost a May election.[40]

Continuing decline in the party's strength convinced the governor that adroit interpretation of troublesome clauses was not enough. Vince Day seconded his conclusion, contending that the rank and file could not understand, defend, or even criticize intelligently the document produced by the convention. He thought the preamble contradicted itself by advocating public ownership in one sentence and a cooperative commonwealth in another. Since the typical Farmer Laborite was not so much opposed to private wealth as to its current distribution and use, Day suggested that the platform be reworked, eliminating its socialistic features and emphasizing the development of private cooperatives.

The state central committee met on April 21 to canvass the whole problem. Apparently the objections to a second convention were considered insuperable, because shortly thereafter Vince Day, Hjalmar Petersen, Frank Starkey, and Harry Boyle began to work privately on revision of the platform. They decided (1) to reprint the document with a brief note of explanation or analysis after each plank, and (2) to segregate the troublesome public ownership clauses from the rest of the platform on the ground that such measures required an amendment to the federal constitution for implementation.

The governor accepted the revised platform enthusiastically, being particularly struck by the ingenious scheme for grouping public ownership planks in a separate section entitled "Ultimate Aims."

This amended version of the party creed appeared for the first time in the May 15 issue of the *Farmer Labor Leader*. An introductory paragraph explained that the state committee was driven to such drastic measures to "overcome the mass of misinformation and deliberate misrepresentation of capitalist newspapers and the capitalist politicians." A second paragraph, in large, black type, announced that "The Farmer Labor party is opposed to state ownership and operation of small business such as grocery stores, meat shops, department stores, millinery establishments, drug stores, and similar enterprises." Fearful lest even these painfully specific words would not exorcise the socialist demon, it went on to proclaim the party the guardian and protector of small business "from the destructive competition of monopolistic institutions."

Following this preamble was a summary of the party's legislative program. It included (1) operation of idle factories, (2) extension of the mortgage moratorium law, (3) exemption of homesteads from taxation, (4) additional taxes on large incomes and inheritances, (5) unemployment, sickness, and accident insurance, and (6) extension of municipal authority to sell power outside the city limits. These proposals would alarm no one; with one or two exceptions they coincided with reform measures pushed by progressives of the 1912 vintage.

The five-thousand-word analysis enabled the Farmer Labor party to amend the original platform beyond recognition without calling a second convention. Within a month after the publication of the analysis, copies of the offensive convention platform had vanished from party headquarters.[41] Thereafter it was available to the voters only when conservative newspapers reprinted it.

The appearance of the analysis touched off a fresh series of attacks by major-party leaders. In unison they loudly insisted that the original platform revealed the true intentions of the Farmer Labor party. After so many years of masquerading, they said, Minnesota radicals had finally torn off the mask, and no amount of explanation could conceal their fundamental position. The *Minneapolis Journal* observed that "at any rate the platform still stands. Regardless of the means now proposed to carry it out, regardless of the quibble about 'immediate' and 'ultimate' objectives, the platform remains as the official program of the Farmer Labor Party in delegate convention assembled. Whether it is to be carried out next week or in the next decade is not so material, the ultimate purpose is the same." [42]

The opposition had no intention of letting the voter forget the original platform. As usual, the *Journal* did the best job of exploiting the instinctive American distrust of public ownership. Starting in early May, it carried front-page maps of the more important Minnesota counties with statistics concerning the employment offered and the wages paid therein by private enterprise. This information was followed by a standard rhetorical question as to whether the voters preferred the present management or a bureau in the state capital.

Republican headquarters cooperated by circulating scare stories about business firms slated to leave the state if the Farmer Laborites returned to power.[43] And the G.O.P. gubernatorial candidate, Martin A. Nelson, solemnly warned the voters that economic measures advocated by the third party would make Minnesota an industrial desert or a plague area.[44]

Olson lashed back at the newspapers and fearmongers in his primary campaign and the *Farmer Labor Leader* sent registered letters to the factories that were said to be leaving the state and printed their denials. With mock solicitude, it also circularized Twin City newspapers to ascertain their plans in the event of Olson's re-election. Some did not bother to reply, but others proclaimed their determination to bear the martyr's cross as long as necessary. None of them even hinted at departure.

Cartoon by Oscar Cesare, from the Minneapolis Journal,
October 8, 1934

Although some of the calamity howling could be laughed off, the systematic renewal of gossip about Olson's private life was more difficult to combat. On the whole, the whisperers presented little material that had not been used against the governor in previous elections, but they revived the controversial Birkeland case in a particularly vicious form.

The essential facts of the case can be simply stated. K. B. Birkeland, a Norwegian Lutheran minister who, rightly or wrongly, was facing reflections on his financial integrity, was found dead in a vacant house under perplexing circumstances. The evidence indicated that Mr. Birkeland had died of a heart attack. It seemed conclusive enough to rule out the possibility of murder, and Floyd Olson, who was then serving as county attorney, in an off-the-record press conference expressed strong doubt that Birkeland had met a violent death.

Just how Olson originally intended to dispose of the case is not clear, but when one of the reporters indiscreetly published his statement, Birkeland's family became upset. On the theory that formal charges of murder would recast the elder Birkeland in the role of an innocent victim, his son Harold was determined to secure prosecution at any cost.

Under ordinary circumstances some face-saving formula might have been devised, but Olson dared not back down after being quoted in print. From this unfortunate situation, which nobody willed, young Harold Birkeland emerged a sworn enemy of Olson. At first he made a strenuous effort to secure Olson's removal from office, accusing the county attorney of conniving with law enforcement officers to blacken the reputation of his father and to suppress information on the murder. Apparently the charges were irresponsible, because Governor Christianson, who wasted no affection on Olson, rejected the ouster petitions.

Then Harold Birkeland went underground. He tried to organize Norwegian ministers and their congregations against Olson by personal persuasion as well as by the circulation of pamphlets. These efforts had no visible effect on Olson's political fortunes in 1930 and 1932. Not only did Birkeland lack organized help, but most people were too preoccupied with the economic crisis to take any interest in personal feuds. However, the 1934 platform made the defeat of Olson a distinct possibility. This may have been enough to arouse Birkeland to a fresh effort, but it is more probable that the Republicans deliberately encouraged him for their own purposes.

At all events, large quantities of Birkeland pamphlets began appearing throughout northern Minnesota late in the spring. Those circulating in the Ninth District, entitled "Governor Floyd B. Olson's First Kidnapping Murder," leveled a variety of irresponsible charges against his character. Farther south, similar pamphlets were distributed to Norwegian ministers, who passed them out surreptitiously among parishioners at church but did not allow the leaflets to leave the premises.[45]

The effect of such literature on the rural imagination is hard to assess. Obviously it meant more than in urban centers, where murder and scandal of one sort or another were a daily staple in the newspapers. Even so, it probably did no more than reinforce a trend.

Olson considered the Birkeland campaign to be hitting below the belt, but he took no public notice of the defamatory pamphlets, wisely confining himself to explanations for his campaign managers. He knew that because the ill-advised platform had made his party vulnerable, the opposition would stop at nothing. A. H. Hendrickson, the Sixth District Farmer Labor chairman, prophesied "the hottest and dirtiest campaign we have ever had."[46]

# Chapter X THE TRUCK STRIKE

THE agitation over the March platform was just beginning to subside when Olson was confronted with the turbulent truck drivers' strike in Minneapolis. He could not escape involvement or control the elemental forces it released. For a time he tried to walk the tight rope of nonpartisanship, but sympathy for the strikers ultimately drove him to risk his personal prestige and political future in their behalf.

The strike grew out of the depressed condition of labor and the stubborn employer resistance to wage increases. Despite substantial economic revival during the spring and summer of 1934, nearly one third of the working class in Hennepin County remained unemployed, while many of those fortunate enough to hold jobs barely earned enough to live on.[1]

Special circumstances tended to aggravate the distress in the Twin Cities. Economic developments had not treated them kindly. Once the center of a great commercial empire, they had begun to lose their preeminent position at the turn of the century.[2] The depletion of timber resources, the exodus of the milling industry, and the rerouting of freight shipments through the Panama Canal slowly destroyed the basis for their prosperity. The relation of the Twin Cities to the hinterland came to resemble that of a huge head to a puny body. Even before the depression it was evident that Minneapolis and St. Paul faced a period of readjustment.

In concrete terms this meant that an ever-increasing labor force bid for the available jobs until despair drove part of it elsewhere. The depression accelerated this trend, creating a great pool of unemployed in the Twin Cities and driving wages steadily downward. For employers this presaged a return to the happy prewar situation when a steady stream of immigrants had provided an abundant supply of cheap labor. But for the unemployed it threatened chronic poverty if not outright starvation.

The organization of labor might have softened the rigors of economic law, but Minneapolis businessmen resolutely opposed any restriction of the open shop. In 1908 they had banded together to form the Citizens' Alliance. Officially dedicated to the maintenance of industrial peace, freedom of contract, and good working conditions,[3] it steadfastly employed tactics designed to keep labor weak and ineffectual. It maintained an elaborate spy system, planted stool pigeons in labor unions, tampered with grand juries, and made generous campaign contributions to antilabor legislators.[4] More than twenty-five thousand dollars was spent to smash a truck drivers' strike in 1916, and on one occasion President A. W. Strong boasted that the vigilance of the Alliance had for a time forced an open shop on the building trades.[5]

Whether this policy contributed to industrial peace was of course debatable, but nobody could deny the sincerity of the eight hundred businessmen who financed it. Their activities were encouraged by popular support or, at the least, popular apathy. The average citizen who paid any attention to labor problems resented unions as an alien importation and cherished the open shop as an embodiment of democratic principles and an essential feature of the free enterprise system. The Citizens' Alliance was accepted rather uncritically as a watchdog of American traditions.

Whatever the spiritual virtues of the open shop, its practical effect on the unskilled or semiskilled workingman was nothing short of disastrous. Defenseless enough in prosperous times, he was reduced by depression to the bleak alternatives of working for a pittance or depending on charity.

Nowhere was the situation more disheartening than in the field of transportation. Taxi drivers received anywhere from

Cartoon by John Baer, from the Farmer Labor Leader,
January 30, 1934

$6.66 to $12.00 for an eighty-four-hour week, while truck operators never got more than $18.00 for a similar period.[6] Almost any measure that would better this state of affairs seemed justified.

The National Industrial Recovery Act passed by the special session of congress in 1933 furnished these depressed classes with their first ray of hope. Tucked away among more spectacular provisions was Section 7a, which gave labor the right to organize and bargain collectively. Had the recovery program not been tossed together with such haste, this revolutionary proposal would certainly have encountered rough going. As it was, the national administration accepted collective bargaining to head off demands for the thirty-hour week rather than because of any settled conviction regarding labor policy.[7]

Section 7a seemed to offer government protection for unions. The implementing machinery was a National Labor Relations Board assisted by a group of regional agencies. The board could investigate industrial disputes, hold elections to determine the appropriate bargaining unit, and punish obstruction with fine or imprisonment. These impressive powers were diluted by restrictions on arbitration as well as by governmental reluctance to test the law's compliance procedures. The enforcement of board decisions depended primarily on public opinion.

None of these considerations dampened working-class enthusiasm. Labor leaders all over the country accepted Section 7a at face value and began vigorous drives to organize unions. By the fall of 1933 this contagion had reached Minneapolis, and appropriately enough, the first efforts were concentrated on truck transportation.

The indispensable role of motor transportation in the commercial life of the city made the truck driver the obvious spearhead for any union drive. By walking off the job he could virtually shut down industrial activity in Minnesota. Such a threat provided powerful leverage to pry union recognition from employers. And success in this venture would open the way for further forays against the open shop. Anticipating the benefits that would be reaped from the organization of this key group, the local teamsters' council designated William Brown, a truck driver of long standing, to attempt the difficult job.

At the outset Brown made two decisions that were to have a profound effect on the labor movement in Minneapolis. He resolved to create an industrial union and appointed the most uncompromising champions of working-class solidarity to organize it. The first decision cost him the support of the parent A.F.L. union, which opposed all efforts to modify the traditional craft structure. Daniel Tobin, president of the International Teamsters' Union, practically ignored the Minneapolis local until the eve of its second strike, when he excommunicated it.

Fraught with even graver consequences was the selection of Carl Skoglund and the three Dunne brothers to organize the truckers. In competence, resourcefulness, and devotion to the labor movement, they were without peers, but unfortunately, the leader of the quadrumvirate, Vince Dunne, belonged to the Trotskyite wing of the Communist party.[8] This exposed him and the union to attack by employers anxious to obscure economic issues. It undermined labor solidarity during the strike, and worst of all, it led to the adoption of doctrinaire class war tactics which culminated in needless bloodshed. But for the moment, Dunne's effectiveness in winning recruits for Local No. 574 was the important consideration.

The decisive event in the rise of the truckers' union was its successful coal strike in February 1934. Drivers of coal trucks and yardmen received as little as thirty-five cents an hour for a working year of five or six months.[9] And the Minneapolis coal companies flatly refused to meet with representatives of the union to discuss wage increases.

Vince Dunne and Carl Skoglund decided to meet this rebuff with a strike. But before calling the men out, they made careful preparations, explaining their strategy to the union members, mapping the coal yards, and drawing up mimeographed instructions for the pickets.[10] This thorough planning paid big dividends. Seven hundred workers walked off the job simultaneously on February 7, tying up coal deliveries completely. The strikers' morale was kept high by nightly meetings, a device that proved valuable later.

The suddenness and effectiveness of the strike caught the employers badly off balance, forcing them to capitulate after two and a half days. They granted recognition to the union and agreed to open wage negotiations with its representatives. The one ominous note was the participation of Sam Levy, a Citizens' Alliance attorney, in the settlement.

The victory of Local 574 over the coal companies stimulated the recruitment campaign and encouraged the union to redouble its efforts. Beginning in March the organizers conducted a series of Sunday night forums, analyzing the coal strike and emphasizing the economic benefits to be derived from a huge union of transportation workers. These meetings were climaxed by a monster rally at the Shubert Theater, with Vince Day substituting for Olson as the principal speaker. Two thousand drivers and helpers were sporting union buttons by the end of April, and nearly seven thousand by midsummer.[11]

The members of the Citizens' Alliance viewed this development with undisguised apprehension. The New Deal recovery program, particularly Section 7 of the N.I.R.A., was abhorrent to them. But Roosevelt's dramatic effort to cope with the depression had caught the public fancy so completely that open criticism was for the moment injudicious if not unpatriotic. So the Citizens' Alliance confined itself to clandestine obstruction. Compliance with Section 7a was evaded by raising a variety of legal objections to administrative procedures.[12]

These delaying tactics did not indicate a lessening of opposition to labor unions, but rather a desire to postpone the conflict until a more favorable occasion. The attitude of the employers was cogently expressed by Charles L. Pillsbury, executive of the Munsingwear Company: "Collective bargaining is all right, but labor leaders have interpreted it to mean that collective bargaining can come only through belonging to a union."[13] The employers would not acquiesce in the new order without a fight.

On April 30 Local 574 felt strong enough to serve a thinly veiled ultimatum on the employers. It announced its demands: the closed shop, shorter hours, an average wage of $27.50 a week, and extra pay for overtime. The employers interpreted the union program as a declaration of war and hastily called a meeting at the West Hotel.

Only representatives of the eleven major trucking firms attended this strategy session, but shortly thereafter a much broader Employers' Committee was organized to conduct negotiations and combat the strike. Actually the Employers' Committee never amounted to anything more than a respectable front for the Citizens' Alliance, which was the prime mover on the side of management.

The first encounter between the employers and the union representatives was inconclusive because the two sides would not discuss the same subject. The employers wanted to debate the right of the union to represent truck drivers, while the labor leaders refused to talk about anything except the union demands.[14]

Thwarted in their effort to drag out negotiations by introducing extraneous questions, the Employers' Committee on May 7 categorically rejected union demands. To convince the public that management was acting from the loftiest motives, H. M. Harden, chairman of the committee, proclaimed the closed shop to be the main issue and explained how it would undermine individual liberty: "The union wants to have the system established whereby no man can get a job driving a truck in Minneapolis unless he belongs to the union. We will never consent to that, and will stand for the system whereby any man competent to work can have a job regardless of whether he belongs to a union or any other organization."[15]

The leaders of Local 574 were fully prepared to try conclusions with the bosses. In a terse statement on May 11 William Brown threatened to tie up "every wheel in the city" unless union demands were met.[16]

With a crippling strike imminent, the ponderous mediation

machinery of the federal government ground slowly into action. The Regional Labor Board began to explore avenues of compromise and insisted on a second conference. The principals agreed to meet, although the Employers' Committee, tartly denying the jurisdiction of the labor board, said it was cooperating only as a matter of courtesy. Such intractability was based on the assumption that in a showdown the public would support the forces of law and order.

While the employers were advertising their recalcitrance, the union leaders managed to create an impression of restraint and moderation. They withdrew altogether the unpopular demand for a closed shop, expressed willingness to arbitrate disputes over wages, and agreed to accept, in lieu of explicit union recognition, a formal contract guaranteeing no discrimination against workers for union activity. In effect, Local 574 was voluntarily waiving the issue which employers had used as a pretext for resisting a settlement, and was demanding only a written promise of compliance with Section 7a.

With cold realism, the employers calculated that even the most indirect recognition of the union would be the prelude to more far-reaching demands. It seemed better to make a resolute stand at the outset, even if it meant flouting the law, than to permit the creation of a monster that could not be controlled later. Accordingly the Employers' Committee spurned the Regional Labor Board and continued to fill the air with abstruse legal objections designed to make the public feel humble and ignorant.

As the zero hour drew near, the employers, despite their control of the principal newspapers, seemed to have the worst of the argument. The Regional Labor Board issued a terse statement that "no conciliatory move was made at any time by the employers," [17] and Governor Olson, who had entered the negotiations at the eleventh hour, minced no words in identifying the obstructionists.

Even so, it would be an oversimplification to say that public sentiment favored the strike. There was a widespread desire to see labor secure its objectives, but also a traditional distrust of the strike weapon. Used effectively, it intruded upon the activities and habits of people having no connection with the dispute. A real tie-up of transportation seemed certain to frighten, annoy, or at least inconvenience consumers. The longer a strike lasted, the more it would be likely to generate frictions and irritations detrimental to the cause of labor.

In the long run, management probably exacted a heavier toll from the average citizen than labor, but its encroachments were piecemeal and cumulative rather than concentrated and intense. Manipulation of markets, price-fixing agreements, and the restriction of competition inflicted inconveniences in an impersonal or indirect way. The end product often seemed remote from the prime mover, whereas a strike abruptly broke the customary rhythm of existence. Inevitably the only weapon that labor could use to enforce its will tended to alienate potential sympathizers.

The position of the union was further impaired by the doubtful legal status of the strike. Judicial decisions during the preceding fifty years had piled up impressive guarantees of individual rights. And American political and constitutional theory reinforced these legal precedents, with the result that the public was conditioned to consider lawless and unjust such interference with business activities as interruption of traffic on public thoroughfares. This way of thinking favored employers in an industrial dispute. Legal and social sanctions supported their strikebreaking activities but hobbled the strike tactics of labor.

Knowing all this, the truck drivers were nonetheless driven by their financial plight to a trial of strength. Despair generated a recklessness that was oblivious to paper calculations of defeat or victory.

Once the momentous strike vote had been taken on May 16, the spotlight shifted to the governor. His constitutional position enabled him to exercise a substantial, if not decisive, influence on events. By calling out state troops to keep the streets open and to maintain the orderly movement of truck traffic, he could unquestionably crush the strike. This was the prescription for industrial disputes which had been regularly applied in the preceding fifty years.

But nobody believed that Olson would voluntarily adopt such a solution. Although he was often branded as a trimmer and opportunist who sought power for its own sake, few questioned the governor's affection for the workingman. His sympathy for farmers and small businessmen grew out of an intellectual conviction that they belonged to the great mass of underprivileged and deserved help, but his sympathy for labor grew out of his own youthful tribulations. He approached labor problems with an uncharacteristic dogmatism and did not hesitate to publicize his uncompromising viewpoint.

As early as 1924 Olson had explicitly pledged himself never to use troops against a peaceful picket line.[18] His praise of the collective bargaining provision of the N.I.R.A. was almost lyrical, and he publicly offered his "wholehearted support" to any group of workmen who wanted to organize.[19] When Local 574 held its great rally in the Shubert Theater, Olson sent a letter commending its activities. Emphasizing the opportunity of labor to organize under Section 7a, he concluded that any group of workers refusing "to take advantage of that right is blind to its own welfare." [20] Privately he was even more outspoken, telling one correspondent that without the long struggle of the trade unions American workers would have sunk to the status of Chinese coolies.[21]

As the champion of labor, Olson had collided often and violently with the Citizens' Alliance. In his feud with that group the note of personal cordiality that so often moderated the political warfare between Olson and his opponents was conspicuously lacking. He could not forgive the Alliance for employing stool pigeons, professional strikebreakers, and legal frame-ups to disrupt the labor movement in Minneapolis. As a fledgling county attorney, he had caught it using an irrespon-

sible dope fiend in a dynamite plot against a union, and his bellicose campaign promise of 1924 "to drive hired thugs and gun-
men from the state" was a scarcely concealed challenge to the
Citizens' Alliance.[22] Even after he moved up to the governor's
chair, Olson doggedly watched its every move. As N.R.A. "codefish" he turned over to the federal district attorney voluminous
evidence on employer violations of Section 7a.[23]

It is not surprising that eliminating Olson from politics had
come to be a major objective of the Citizens' Alliance, second
only to the dissolution of unions. And the truck strike presented
an excellent opportunity to maneuver him into the union camp
and then smash both enemies simultaneously.

By refusing to recognize or deal with union leaders, the
Citizens' Alliance could virtually assure the outbreak of violence, and this would force Olson to choose between the strikers
and the general public. If he used troops to support the workers,
he would face the defection of moderates; if he used them to
break the strike, his labor following would splinter hopelessly.
By systematically fanning the flames of class war, the employers
could turn Olson from arbitrator to participant and impale him
on the horns of an insoluble dilemma. And they could do this
simply as a by-product of their efforts to smash Local 574.

Within twenty-four hours of the strike declaration, pickets
had occupied key points in the city and cut down truck transportation to a trickle of necessities such as ice, milk, and other
food. Applying the lessons learned in the coal drivers' strike the
preceding February, Local 574 functioned with unprecedented
efficiency.[24]

An abandoned garage at 1900 Chicago Avenue was converted
into strike headquarters, where leaders received progress reports and dispatched pickets. Here, too, strikers with their
families ate and slept, and daily pep rallies were held to keep
the rank and file posted on the latest developments. Even the
sick or wounded received medical care on the premises.

These devices boosted morale and gave a martial air to the

enterprise. By bringing the women to headquarters and allowing them to participate in the common task, much of the usual
pressure for settlement on the bosses' terms was eliminated. The
frequent mass meetings to discuss objectives and strategy also
proved an excellent antidote to the defeatist propaganda of the
metropolitan press.

More questionable was the decision to take care of strike
casualties at headquarters. Although leaders justified it on the
ground that in the city hospitals key strikers would be detained
indefinitely for minor injuries, the facilities set up for the care
of sick or wounded pickets were entirely inadequate. When the
National Guard raided strike headquarters on August 1, it found
the patients convalescing under very unsanitary conditions.[25]
Nevertheless, the conversion of 1900 Chicago Avenue into a
bristling fortress was the key to the extraordinary militancy and
discipline of the strikers.

Indecision characterized the employers during the opening
days of hostilities because of divided counsels as to how the
strike should be met. Several of the major trucking companies
kept their vehicles off the streets, apparently on the theory that
an outraged public would demand the immediate restoration
of normal traffic. And in the beginning, complaints from
farmers, filling station operators, and other retailers seemed to
justify these tactics. But the public in general remained disap-
pointingly apathetic. Even the *Minneapolis Journal* reported the
strike with commendable detachment. As late as May 18 its
editorial page was still focused largely on such world topics as
"An Arms Embargo to Halt War" and "Why Finland Pays Her
Debts."

Unable to arouse widespread public protests or shake the
grim determination of the union, the more cautious employers
fell in with majority plans to use force against the strikers. After
a council of war at the West Hotel on May 17, the Employers'
Committee issued a sharp statement about the irresponsible
group of men who "have seized the city and dictated how,
where, and when we are to obtain the bare necessities of life." [26]

They called for police intervention to remedy the intolerable conditions.

In plain words, this was a request for armed convoys that would move trucks through picket lines. Mayor A. G. Bainbridge of Minneapolis responded promptly, offering blanket protection and authorizing the oil operators to recruit special deputies, provided the industry paid for them.

Alarmed by this ominous turn of events, Olson lent his support to the faltering negotiations that were being conducted through the Regional Labor Board. On May 17 he shuttled tirelessly between the two camps from midnight until 6:00 A.M. Although unable to effect a settlement, he managed to keep the conversations going Friday and Saturday. The strikers were willing to arbitrate the dispute, in spite of their fear that the Regional Labor Board would be unable to enforce an agreement,[27] but the employers refused to retreat an inch.

Finally, on Saturday night the employers abruptly broke off all discussion and issued a public statement to the effect that they were ready at any time to recognize and bargain with duly accredited workers' representatives selected by employers "provided they did not have to enter into any written agreement with any organization of any kind or nature." [28] That is, they were ready to make a settlement provided it was not binding.

Olson, with some justification, interpreted this statement as an incitement to bloodshed and threatened to use the last weapon at his disposal: martial law. In a prepared statement he declared that the National Guard would be called out to keep order and ensure the distribution of foodstuffs in the event of violence. He made it absolutely clear that troops would not be used to convoy employer trucks, but would handle the distribution of food if necessary.

At the threat of martial law, the strikers announced that they would throw their "whole force into the battle" unless the governor stopped the local police from interfering,[29] while the employers termed the strike "an outrage on the rights of Minneapolis citizens" and demanded the proposed intervention of troops.

Slowly but surely Olson was being maneuvered into a position where he would have to choose sides. Thus far the strike had not irritated the public in any definite way, but each day it was certain to cause more and more inconveniences. Violence would accelerate the process and double the pressure on Olson to turn the troops against the workers. As one union leader laconically put it, "The governor was sitting on the middle of a picket fence." [30]

Even before negotiations broke down, violence began. On Saturday the employers moved a decoy truck full of heavily armed men and mercilessly beat the men and women pickets who tried to stop it. This warned the strikers that they could no longer afford to go unarmed, so they spent the weekend accumulating a supply of clubs and blackjacks.

The employers at the same time were recruiting a citizens' army of doctors, lawyers, clerks, and college students and hiring three hundred and fifty extra police for the impending battle. The strikers were almost certain to consider the citizen soldiers, who wore everything from jodhpurs to jeans, as strikebreakers whether they were formally deputized or not. Many of the latter did not foresee this development and were unpleasantly surprised when confronted by strikers in the market area. In the meantime, however, they talked with naive enthusiasm about the sacred duty of convoying food to a starving population. The leaders of the employer army set up a headquarters of their own at 1328 Hennepin Avenue and spent most of Sunday formulating plans to move trucks the following day.

The rival armies gathered as if by prearrangement at the market area early Monday morning. More than any other spot in Minneapolis, it symbolized the low wages and bad working conditions against which the men were striking. If the sixteen market firms could not be brought to terms, the whole unionizing drive faced complete defeat. It was no accident, therefore, that the employers chose to move trucks in this area and that the strikers prepared to resist with all their resources.

In the predawn light a battalion of pickets six hundred strong, armed for the most part with clubs, marched four abreast to the market place. Their sober discipline and military precision terrified the waiting citizens' army, which broke into headlong flight with hardly a scuffle.

The uniformed police proved to be a more difficult obstacle. By forming a hollow square and holding their guns in firing position, they prevented the strikers from moving in close where clubs could be used to advantage. Finally the strikers conceived the brilliant idea of driving a picket car straight at the police. Faced with certain death, the men in the path of the oncoming vehicle broke formation, and the strikers closed in for a hand-to-hand encounter. The resulting skirmish injured some thirty-seven, mostly police. Both sides claimed victory, but the union forces retained the field of battle and held truck movements to a trickle for the fifth successive day.

The following day thousands showed up for the return engagement, including strikers, police, members of the citizens' army, and a number of curious spectators. Radio station KSTP even set up microphones in the market area, so that those unable to attend personally would not miss the show.[31] The public had come to view this elemental economic struggle as a kind of glorified sporting match. But the events of the day shattered this mood.

Both sides seemed reluctant to start the fight and faced each other warily until an unidentified person touched things off by throwing a crate of tomatoes through a grocery store window. The encounter that followed lasted no more than an hour, but it ended in the death of two members of the citizens' army, one of whom was C. Arthur Lyman, vice-president of the American Ball Company and a prominent Minneapolis citizen.

Coupled with the complete victory of the strikers, who triumphantly roamed the streets until 10 P.M., the death of Lyman made some of the employers afraid for their lives and others recklessly determined to continue the fight whatever the odds. A few of the first families actually thought of fleeing the city,[32] but the majority talked grimly of throwing more police into the fight though they were already losing thousands of dollars daily.

Success made the strikers more hopeful about their prospects and so less amenable to compromise. They used the prestige of their victory to secure new allies. The taxi drivers were persuaded to walk off the job, and the building trades promised a sympathy strike. Some began to agitate for a general strike to shut down everything.

As the gulf between employers and strikers widened, the average citizen, who had no direct stake in the outcome, began to stir uneasily. Initially inclined to view the conflict with amused tolerance, he was startled by the loss of human life and frightened by the threat of a general strike. The broadening scope of the struggle destroyed the comfortable fiction that he was an outsider looking in. He became less inclined to consider the issue on its merits and more insistent on the re-establishment of law and order. As yet, this sentiment remained largely inarticulate, but the gradual shifting of public opinion could not be ignored.

More positive was the reaction of near-by truck farmers, whose anger reached the boiling point when pickets stopped their produce trucks at the edge of town. Rudolph Lee gleefully observed that "Farmers were classed as employers and turned back just the same as drivers of other trucks." [33]

After the two-day battle in the market area, Olson responded to increasing public pressure for a settlement and secured a forty-eight-hour truce, which permitted grocery and produce trucks to operate. Even so, his intervention only brought him abuse. Conservatives indignantly condemned him for not calling out troops to curb the disorder. Ward Senn, Republican chairman in Hennepin County, charged him with personal responsibility for the bloodshed, claiming that "had he taken definite action, instead of pussy-footing around, the death of a Minneapolis businessman and the injury of scores of others could have been prevented." [34] The *Chicago Tribune* amplified the accusation, saying that Olson's public acts and speeches were "an invitation to disorder." [35]

At this point the employers were acutely embarrassed by a peremptory order from the National Labor Relations Board to terminate the strike. To sign an agreement in accordance with Section 7a was to concede the major strike objectives. On the other hand, to flout the board seemed certain to alienate public opinion, which had begun to shift in favor of management.

In the end, with thirty-seven hundred national guardsmen mobilized for possible use in disarming strikers and police alike, the employers decided it would be prudent to reopen negotiations. The union leaders were so suspicious of this gesture that they refused to enter the Nicollet Hotel until police and private detectives had been removed.* For their part the employers refused to deal directly with union negotiators, using members of the Regional Labor Board to shuttle proposals back and forth.

Almost immediately a new deadlock developed. The employers' representatives ostentatiously signed the agreement to end the strike, observing with irony that they hadn't favored it in the first place. But the union leaders withheld assent on the ground that the agreement did not specifically guarantee recognition of Local 574 or concede its right to speak for inside workers. Federal mediators patiently worked out alternative versions, only to have the employers reject each draft that made their obligations more explicit or precise. Even a twenty-four-hour extension of the truce failed to break the deadlock, which had focused on the definition of "inside workers."

With the mediators on the verge of giving up, Olson drove to strike headquarters for a final exploratory talk. Exercising all his charm and persuasiveness, the governor prevailed upon the leaders to accept a somewhat ambiguous description of inside workers as "truck drivers and helpers and such other persons as are ordinarily engaged in trucking operations." Neither side

* Warrants had been issued for the arrest of strike leaders in the event that they entered the hotel. (C. R. Walker, *The American City*, p. 123.)

was quite certain what the phrase "other persons" meant, and the strikers, fearing future trouble over interpretation, ratified the Olson compromise only after an acrimonious discussion. There was substantial sentiment among them for continuing the strike.

The subsequent refusal of employers to abide by the Olson definition of inside workers led Stalinist Communists to charge that the Trotskyite leaders of Local 574 had deliberately betrayed the workers.[36] They also condemned the governor as a bourgeois trickster who wrecked the strike to further the interests of his own class.

Olson must have recognized the ambiguities in his formula covering inside workers. That he endorsed it unreservedly suggests his preference for half a loaf rather than renewal of the strike. The agreement, signed on May 26, committed employers to arbitrate differences with union representatives whenever they were selected by the workers. This was a far cry from the closed shop, but it granted union recognition of a sort. To a political realist like Olson even such a minor concession provided a toehold for a further offensive. If the employers refused to follow a reasonable policy regarding inside workers, the question could be reopened later when the union had consolidated its position.

In retrospect the concessions of May 26 were to appear empty and illusory, but at the time they seemed to provide a solid foundation for future progress. The *Minneapolis Labor Review* hailed the agreement as "the greatest victory over the Citizens' Alliance that organized labor had gained in the history of the city."[37] Union leaders as a whole believed that at least a hopeful beginning had been made.

The May 26 peace all too soon degenerated into an uneasy truce because of deliberate bad faith on the part of the employers. An important permissive factor in this development was the inability of the federal government to police the settlement it had arranged. Since the main theme of the N.I.R.A. was voluntary cooperation, Washington hesitated to resort to its uncertain powers of compulsion. This manifest weakness of the government's policy gave the employers virtual immunity from legal coercion and thus encouraged them to violate the settlement.

Almost before the ink was dry, the pattern of piecemeal repudiation began to emerge. Wages, which had been raised to $17.00 for a thirty-four-hour week, gradually dwindled to $12.40 for a forty-one-hour week.[38] In the market area, checks for higher wages were made payable at the payroll window only, where they were uniformly cashed for smaller amounts. Employers persistently refused to select their representatives for the arbitration board on the ground that the relevant clause was in the singular and so sanctioned bargaining by individual employers rather than groups. This interpretation sabotaged arbitration and prevented any orderly redress of grievances.

Employers avoided the rehiring of strikers by calling them back to the job and then announcing that no work was available.[39] Worst of all, they hamstrung union efforts to organize inside workers by placing the narrowest possible construction on that clause of the settlement. The mediators, anticipating trouble with this issue, had appointed a three-man committee to define the categories covered by the phrase "other persons." The committee divided two to one, with Governor Olson and the labor representative defining the term broadly to include all employees whose work facilitated the movement of merchandise by truck and the management representative contending that "other persons" simply meant bona fide truck operators.[40]

It was hoped that both parties would feel morally obligated to accept the majority decision, but the employers blandly ignored it. Some basis existed for their attitude. The broad definition of warehouse workers ignored their hybrid character as shipping and clerical personnel. Moreover, the impartiality of a committee which gave Olson the casting vote was certainly in question. Even so, the employers could have reached an understanding with Local 574 on this vexing question if they had not preferred to make it another instance of covert opposition to the union.

The union showed commendable restraint in the face of all these stalling tactics, carefully avoiding provocative acts that would give employers an excuse for noncompliance. But when the five-day deadline for the creation of an arbitration board had been lengthened to a month without action, its patience gave out. The union leaders called a mass meeting on July 6 and found sentiment overwhelmingly in favor of a showdown. It was decided to serve employers with an ultimatum calling for (1) recognition of the union as bargaining agent, (2) immediate negotiations concerning wages, hours, and working conditions, and (3) a wage increase retroactive to May 26. The union made it clear that refusal to comply with these terms would precipitate a strike vote.

The threatened renewal of class warfare galvanized the federal government into fresh activity. E. H. Dunnigan, a crack mediator, was sent to Minneapolis to begin conferences with both sides, while the dispirited Regional Labor Board reworked the old compromise proposals. But these efforts were futile. The employers had merely used the breathing spell to reform their lines; they had abandoned no fundamental convictions.

Governor Olson, who had been recalled from a vacation at Gull Lake to participate in the negotiations,[41] took the measure of employer intractability in a strongly worded statement. A strike could be averted if management would accept the recommendations of the Regional Labor Board, he said, adding that "some tribunal must settle this and it would be better to settle it before the strike than after." [42]

These sober words of warning were ignored by both sides. At a second mass meeting the union voted to strike at midnight on Monday, July 16.

During the three weeks before the second strike both sides engaged actively in propaganda to win public support. The most damaging charge the employers made against Local 574 was that it provided a front for the operations of communists seeking to subvert American institutions. In reworking this theme, with the cooperation of the press, management devoted much attention to the denunciation of Local 574 by Daniel Tobin, president of the International Teamsters' Union, who concealed his opposition to industrial unions by condemning the truckers on ideological grounds.

Use of the communist issue reached its peak on the eve of the strike when a full-page paid advertisement appeared in the *Minneapolis Journal* charging the union with a plot to set up a local Soviet Republic. This sensational accusation was repeated on the editorial page with the statement: "The real objective of the Communists is to enlist Minnesota in the revolution they hope to start in this country for the overthrow of the constitution and the laws of the land."

The hysteria campaign against the union had just enough basis in the facts to make it dangerous. Although communism boasted few converts among the union members, it was generally known that Vince Dunne, the ablest strategist of Local 574, belonged to the Trotskyite wing of the Communist party. There was at this time no evidence that he sought to use the strike for any end other than the immediate welfare of the workers, but his conspicuous role in the formulation of union policies inevitably laid the truck drivers open to suspicion.

In fact, the communist problem, interacting with the issue over craft unions, divided the house of labor against itself. The St. Paul truckers, who had won recognition from the parent body, refused to walk out with their Minneapolis brethren, while the Central Labor Union, composed of sixty A.F.L. unions, refused a sympathy strike. It never actually opposed Local 574, but it pursued very different tactics during the strike to secure a labor victory.

Another phase of the preliminary war grew out of the necessity for employers to prove that the union had broken the May 26 agreement. Here their most dramatic gesture was a public offer of one thousand dollars to the union treasury if it could prove that management had not lived up to the agreement.

Local 574 rejected this specious proposal because there was little chance that the Hennepin County judges, who had been suggested as referees, would find for the union under any circumstances.

Finally, management indicted the union for ruining business in Minneapolis and depriving workers of desperately needed wages. The paralysis of industry by strikes was represented as an illegal interference with individual rights which a patriotic and disinterested group of employers would not tolerate.

This attitude represented firm conviction rather than mere propaganda to hoodwink the public. Many employers would have sincerely denied that economic considerations influenced their attitude. A. W. Strong, the president of the Citizens' Alliance, showed a deep paternal concern for his employees at the Strong, Scott Manufacturing Company as long as the threat of unionism did not present itself. With Strong and others like him an honest belief that strikes jeopardized the traditional values of American life lent a crusading ardor to the struggle against Local 574.

Limited resources severely handicapped the union in its effort to counter the propaganda of management. Employers and their sympathizers controlled practically all the agencies for disseminating information. The metropolitan dailies and the local radio stations were uniformly hostile. The principal labor journals were published only once a week and hardly met the requirements of the union. They could not keep the members up to date on developments or be depended upon to endorse every move of the militant truckers' union.

Local 574 partially met this deficiency by launching their own newspaper, the *Organizer*. It appeared first on June 25 and at irregular intervals thereafter until the second strike, when it became a daily. It carried brief accounts of prestrike negotiations and editorials expressing the union viewpoint. It exposed the machinations of the employers in colorful prose and satirized them in clever cartoons. After the resumption of hostilities, the *Organizer* became the chief source of information for the

*Cartoon by John Baer, from the* Farmer Labor Leader,
*April 30, 1934*

strikers, but it never had a wide enough circulation to influence noncombatants.

The union simply could not match the propaganda program of the employers once they discovered the importance of selling their cause and began to use the immense facilities at their disposal. The only hope for the union lay in the prevailing sympathy for the underdog.

The opening days of the second strike followed closely the pattern established in the first. Truck traffic was quickly shut down and scores of pickets roamed the streets. With this initial advantage, the union worked to win new allies. It urged the unemployed to sign up for picket duty and tried to soften rural opposition by permitting members of the Farm Holiday Association to set up a produce market on the outskirts of the city. This gesture paid dividends in the form of substantial food contributions to the union commissariat. It also created an illusion of farmer-worker solidarity that was helpful to striker morale. Actually members of the radical Farm Holiday Association distrusted the workers and gave food so generously only because it brought nothing in the market.

Meanwhile, in spite of the danger of wholesale bloodshed, the employers, convinced that it would take strong measures to smash the strike, were preparing to support truck movements with lethal weapons.

This momentous decision was reached after Police Chief Mike Johannes promised truck convoys up to the limit of his equipment. Driven by a fanatic conviction that it was his duty to keep the streets open, Johannes requested a special allotment of $33,200 to outfit eight hundred men with shotguns, bayonets, steel helmets, and riot clubs. Mayor A. G. Bainbridge further emphasized the city administration's support of the employers by a formal request that Governor Olson call out the state militia to assist local police in protecting life and property.

Once again Olson faced the same old dilemma. He could not afford to ignore disorder and bloodshed. On the other hand, he could not mobilize troops to supply essential services for Minneapolis without acting in effect as a strikebreaker.[43]

Characteristically, Olson responded with a halfway measure. He ordered one unit of the state guard mobilized at the Minneapolis Armory and called up two thousand men for riot drill at Camp Ripley, which was four hours away. But he accompanied these military preparations with an emphatic reiteration of neutrality: "I will not take sides in the strike, nor will I hesitate to discipline either or both of the conflicting groups if circumstances require." [44] This statement led the employers to sneer at his irresolute measures, while the *Organizer* tartly observed that strikers expected more than neutrality from a Farmer Labor governor.[45]

Collaborating with the Reverend Francis J. Haas, who arrived to reinforce him on July 18, E. H. Dunnigan worked hard to find some acceptable compromise formula. The mediators requested Chief Johannes to suspend truck convoys while the avenues of accommodation were being explored lest an overt act wreck the negotiations completely. But he stubbornly refused, observing that "it's law and order with me." [46] Father Haas and Governor Olson thought they had extracted a forty-eight-hour truce on July 20, but Johannes later denied making such a commitment. In any case, he did not suspend his efforts to move trucks.

The same afternoon the inevitable catastrophe occurred. A decoy truck accompanied by fifty heavily armed policemen started to move across the market area. Challenged by a picket car which cut across their path, the police promptly opened fire with shotguns, wounding sixty-seven persons, two of them fatally.

The first newspaper accounts stated that police shot the pickets without provocation. Later editions were altered to read that they fired repeatedly into the air and shot point-blank at the pickets only after a policeman had been attacked.[47] An investigating committee reported to Olson that twenty-five strikers had been shot in the back while trying to run away and four others while aiding the wounded. This version tallied with the account of several eyewitnesses.[48]

In retrospect it became clear that the employers and city officials had deliberately planned an incident to try conclusions with the union. They felt certain the picket armies would melt away when threatened by actual loss of life. Moreover, unyielding partisanship had so completely warped their sense of values and anesthetized their humane instincts that they came to consider victory sufficient justification for extreme measures.

The irresponsible recklessness of the employers tended to obscure the equally reprehensible role played by strike leaders in Friday's encounter. The intention of employers to move decoy trucks was no secret. It had been exposed the preceding day in the columns of the *Organizer*.[49] Even the specific strategy had leaked out, because newspaper reporters and cameramen were stationed at the fateful spot in plenty of time for the encounter.[50] On the chance that union headquarters lacked information regarding the decoy, Adjutant General Ellard Walsh phoned the strike leaders to tell them the employers were planning to move a truck full of police and warn them not to interfere with it. Yet the unsuspecting pickets were promptly dispatched to probable injury and possible death.

One is driven to the conclusion that the strike leaders deliberately sought the shedding of blood to reinforce working-class solidarity. Marxist doctrine laid great stress on tactics designed to widen the gap between capitalists and proletariat. The ideal strike was one conducted like a war with street fights and barricades. By intensifying labor militancy and aggravating its sense of grievance, the way would be cleared for the most effective weapon of class warfare: the general strike.

Up to this point the devotion of union leaders to Marxist principles had not expressed itself in a manner detrimental to the welfare of the truckers. But the application of the more extreme communist tactics in the Friday encounter exposed a divergence of interests within the union. Rank-and-file union members were seeking the redress of specific grievances. They were at war with a few employers rather than with all defenders of capitalism. Their success depended upon the sympathy of countless little people who believed in the existing economic system, and victory was out of the question if this group came to consider strike tactics a threat to the capitalist system.

The influential communist clique in the union had very different objectives. Their devotion to Local 574 was beyond dispute, but they never lost sight of their ultimate goal, the emancipation of the toiling masses everywhere. They were under constant temptation to turn every labor dispute into a general class war, without regard to the effect on the original strike. Apparently they believed the martyrdom of a few pickets would stir up enough active antagonism to create a revolutionary situation.

As in fact it seemed to do. The evening after the massacre a monster protest meeting generated such frenzied indignation that it ended in a march on the city hall to lynch the mayor and the chief of police.[51] Only the timely action of General Walsh, who had ordered a detachment of troops from Camp Ripley immediately after the afternoon encounter, averted an irresponsible act of retaliation. In the days that followed, union leaders made further efforts to capitalize mass resentment, issuing impassioned pleas for a general strike and turning the funeral of Henry Ness, one of the martyred pickets, into a demonstration of working-class solidarity.

These tactics did not help the cause of Local 574 with the public. They merely frightened sympathizers in the capitalist class, whose convictions had already been partially undermined by the steady communist harping of the metropolitan press. And as labor militance alienated those potential supporters, it became increasingly difficult for Governor Olson to withstand pressure for breaking the strike.

These developments pleased the employers. By encouraging extremists in the camp of labor, they could vitiate the compromise efforts of the mediators and evade their obligations under the law without seeming to do so. They self-righteously prepared to move trucks once again, hoping that public opinion would force the governor to turn against the strikers.

Olson was left no choice but to intervene. Until the bloodshed on Friday he had hoped to avert violence with a compromise formula. Indeed, he was actually talking optimistically over the phone about the prospects of an early settlement when informed of the shooting. Concealing his disappointment, he issued a public warning that he would make Minneapolis "as quiet as a Sunday School picnic" in the event of fresh disturbances.[52] Then he prodded the weary mediators into drafting a settlement proposal that he could endorse.

Known as the Haas-Dunnigan plan, it simply restated the terms of the May 26 compromise. The union accepted it, but the employers still felt confident they could blast the pickets off the streets. Olson subjected them to the most intense pressure, even crashing a secret strategy session with the solemn warning that any future violence would be their responsibility.[53]

Nonetheless, the Employers' Committee flatly rejected the Haas-Dunnigan plan in a letter to the governor that crackled with their anger. After charging that he had obstructed rather than aided local authorities in maintaining law and order, it accused him of threatening martial law "to force a settlement which will leave the issue and the methods of the present strike wide open for repetition in the future."[54]

Abruptly dropping the pose of impartiality, Olson dictated a reply that relieved all his pent-up indignation. "I do not agree," he wrote, "that the plea for a living wage by a family man receiving only $12.00 a week is answered by calling him a communist. Neither am I willing to join in the approval of the shooting of unarmed citizens of Minneapolis, strikers and by-standers alike, in their backs in order to carry out the wishes of the Citizens' Alliance."[55] The agencies of government belonged to the people rather than to a selfish clique, he said, and pledged himself to use those under his jurisdiction for the benefit of all.

Shortly after sending this letter to the Employers' Committee, the governor issued a proclamation of martial law, opening a new and unpredictable phase of the strike.

The establishment of military rule did not add greatly to the inconveniences already being suffered by consumers. There was a twelve o'clock curfew, a ban on liquor sales after 9 P.M., and a prohibition of parking in downtown Minneapolis. Far more significant, though not of immediate consequence to the public, was the regulation that suspended picketing and forbade truck movement without military permit. In effect it substituted state troops for pickets as the arbiters of city traffic. This reflected Olson's determination that troops should not be used to help either employers or strikers, but to protect "the citizens of Minneapolis from both if necessary." [56]

The employers were infuriated by the governor's interpretation of his responsibilities. When they had clamored for state troops, they had not anticipated their use for anything but to break the strike. Olson's decision to mobilize the militia for duty as an umpire instead upset their calculations. They had felt the strike was breaking up as a result of the Friday shooting[57] and the replacement of pickets with state troops seemed to be snatching victory from their fingers. They began a frenzied effort to blacken Olson's reputation and impugn his motives.

They opened the campaign with wild charges of censorship. Seizing upon a clause of the martial law proclamation which made it unlawful "to publish or transmit within said areas notices, handbills, documents, or newspapers defaming the state of Minnesota or any member of its national guard in the field," [58] the Employers' Committee wrote the governor a sarcastic letter asking whether it was possible for them to speak freely.

In reply Olson graciously assured them that they could address him with complete immunity from military regulations and state laws on libel, then warned them with mock solemnity "to refrain from stating anything that will frighten the children of Minneapolis." He urged that they and their "many collaborators" find some other description for himself and the underpaid workers than the term "Communist." And in conclusion he expressed delight at the prospect of further communications and "the supporting editorials of the *Minneapolis Journal*." [59]

Thereafter the press and radio provided the principal medium for the anti-Olson campaign. And the censorship charge was soon abandoned. After the troop commander, General Ellard Walsh, complained about an editorial in the *Minneapolis Star* ridiculing the military forces, the newspaper ran an article of retraction and its editor, G. H. Adams, wrote Olson a letter of apology. [60] The issue had lost its drama and gradually disappeared from the papers.

Much more effective was the steady barrage of editorials pillorying Olson as a defender of lawlessness and mob rule. The *St. Paul Pioneer Press* denied his right "to say who shall use the streets and who shall not." [61] And the *Minneapolis Tribune* charged that the governor was taking his ease at Gull Lake or the Athletic Club while the city writhed in agony. [62] This sort of propaganda was difficult to combat. The shortages that developed in line after line of consumer goods irritated the public and made it increasingly susceptible to the employers' claims. General Walsh found sentiment hardening against the strike after a week of martial rule, and Vince Day expressed concern over the increasing effectiveness of radio attacks on Olson and the truck drivers. [63]

The union itself was far from grateful for Olson's action. Its leaders denounced martial law as a deliberate attempt to break the strike. At first their objections seemed based on a Marxian enthusiasm for street fights and barricades which the disaster of "bloody Friday" had not dampened, but later abuses of the truck permit system seemed to justify their fears.

Martial law succeeded in preventing bloodshed, but it created administrative problems whose solution proved detrimental to the strike. Foremost of these was the classification of goods eligible for movement under military permits. The strikers had limited transportation strictly to necessities such as food, milk, and funeral cars. But the strikers dared to ignore the convenience of citizens; the governor could not. Through his troop commander he was now accountable for the type and quantity of goods reaching consumers, and some relaxation of the pickets' strict interpretation of necessities was inevitable.

Even more difficult from an administrative standpoint was the institution of adequate controls over truck movements. To avoid raising a federal question, permits had to be issued wholesale to postal trucks, trailer vans that moved across state lines, and trucks hauling necessities as defined in official orders. The most conscientious administration of official policy could not have plugged up all the possible loopholes. But whereas reasonable vigilance seemed likely to ensure a seventy-five percent shutdown of truck traffic, the actual curtailment was much less.

Permits were issued too liberally — owing less to deliberate treachery than to the unsympathetic attitude of those who administered the permit system. General Walsh, the troop commander and a personal friend of Olson, performed his difficult duties with distinction, but it was physically impossible for him to supervise the issuance of permits. This task fell primarily to National Guard officers, and most of them were professional men with a strong antilabor bias. Even where this was not a dominant factor, the officers often stretched a point to accommodate friends who wanted to move trucks.

In still other ways the variable human factor vitiated careful calculations. It proved virtually impossible to rebaptize troops as pickets or inoculate them with class consciousness. They lacked the incentive of impending starvation to make them vigilant against illegal truck movements. Indeed, for some of them the strike provided a welcome release from a humdrum daily existence, and they cared little about its purposes or implications.

The final factor in the breakdown of the permit system was the shortage of personnel and equipment. The guard units called up for duty simply could not cope with the tremendous job of checking all truck movements. Often tips on violations phoned in by zealous union sympathizers could not be followed up for lack of patrol cars. Before the first week of martial law ended, it had become clear that Governor Olson's measures to protect the strikers were breaking the strike. By July 29 truck traffic reached sixty-five percent of its normal volume.[64]

The union held a mass meeting the same day. President William Brown denounced the Farmer Labor administration "as the best strike-breaking force our union has ever been up against" and pushed through a resolution to stop truck movements by force unless the permit system was brought to an end within forty-eight hours.[65]

When the deadline had expired without a satisfactory response from Governor Olson, a second meeting was convened Tuesday night to perfect plans for mass picketing the next morning. Formal notice of this intention was given to military headquarters by Miles Dunne. Over the telephone he bluntly told the provost marshal to get his tin soldiers off the streets before they were thrown off.[66]

It was ironical in the extreme that the policy Olson had inaugurated to save the strike actually tended to break it. In proclaiming martial law Olson had mortgaged his political future for the welfare of labor, only to find that its support was also lost. He was paying the price that all moderates pay in time of stress. The employers could not forgive him for sympathy with working-class aspirations, nor the leaders of Local 574 for refusing to join them behind the barricades.

Olson knew that he must uphold the state's authority, but he suffered great emotional turmoil in bringing himself to the actual decision. Only after a long conference with General Walsh did he consent reluctantly to punitive measures against the union. Then, incapable of participating in the round-up of strikers, he left Minneapolis to spend a sleepless night at the Lowry Hotel in St. Paul.

After his departure General Walsh raided strike headquarters at 2 A.M., arrested William Brown and Miles and Vince Dunne, and imprisoned them in the stockade at the fair grounds. Simultaneously state troops disarmed the rank-and-file strikers, who had been scheduled to re-establish picketing in the morning. This operation was carried out so quickly and efficiently that they had no opportunity to resist. Deprived of their headquarters and their leaders, the strikers roamed the streets angry, confused, and defiant. Strategy sessions were held by subordinates on sidewalk curbs, but beyond securing pledges not to return to work they accomplished little.

Olson's friends subsequently explained the raid on strike headquarters as a political gesture to pave the way for a similar raid on the Citizens' Alliance a few days later. Charles R. Walker in his book *The American City* suggests that Olson acted in the belief that the strike would be more easily settled with the communist leaders removed.[67] Both these explanations suggest a balancing of political alternatives that was missing from this particular decision. The governor acquiesced in the raid only as a grim necessity. Other considerations may well have suggested themselves at a later date, but at the zero hour General Walsh's insistence on vindication of the state's authority was decisive.

The statement issued by Olson after his return to Minneapolis bears out this interpretation. After deploring the attempt by union leaders to defy military orders, he concluded that "the guard had no alternative but to proceed as it did this morning. Otherwise there would be no guard." [68]

This explanation made no impression on the strikers and they spent the day loudly demanding the release of their leaders. Curiously enough the strikers' wives felt more relief than indignation. Far from being resentful over the imprisonment of her husband, Mrs. Vince Dunne thought the governor had acted conscientiously to prevent bloodshed.[69] Even Vince himself accepted confinement philosophically.

However, within twenty-four hours it became apparent that the raid had created chaos. The subordinate leaders of Local 574 simply could not control their followers. This hard fact drove Olson and Walsh reluctantly to the conclusion that liberation of William Brown and the Dunne brothers was an essential prerequisite to any settlement. Accordingly, they were released the morning of August 2 after promising to observe military regulations.

In order to recover his prestige with the strikers, Olson ordered a raid on the Citizens' Alliance headquarters the following day. It was directed by Lieutenant Kenneth Haycraft of the National Guard, who captured documents revealing a close connection between the Employers' Committee and the Citizens' Alliance. He also uncovered plentiful evidence of the employers' plans to obstruct federal mediation.

Nonetheless, the catch was disappointing. Haycraft had hoped to secure a list of labor leaders and stool pigeons on the Alliance payroll, but found only a disappointing book of stubs containing serial numbers of checks paid out. It was learned later that the Citizens' Alliance had been tipped off about the raid and had shipped out four files the preceding day.[70]

Meanwhile, Olson was groping his way toward a new policy. The issuance of permits had got so far out of hand that truck traffic climbed back to seventy percent of normal during the first days of August. Plainly the only way to shut down this traffic short of removing the troops was to cancel all permits and start over again.

The chief difficulty lay in finding an adequate excuse for such a step. Vince Day and Holberg of the United Press thought they had an ideal one. They proposed that truck permits be tied to the acceptance of the Haas-Dunnigan plan, which the employers had already rejected.[71] Olson promptly converted this formula into an ultimatum. Employers were notified that unless a settlement was reached by midnight on Sunday, August 5, all truck permits would be revoked except those held by companies that were transporting necessities or that had signed the Haas-Dunnigan agreement. Some forty-seven firms signed up, but the rest refused, denouncing the governor for illegal discrimination against them.

The employers played their final trump card on August 6. It was a petition to the United States District Court for an injunction suspending martial law as a violation of the due process clause of the Fourteenth Amendment. Specifically the employers' brief contended that interference with the use of equipment on the streets prevented the conduct of legal business and hence in effect deprived citizens of their property unconstitutionally.

Olson decided to argue the case for the state personally, and managed to secure a two-day postponement while he participated with President Roosevelt in ceremonies honoring the famous Minnesota surgeons, Doctors William and Charles Mayo. On his return from Rochester Wednesday night, the governor held a long strategy session with General Walsh. Neither of them believed there was the slightest possibility that the Republican judges would sustain the state. But they were convinced that anarchy and bloodshed would follow the removal of troops, so they decided to keep them on the job regardless of the court decision.[72]

Despite the strain of recent weeks, Olson was at his best for the court hearings. Calm and self-confident, he fulfilled his promise to give the Citizens' Alliance attorneys a lesson in law. Brushing aside their contention that the liberty of corporations or persons under the Fourteenth Amendment had been abridged, he contended that executive judgment as expressed in martial law was not subject to review.

Citing the Supreme Court decision which had upheld Governor Peabody of Colorado for imprisoning a coal mine union leader two and a half months to avert violence, Olson argued from analogy that he could lock trucks up in a garage to protect drivers and citizens from bloodshed. And, he maintained, executive discretion would empower him to ignore any court decision finding his proclamation illegal. In conclusion he told the court that if it questioned his reasonable judgment "as to the means of protecting life and property, and preserving peace" he would not be responsible for the consequences.[73]

This last argument annoyed but impressed the judges. Even though the strike threatened traditional legal and economic concepts at every point, they were not willing to be responsible for what might follow a decree withdrawing the troops.

So the court prudently handed down a decision sustaining Olson's right to declare martial law and conceding that his action was not subject to review. But with human irritation at their own helplessness, the judges added the barbed comment that "while we may personally disagree with Governor Olson as to the manner in which he has handled the entire situation, that will not justify nor permit the relief prayed for." [74]

Throughout the legal controversy, the union persisted in its unrealistic attitude of welcoming a setback for Olson. Albert Goldman, attorney for the truck drivers, insisted that the court's granting an injunction would rejuvenate the strike and permit Local 574 to determine "who shall and who shall not operate trucks." And the *Organizer* boasted that "Local 574 is perfectly capable of stopping scab truck movements without military aid." [75]

After the refusal of the court to grant an injunction, the strike settled back into a war of attrition once again, with employers complaining about communists and the union about chiseling under the permit system. The combatants were nearing mutual exhaustion, however. Many employers were losing thousands of dollars daily and continued the fight only because Twin City bankers threatened to call in the loans of those who capitulated.[76] And the raid of August 1 had disclosed deplorable conditions at strike headquarters, where pickets were convalescing from wounds without proper diet, ventilation, or sanitation. Cash contributions from other unions ran out and food supplies dwindled, so that strikers and their families had to subsist on less and less.

The patience of consumers also began to give out as inconveniences multiplied. Vince Day heard loud complaints about profiteering in scarce commodities and the heavy costs of maintaining the state troops.[77] The employers stood to gain from this increasing unrest and missed no opportunity to feed public discontent. They even went so far as to petition Washington for new federal mediators on the ground that Haas and Dunnigan had sold out to the radicals and were obstructing a settlement.

In response to this criticism, the mediators drew up a modified Haas-Dunnigan plan much more favorable to management. In effect it eliminated the minimum wage provision and permitted employers to use their own discretion about rehiring strikers. These concessions were sufficient to assure prompt acceptance by management, but the strike leaders indignantly rejected the compromise.[78]

The National Labor Relations Board as a last resort called for an election to designate the appropriate bargaining unit. Seemingly, this order favored Local 574 because it gave workers an opportunity to vindicate union claims, but the strikers feared that P. A. Donoghue, the government representative, would accept payrolls padded with scabs as the official list of eligible voters.[79] And even if he conducted an honest election that resulted in a union victory, he did not have the authority to force the arbitration of issues. So the union felt it had little to gain by an election.

The deadlock over the election lasted four days. Then the whole strike controversy ended abruptly at 10:30 P.M. on Tuesday, August 21.

When the terms of settlement were made public, they indicated an overwhelming victory for the union. Employers conceded virtually everything required of them under the original Haas-Dunnigan plan, including (1) immediate re-employment of strikers, (2) minimum wages of fifty cents an hour for truck drivers and forty cents for inside workers, with overtime as prescribed in N.R.A. codes, (3) arbitration within two days of disagreement, and (4) an election procedure that ensured recognition of the union.

The sudden settlement with such terms caused general surprise. Walker hinted at "mysterious pressure from Washington" but did not elaborate.[80] Subsequent investigation has confirmed his surmise, although none of the principals ever saw fit to publicize the details.

Actually the foundations for the settlement were laid on August 8 during Roosevelt's visit to Rochester, Minnesota. Olson conferred with the President privately and briefed him on the strike controversy. The same day a delegation of the Central Labor Union headed by Robley D. Cramer also attempted to call on Roosevelt. Failing to reach him, they secured an interview with his secretary, Louis Howe, who was lying ill in a Pullman car. When Howe assured them that a written statement of labor's viewpoint would be placed before the President, Cramer typed up a scorching indictment of the employers which included everything from their obstruction of federal mediation procedure to their uncomplimentary personal remarks about Mr. Roosevelt and his wife.[81]

The Central Labor Union took this action in spite of the fact that it distrusted the communistic leaders of Local 574, disliked their strike tactics, and disapproved of their attempt to create an industrial union. It had steadfastly resisted a general strike but it had never suspended the battle against the Citizens' Alliance and the open shop.

The appeals to President Roosevelt bore fruit in an order to the Reconstruction Finance Corporation to withdraw its loans to banks that were financing employer resistance.[82] This pressure proved decisive because Twin City banks had served as the principal coercive agency of the Citizens' Alliance. Deprived of life-and-death financial power over debt-ridden employers, the Alliance could not keep the strike from collapsing.

Olson emerged from the strike with enhanced prestige. At first the leaders of Local 574 ignored his contribution, boasting that they had won despite the governor. But the sentiment of union members eventually forced them to change their tune, and on September 28 Miles Dunne seconded a Central Labor Union resolution commending Olson for his handling of the strike.[83]

The Olson contribution to union victory will always be a matter of dispute. His well-meaning attempt to end bloodshed with state troops almost broke the strike, and his acquiescence in the arrest of Brown and the Dunne brothers deprived Local 574 of leaders when they were most needed. Yet nobody can honestly dispute his devotion to labor or deny his courage in calling out troops for the protection of strikers rather than for the restoration of law and order in the accepted sense.

If it is understood that Olson forthrightly endorsed labor organization and sought to implement the collective bargaining provisions of the N.I.R.A. long before responsible national leaders took a definite stand, then the pioneering aspects of his work become apparent. He helped orient people to the revolutionary concept that labor as well as management deserved legal protection of its rights. His resolute defense of the workers when the political risks were incalculable paved the way for more cautious leaders to pass the Wagner Act.

# Chapter XI THE 1934 ELECTION

$A$T THE time the governor embarked upon his last campaign, all the qualities that fed the legend of Olson as the master politician had been developed. Contemporaries marveled at his ability to cut through the baffling complexity of political problems and reduce them to simple terms that even the most unsophisticated voter could comprehend. Olson never permitted the complicated nature of an issue to betray him into outward embarrassment and vacillation, whereas his opponents often lost public confidence by their irresolute approach to political issues.

Accompanying his talent for lucid exposition of a problem was a well-developed flair for telling attacks on opposing institutions and individuals.[1] Indictments of the chain stores, the chain banks, and the steel trust were a staple of nearly every Olson speech. He poured withering sarcasm upon his political foes. When Senator Schall congratulated him for resigning from the N.R.A., Olson paid him back with interest. He noted that the senator's absence from congress on the day of the N.I.R.A. vote had been ascribed to his unwillingness to take a stand, then, solemnly dismissing such a low motive, suggested instead that Schall's "absence was due to onerous duties as a member of the Nicaragua Canal Committee."[2] He added that "the senator could render a valuable contribution to the people by taking a definite stand with reference to some plan that would help them."

On a later occasion when the hapless Judge Nordbye gave a speech defending his antilabor decision in a strike case, Olson publicly proclaimed that Nordbye had legally and morally disqualified himself from ever sitting as judge in a labor dispute: "Judge Nordbye has thrown his judicial robes in a partisan ash can. Let him leave them there and become the Republican candidate for office — any office. I will be glad to discuss his judicial record and fitness for office with the people of Minnesota." [3]

Even the publisher of the *Chicago Tribune*, Colonel Robert R. McCormick, who was no novice at vituperation, came off second best in an encounter with Olson. The murder of a hard-hitting newspaperman who had repeatedly attacked the governor in his columns encouraged McCormick to state that Olson was giving assistance to gangland in its campaign of killing honest men who sought to expose its activities.

From a hospital bed Olson dictated a scorching reply. Jeering at McCormick's alleged championship of a free press, he noted that "dozens of papers have been suppressed because of economic views expressed, without a word from Bertie. It is only when a scandal sheet has difficulty that Bertie comes to the rescue. That is because he is owner of the world's leading scandal sheet." Alluding to the outbreak of amoebic dysentery at the Chicago World's Fair, which resulted in hundreds of deaths but was not reported in the papers, Olson suggested that "if McCormick has a conscience, it should be crawling with dysentery germs." As a parting shot he said that in any list of infamous persons "Bertie McCormick would be at or near the top." [4]

Olson had several brushes with the courts, but never did he give his sarcasm freer rein than when the state supreme court invalidated the tax on intangible property. Especially irritated by the judicial interpretation of legislative intent, he congratulated the court for its ability to read the minds of the legislators and thus save the corporations millions of dollars. He urged the corporations to "manifest their gratitude by endowing a university course in crystal gazing." [5]

Reading these impassioned attacks on political opponents, one would suppose that the deepest personal hatred animated Olson. Normally this was not the case. He could denounce a man unsparingly and greet him ten minutes later as a friend, joking over the vigorous language he had used. He did everything in his power to drive an opponent to cover, but once the battle ended "he was mercy incarnate." [6] And he never picked on an opponent who was not his size. He loved to hit and expected to be hit in return.

Occasionally, however, there was real bitterness in his attacks. He felt a fierce, uncompromising hatred toward those who whispered behind his back and maligned his character. He expected his opponents to fight fairly in the open and was deeply wounded by the underhanded attacks of men like Harold Birkeland and Vin Weber, the Slayton newspaper publisher. Olson could not tolerate foes that broke the unwritten code of sportsmanship.

With the reporters and writers on the opposition newspapers, Olson maintained cordial personal relations. Cheney says in his memoirs that he and the governor "were friendly enemies." After a particularly bitter campaign, Olson made a special trip to the office of the *Minneapolis Journal* to thank Cheney for fair treatment.[7] And even at the height of the governor's feud with the *Journal* over the Austin strike, Cheney did not hesitate to phone Olson some helpful information about his political enemy, Senator Schall.[8] Jack Mackay, the Associated Press statehouse reporter, tipped the governor off about leaks in the Capitol switchboard, and Olson reciprocated with small favors.[9] Nothing done by the correspondents escaped his attention. When Herbert Lefkovitz, political editor of the *St. Paul Pioneer Press*, wrote a series of articles on the farm crisis, the governor took time to write him a personal letter of commendation.[10]

Olson had a gift for taking on the color of his surroundings and saying the proper thing at the proper time. He could speak to a labor meeting in midafternoon, chewing sandwiches as he talked, then don a tuxedo for a dinner address before the State Bar Association, and finish the evening contentedly rocking a schooner of beer and talking Yiddish at a "north-side" American Legion party.

Many political leaders have met with groups of similar diversity on a single day, but few with the obvious relish of Olson. He had no poses or mannerisms consciously cultivated to appeal to the social prejudices of any particular group. He did not lapse into grammatical inaccuracies at a labor meeting or wear work clothes when addressing farmers. Indeed, he sometimes dared the fates by wearing spats in rural areas. Olson was at home in any situation and immediately put his auditors at ease.

His ability to convert the most hostile audiences never ceased to amaze contemporaries. The *Windom Reporter* once complained that Olson had given such an appropriate speech on a nonpartisan occasion that he gained votes in a critical area.[11] His veto of the 1931 Truck Bill angered many of the railroad workers, and shortly thereafter when he entered the Northern Pacific shops at Brainerd the atmosphere was heavy with resentment. But when Olson rose to go after half an hour of informal conversation, the men were clustered about him on the floor in high good humor. Herbert Lefkovitz recalled that Olson ended a period of hard feelings between them by sailing his hat into the office first, then entering a few seconds later with a wide grin and the remark that if he were unwelcome the hat would have sailed back out.

With equal facility, he could take the edge off a public crisis. A notable instance of this was the Minnesota-Iowa football game in 1935, which seemed likely to end in violence. Considerable ill feeling had been generated the preceding year because Iowa fans believed their star Negro halfback, Ozzie Simmons, had been roughed unnecessarily. Governor Herring of Iowa even allowed himself to be quoted as saying, "If the officials stand for any rough tactics like Minnesota used last year, I'm sure the crowd won't." [12]

The controversy took on an official character when the Minnesota attorney general, H. H. Peterson, wired Herring that his remarks were a breach of his duty as governor and showed "an unsportsmanlike frame of mind." [13] The rising tension made it likely that the game would have to be played under police protection. The sheer lunacy of this teapot tempest was apparent to any reasonable person, but neither side could retreat without loss of face.

At this stage Olson took a hand in the quarrel and eased the tension with a gesture. He issued a statement that he believed Herring had been misquoted and solemnly offered to bet his fellow governor a Minnesota hog against an Iowa porker on the outcome of the game. Herring gratefully accepted this face-saving proposal and good humor was quickly restored all around.

The game went off without incident. Iowa lost thirteen to six, and Governor Herring paid off his bet in person at St. Paul, delivering to Olson a prize porker dubbed "Floyd of Rosedale." While "Floyd" ambled delightedly among the spectators at the Capitol, Herring made a humorous speech of presentation and Olson replied in kind. Thus an exceedingly disagreeable incident closed on a friendly note, and athletic contests between the two institutions were entirely free of antagonism in subsequent years.

When opponents on one occasion criticized Olson for lowering the dignity of his office by writing a series of newspaper articles, his response was unforgettable: "I have always thought that the main thing in public relationships is to be genuine, to be yourself; and so, if one is genuine, courteous and decent, he has dignity." [14] His behavior reflected faith in this basic philosophy. He attracted people from every walk of life, recalling their names and faces easily because the personalities behind them were really alive to him. He was gregarious to a fault, losing all sense of time in the pleasures of conversation and good fellowship. One day while political leaders paged him frantically in the hotels and restaurants of Brainerd, he sat in the kitchen of the Norwegian Lutheran Church, talking to the ladies and jotting down recipes for his wife.[15] On another occasion, he left for the office at 8:45 A.M. to keep a crowded schedule of appointments, only to tarry for half an hour at the corner lot tossing a football with some children.

Out of this zest for the commonplace activities of life, Olson won a multitude of friends representing every shade in the political spectrum. Men like R. C. Lilly, the St. Paul banker, and Ellard Walsh, the adjutant general of Minnesota, were intimate with the governor although they belonged neither to the Farmer

Labor party nor to the all-party committee. Lilly actually voted against Olson three times. But it never made any difference in their relationship. Each respected the intelligence of the other, and they spent many happy hours debating the issues of the day.

With the exception of the "bitter enders" from the Citizens' Alliance, businessmen found Olson so gracious and approachable that they unhesitatingly presented their views to him. In fact, many of them expressed their liking tangibly in campaign contributions. A close friend recalled that Olson once chatted with a New York theater operator for fifteen minutes about bridge, golf, and the show business. Whereupon the latter took out a hundred-dollar bill, saying, "Floyd, I don't know your Minnesota politics, and I've almost forgotten what you're running for, but here's something for your campaign." [16] It was a political miracle that year after year an all-party committee of well-to-do citizens could be organized for Olson, despite his truculent indictments of entrenched wealth.

With all his attractiveness and poise, Olson never managed to shake off completely the rough manners of his youth. His conversation was apt to be generously punctuated with profanity. But it flowed out so naturally and easily that his auditors took no offense. There was something spontaneous and natural about the Olson phraseology that set him off from the politician who swore simply to prove that he was a good fellow.

Another habit from which all the years in polite society failed to free Olson was tobacco chewing. Often after a conference had cluttered up the floor of his office with little pieces of paper, he would lean across his desk and aim at them with puckish delight.[17] Frequently the tobacco found its target, leaving the place looking more like a poolroom than a governor's office.

Part of Olson's success on the hustings was due to the fact that he cut such a handsome figure as a campaigner. Double-breasted suits hung elegantly on his huge frame, and heavy side jowls imparted distinction to his well-proportioned Nordic features. The impact of this striking physical presence was heightened by his overflowing vitality. Indeed, he made such an impression on women that perfumed letters requesting private interviews followed almost every address.

Olson was a perfect technician on the platform, modulating his rich voice to achieve just the maximum effect. In fact, his oratory was sometimes a handicap. It charmed audiences into a momentary acquiescence that often disappeared on sober afterthought. As a result the governor was apt to be deceived by his soundings of public sentiment. During the torrid 1934 campaign, more people cheered him to the echo in the armory at Owatonna than voted for him in all of Steele County, where the town is situated.[18] Misled by such deceptive bits of evidence, he entered the final days of the campaign confident that he would have a plurality of 150,000, whereas he was lucky to win by half that margin.

The governor reinforced his natural speaking ability by time-honored political techniques. He always studied the community before giving a speech, mastering local economic problems and learning a few phrases of greeting in the language of the majority's homeland, as well as appropriate dialect stories. He always had half a dozen talks prepared, and if one topic failed to elicit the proper response he could shift to another simply and easily. He showed extraordinary skill in handling hecklers, building up crowd sympathy by insisting on their right to be heard. The device worked so well that he sometimes planted hecklers in the audience to create an opportunity for exhibiting his magnanimity.[19]

He enjoyed the rough and tumble of a political speech immensely, but found handshaking something of an ordeal. Farmers tortured him with their steel grips and callused hands. Eventually he developed the practice of grabbing their hands first, which reduced the pressure and made the receiving line more tolerable.

Olson's effectiveness as a campaigner reflected his acute sensitivity to public opinion. He recorded the rumblings of the electorate like a political seismograph. Sensing with astonishing accuracy the appropriate tactics to be applied in a particular situation, he knew just how far he could go without stirring up a hornet's nest. Seldom did he fail to anticipate which policies and actions would breed trouble. He called off an attractive junket to the Yorktown Sesquicentennial Celebration because he feared it would be criticized as a needless extravagance in time of depression.[20]

But Olson was never paralyzed by timidity. If he was convinced that strong tactics would succeed, he pushed them uncompromisingly. When confronted with an incipient revolt by Townley and a left-wing faction of patronage purists in September 1934, he met the challenge resolutely. A committee of one hundred had been named to present the demands of the dissidents to Olson and warn him that unless substantial concessions were made on patronage Townley would file for governor. Since the election was already in jeopardy, further defections would be dangerous, but Olson had taken his soundings and decided that Townley was not a real threat.

So when the committee of one hundred had assembled in the main reception room of the governor's office, Olson emerged from a side door shaking his finger fiercely and delivering a lecture on party loyalty. The crowd of dissidents gradually melted from the room. By the time Olson had finished his lecture, only twelve remained. These timidly shook hands and departed without daring to say a word of the mission on which they had come.

Subsequent developments fully justified the governor's uncompromising attitude. Townley did file as an independent, but he carried only a corporal's guard with him in revolt.

Behind the more obvious characteristics that made Olson so effective a propagandist and leader of men were others not quite so apparent to the public but equally important. He had a kind of innate humility that enabled him to accept advice cheerfully. He recognized the inadequacy of his training and sought the aid of specialists. He could abandon even a pet project once he was convinced of its unwisdom. He was much taken with the state bank scheme in North Dakota and planned to endorse it in his

1933 inaugural address, but deleted the paragraph at the suggestion of Commissioner Peyton.

Guy Stanton Ford of the University of Minnesota praised Olson for recognizing "often and consistently" the value of the expert knowledge that resides in the staff of a great university.[21] Time after time the governor called on the state university for studies of pressing social and economic questions, and he conscientiously tried to implement the recommendations whenever they could be tailored to fit political realities. Many radicals were critical of the university's research because they assumed that the conservative board of regents would prevent disinterested advice. But Olson did not allow this notion to chill his enthusiasm for technical guidance or to mar his cordial relations with university officials.

Coupled with this willingness to follow the lead of experts was an extraordinary capacity for assimilating information rapidly. Olson literally absorbed facts like a sponge. When the bank panic broke in the winter of 1933, he knew almost nothing about the technical aspects of the situation, but after some hurried briefing by Peyton he was able to weigh alternative policies with a professional competence that amazed the banking fraternity. And when he first sat in on the conferences for setting up the state printing bureau, his knowledge of printing processes was quite superficial, but in the first half hour he acquired such a grasp of the subject that it seemed he had been in the business all his life.

He also possessed the happy faculty of pulling the key points from lengthy reports in a matter of minutes. When Henry Arens decided to run for congress instead of for a second term as lieutenant governor, he handed Olson a paper listing all the arguments to justify his switch. The governor did not like the idea of losing an authentic dirt farmer like Arens from the state ticket, so he gave the list only a hasty glance. But when Arens indignantly protested such a cavalier disregard of his political aspirations, Olson slowly and deliberately repeated the contents of the brief almost word for word.[22]

This seemingly effortless mastery of facts and details provides the real explanation of Olson's ability to keep abreast of his work despite frequent intervals of enforced inactivity. Without a lightning power of analysis and a photographic memory, he would have been forced to delegate important segments of policy to subordinates and risk the loss of his control over the state administration. As it was, even short periods of work compensated for his protracted absences from the office.

Although he undoubtedly took his work seriously, Olson never became too grim about it to appreciate a joke even when he was the victim. When he asked Cheney what he thought of the new commissioner of agriculture, the reporter answered, "He went broke farming, but you picked a busted banker for commissioner of banks, so this was a logical choice." [23] Olson responded by throwing back his head and laughing heartily. He handled tactless references to his private life with the same good humor, although they irritated him. One inquisitive woman was shut off with the bantering retort, "Madam, that is the cross I have to bear." [24] A solemn warning about the baleful political effect of uncontradicted rumors of his drinking elicited only the breezy reply, "I'll have the drinkers' votes anyhow." [25]

The same quick wit often flashed out in a heated personal debate. After an all-night argument with the alleged British communist, John Strachey, Olson offered him a ride home.* When Strachey, accepting the offer, named the exclusive Minnesota Club as his residence, Olson snorted indignantly, "You bloody bourgeois!" [26]

Not all the governor's joking was at a sophisticated level. He won the affection of the custodial staff at the Capitol by his lighthearted banter. The elevator boy, who promised to deliver rural Hennepin County for Olson in 1932, was teased unmercifully by the governor for permitting Brown to get ten votes in

* John Strachey visited the Twin Cities in February 1935 during a lecture tour of the United States, speaking at a University of Minnesota meeting and before the Woman's Club of Minneapolis and the St. Paul branch of the Foreign Policy Association. He was arrested shortly thereafter by federal authorities for deportation as a communist.

his township,[27] and Billy Williams, the Negro receptionist, and Olson habitually joked about their respective athletic careers. He got a whimsical pleasure out of cutting short the importunities of job seekers by kicking his huge mastiff Rolf, who was coiled up under the desk and responded with a fierce growl.

It was Olson's buoyancy and enjoyment of a jest, more than anything else, that prevented his taut nerves from snapping completely. Without an active sense of humor the heavy responsibilities of his office would have become unendurable.

To many of his contemporaries Olson seemed an unyielding partisan, preoccupied with the retention and consolidation of political power. This impression was heightened by his willingness to use the weapons of his adversaries. Olson could play the game gently, but he could also be as ruthless as his opponents. In his ten years as county attorney the perpetual battle of wits with crooks, gamblers, and confidence men gave him insight into all the unsavory methods of manipulation and made him exceedingly fast on his feet. He came to understand the techniques of corruption with a thoroughness that terrified his enemies. And he learned from experience that the lawless elements in a community could not always be routed by strictly legal methods.

Olson never transgressed his code of personal behavior to indulge in petty, spiteful retaliation, but he did not hesitate to use whatever methods seemed necessary to gain his ends. When Senator Gustaf Widell began what Olson believed to be a highly partisan investigation of the Highway Department, the governor — proclaiming his determination "to fight fire with fire" — ordered Commissioner Elsberg to examine the circumstances surrounding the award of a bridge contract to a firm in which the senator was interested.[28]

On another occasion when Olson heard that a representative lined up for an administration bill had been bribed into switching his vote, he called the culprit into his office, reviewed the arguments in behalf of the bill, and courteously reminded the legislator that his vote had been pledged for the measure. Finding the man still intractable, Olson told him with icy calm that he would either vote for the bill or find the bribery story in his hometown paper within twenty-four hours. The hapless legislator stumbled mechanically from the governor's office without a word, but the next day he voted as Olson had demanded.

Such incidents spread the feeling among Olson's opponents that he would use any means to accomplish an end. This attitude reflected their chagrin at his effectiveness as a politician. Left-wing leaders were usually amateurish and naively idealistic in their political activities, but Olson was a clear-headed realist who could use the enemies' methods to as good an effect as they could themselves. So they called him cunning and unscrupulous.

Like most aggressive political leaders, Olson exercised initiative and accepted sole responsibility for major decisions. He rarely convoked general meetings of his staff to debate and hammer out the administration program. No major, over-all adviser stood by his side. He enlisted many special talents in the preparation and execution of his policies, but he assigned only individual fragments to each one, keeping the task of synthesis and decision in his own hands. Under such a system, the governor could have no real colleagues, only willing subordinates.

This aspect of his administration lent some plausibility to descriptions of Olson as a crafty despot who ran the Farmer Labor party to suit himself. Actually there is no evidence that he adopted policies arbitrarily or in defiance of the rank and file. He subjected them to thorough preliminary criticism but not in the accepted way, preferring to put his trust in personal friends like Charles Ward, the wealthy head of the Brown and Bigelow company of St. Paul, Richard Lilly, and Ellard Walsh, who were more remote from partisan politics than the average party leader.

Even with these friends Olson seldom discussed specific issues. Instead he drew them into long debates on a wide range of abstract questions. During the course of an evening they might canvass such diverse subjects as planned economy, religion, and imperialism. Olson relished such a session. It gave him a chance to test and defend his ideas under the relentless cross-examination of minds as fine as his own. From these informal discussions of general principles, he reached conclusions which he applied to a concrete situation. But always the decision was his own. Even Mrs. Olson could not recall an instance when the governor asked her advice on a political question or on the delicate problems of human relations arising therefrom.

There was something paradoxical in Olson's determination to keep his own counsel. A man of a thousand friends, genial and gregarious to a fault, he nonetheless refused to share his staggering burdens with anyone. At first this aloofness had a touch of majesty about it, but as the ravages of ill health increased, his self-imposed isolation became rather pathetic. Had he been able to pour out his heartaches and frustrations to a friend, perhaps he would have obtained relief from the intolerable tensions that generated his physical distress. There can be little doubt that, for all his mask of jaunty amiability, Olson suffered a great deal of inner turmoil and nervous excitement.

His disposition varied directly with the seriousness of the problems that confronted him. As they grew more difficult, he became outwardly calmer. This external poise may well have been purchased at the price of great internal strain, but it strengthened the morale of his supporters and confounded the opposition. Hjalmar Petersen recalled how Olson raised the drooping spirits of Farmer Laborites by closing a gloomy strategy session on the 1934 platform with the breezy remark, "We'll manage okay." [29] And his foes will never forget the glacial composure with which he argued the injunction case in federal court during the tense days of the truck strike. Those who dealt with Olson personally soon learned that if he was loud and blustery they had nothing to fear, but that if he acted cool and unruffled it was time to run for cover.

Olson invariably irritated opponents by his skill in dodging explosive political issues. He often pursued a policy of deliberate inactivity on the assumption that a troublesome situation might eventually subside if studiously ignored. He had such strong faith in this technique that he left standing orders with his office staff to answer routine letters immediately but to bury the difficult ones in the bottom of the basket for two weeks. As a rule he waited until the last minute to declare himself on a ticklish question, and sometimes he managed to evade a stand of any kind. Neither wets nor drys knew where he stood on the controversial liquor control issue because he forwarded the report of the investigating commission to the legislature without personally committing himself.

Of all the ambiguities and paradoxes in the governor's personality, none evoked such divergent conclusions as the question of his personal integrity. Many intimate associates were positive that he never broke a pledge. Richard Lilly found him always scrupulous about fulfilling his promises, and President Lotus D. Coffman, recalling his contacts with Olson on university business, said, "I came to know that I could depend on his word." [30] Olson revealed his own standard, perhaps, once when Julius Schmahl, the Republican state treasurer, accused him of evading a pledge. Showing a genuine desire to clear himself, the governor wrote, "I am not concerned with political differences that may arise between us, but I would not under any consideration have you believe that I would break faith with you." [31]

But others who dealt with Olson got a quite different impression. Many Farmer Laborites, as well as Republicans, considered him shifty and devious. The complaints varied, some contending that he repudiated pledges completely and others grumbling that he framed commitments loosely enough to permit evasion.

In all probability, the truth about Olson lay somewhere between the two extremes. Like all astute politicians, he tried to perform the impossible task of satisfying petitioners without granting their requests. In his effort to please, he slipped occasionally into the dangerous practice of giving qualified approval to projects which he actually opposed. The temptation was all the greater because people succumbed so readily to his charm. Doubtless Olson had a very positive notion of just how much he was promising, but his less sophisticated auditors understandably confused cordiality with commitment. The result was a great deal of uncertainty that bred hard feelings. Moreover, those whom the governor outsmarted tended to salve their self-esteem by charging him with bad faith even when they were clearly in the wrong. Discounting the element of personal pique, one is led to the conclusion that Olson did not deliberately break his commitments, but that he sometimes loaded them with enough reservations to impair their usefulness.

The one fact about the 1934 campaign that overshadowed all others was Olson's vulnerable position. The utopian enthusiasts at the Farmer Labor convention in the spring had unwittingly accomplished in a few hours what Olson's bitterest critics had failed to do in four years of methodical scheming: they had forced him into a grueling defensive war.

Even with the analysis and explanations later circulated to counteract its disastrous effects, the platform drafted by the March convention provided campaign issues that were tailor-made for the Republicans. They had been protecting Minnesota from baleful economic reforms since 1896, and always seemed to exhibit their maximum resourcefulness and animation as defenders of the status quo. On the congenial theme given them by this Farmer Labor platform they devised endless variations: The small businessman was to lose his factory or store, the farmer his plot of land, and the consumer his hard-earned savings. All would disappear down the voracious maw of the state. And the loss of property would be followed by the loss of freedom as the Farmer Labor machine entrenched itself through control of public funds and the educational system.

This propaganda was difficult even for the persuasive Olson to counteract. The one hope from the Farmer Labor standpoint was the rebellious mood of the country. Although unprepared for a dose of pure socialism, the multitude wasted no love on the status quo. Everywhere in Minnesota angry men demanded measures to ensure them a larger share of the wealth of society. The urban masses agitated for jobs and better wages, striking in some cases when their pleas were ignored, while farmers in the western counties called urgently for government aid to combat drought conditions that had turned the upper Minnesota River Valley into a desert.

While the Farmer Laborites sought ways of mobilizing this protest vote, the opposition completed preparations for the campaign. The Republicans nominated Martin A. Nelson for governor. An Austin lawyer, war veteran, and former congressional candidate, he possessed the virtue of party loyalty without the liability of a public record. Although he lacked personal magnetism and political seasoning, he partially made up for these deficiencies by hard work and attention to detail. His speeches read well on paper, but they lost some of their effectiveness in delivery because of his high-pitched voice. Party leaders rested their hopes on Nelson's reputation for respectability and the sensational material available for campaign purposes.

The Democrats again selected John Regan as their standard bearer. Two years had done little to mellow him or heal the party breach. His feud with National Committeeman Joseph Wolf over patronage had reached such proportions that he advised Rice County Democrats who wanted jobs to "go to Wolf and tell him you didn't vote for John Regan — in other words, tell him you didn't vote for the ticket."[32] This split seemed to preclude a November victory despite the popularity of President Roosevelt and the rejuvenation of the Democratic party nationally.

The senatorial contest deserves only passing comment. The Republicans thought the nomination worthless and gave it to N. J. Holmberg, the former secretary of agriculture, although Tom Davis, who professed to be shocked by the Farmer Labor platform, campaigned strenuously for the honor. The Democrats were apparently more optimistic about their chances of beating Shipstead because they prevailed upon Einar Hoidale to leave a relatively safe congressional seat and make the race.

A certain amount of preprimary high jinks was provided by the staff of the *Fairmont Sentinel*. They prevailed upon a poor simple farmer bearing the name of John Lind, the illustrious governor of the Populist era, to file against Olson on the Farmer Labor ticket and paid his legal fees.[33] Lind took his candidacy seriously enough, but his sponsors had no other purpose than the embarrassment of Olson. In this they failed, because the governor paid no attention to his rival. The metropolitan dailies professed to interpret the fact that Lind piled up several thousand votes in the primary as an indication of party dissension, although most Lind supporters probably thought they were voting for the dead governor.

The Democratic and Republican candidates opened their campaigns much earlier than Olson. Regan and Nelson were making the rounds of county picnics while the governor was still working under terrific pressure to end the strike in Minneapolis. Except for a few engagements contracted earlier, Olson refused to campaign systematically until late September. Although sheer exhaustion accounted in part for this inactivity, he worried less about election prospects than most of his immediate entourage. He never doubted that he would ultimately prevail.

Recognizing that the March platform wasn't "so damned funny any more," [34] the governor devoted speech after speech to minimizing the stigma of radicalism. His keynote address painstakingly distinguished between communists and Farmer Laborites:

"The Communists believe in the abolition of private property. We believe in its creation. The Communists would confiscate whatever little private wealth the ordinary man has. We would give him an opportunity to earn more. The Communists believe the individual is created for the service and benefit of the state.

239

We believe that the state is created for the service and benefit of the individual. The Communists would abolish Christian morality. We would give Christian morality the first real test in commercial relations it ever had. The Communists would reduce all people to a dead level. We would uplift all people to a happier life." [35]

More effective than abstract arguments were his homely antidotes for hysteria. Reminding a St. Cloud audience that in their community the government operated a beef-canning factory for the unemployed, he asked whether this kind of relief had brought communism to the town. Elsewhere he used elementary illustrations like post offices, roads, and bridges to prove that socialism was not a stalking horse for communism.

Olson expended equal energy assuring voters that the Farmer Labor party stood for exactly the same things as the national administration. He insisted that the Farmer Laborites were fighting alongside Roosevelt for lower interest rates, public ownership of utilities, and government operation of idle factories. Even the analysis that replaced the March platform contained the statement that the "red scare" attacks against the Farmer Labor party were "part and parcel of the Republican campaign against the Roosevelt administration." [36] These efforts to exploit the popularity of the President for the benefit of the Farmer Labor party began to pay dividends in late summer, scaring Martin Nelson into assuring voters that a Republican state victory in 1934 would not injure the President's chances in 1936.

The Regan Democrats angrily resented Olson's assumption of the Roosevelt mantle in Minnesota, and they anxiously examined each gesture from national headquarters for signs of recognition or approval. Roosevelt's visit to Minnesota in mid-August was a blow to their hopes. His refusal to endorse Democratic candidates indicated a tacit approval of Olson, which was strengthened by his remark in Rochester that Olson should join him in Washington and leave a secretary to govern Minnesota. [37]

The Democratic national chairman, James A. Farley, was not

much more encouraging. When he endorsed the Minnesota Democratic ticket, he mentioned Hoidale by name but pointedly ignored Regan.[38] In fact, the only recognition from national headquarters came during the closing days of the campaign when Emil Hurja, Farley's executive assistant, gave five speeches in Minnesota and specifically called for the defeat of Governor Olson. The Democrats were jubilant at this eleventh-hour recognition, and Cheney of the *Minneapolis Journal* ventured the speculation that Roosevelt had finally been estranged by Olson's attacks on federal farm policy, his extreme radicalism, and his involvement in relief scandals.[39]

The elation was short-lived. Hurja was suddenly recalled, and shortly thereafter Ernest K. Lindley, a newspaper correspondent commonly believed to have access to the President, wrote an article in the *New York Herald Tribune* insisting that Roosevelt favored Olson:

"Mr. Hurja's self-appointed visit to Minnesota to talk for the state Democratic ticket against Governor Olson and Senator Shipstead was not only unauthorized, but met with utter disfavor from the White House. . . . The President is known to be particularly fond of Governor Olson, whom he considers a very close personal friend. The President has been noncommittal on the candidacy of Governor Olson because of his present hands off policy on state campaigns, but it is a well-known fact among his intimates that the President is very strong for Governor Olson and is anxious to see him re-elected." [40]

To complete the discomfiture of Regan supporters, Democratic National Committeeman Joe Wolf announced after a visit to the White House that the Minnesota gubernatorial race was between Olson and Nelson.[41] The effect of the national administration's attitude is hard to assess, but the ride on Roosevelt's coattails may well have saved Olson.

The opposition parties might have unseated Olson had they been able to join forces in support of one candidate. Both Republicans and Democrats paid lip service to such fusion from

April to September, but neither Nelson nor Regan would agree to step aside for the other. So the two parties organized separate campaigns against Olson. The Republicans showed the most aptitude at this game, generating tremendous controversy over a plank in the Farmer Labor platform which endorsed the state printing of textbooks.

On the surface nothing could have been more innocuous. The Republican legislature of 1877 had awarded an exclusive contract for printing textbooks to a St. Paul firm that underbid other firms by fifty percent. A popular vote ratified the arrangement, which lasted fifteen years. Shortly thereafter Governor John Lind reopened the question in his inaugural address, proposing that the state print textbooks. The legislature ignored his recommendation, and subsequent governors did not attempt to press the issue. It lay virtually dormant until revived in the 1934 platform.

There is no evidence that either Olson or his more radical followers acted from any sinister motive in reopening the textbook question. The relevant plank merely reflected the over-all Farmer Labor belief that the state could perform many functions more economically and efficiently than private enterprise.

The effectiveness of the Republican attack lay not so much in straightforward objections to the extension of state activities as in deliberate misrepresentation of the Farmer Labor proposal. Republican spokesmen expressed fear that the administration intended to rewrite all textbooks, filling them with dangerous un-American doctrines, and professed to find confirmation of this suspicion in the survey of the social science curriculum sponsored by the state Department of Education and conducted by such respected educators as Dr. August C. Krey and Dr. Edgar B. Wesley of the University of Minnesota.

The *Minneapolis Journal* touched off the organized drive on this issue on October 3 with a sensational front-page cartoon depicting a dishevelled, sinister-looking individual rewriting textbooks from an open volume of Karl Marx, while copies of the United States Constitution, Folwell's *History of Minnesota,*

REWRITING THE SCHOOLBOOKS

Farmer-Labor Platform—"Textbooks to be published by the State"

*Cartoon by Oscar Cesare, from the* Minneapolis Journal, *October 3, 1934*

and a McGuffey's reader lay mutilated on the floor or in the wastebasket. Thereafter almost every day the Twin City newspapers carried front-page editorials or statements from clergymen and educators denouncing Farmer Labor efforts to drag textbooks into politics. These efforts were ably supplemented by campaign speeches at a thousand crossroads towns.

It was one thing for Republicans to denounce state printing of textbooks, but quite another matter when Lutherans, Baptists, and Methodists took up the cry. If the religious vote lined up solidly against the Farmer Labor party, the election was lost. This threat galvanized Olson and his associates into a strenuous counterpropaganda drive.

Hardly a major campaign address during the last two weeks omitted an explanation of the textbook issue. Ministers favorable to the Farmer Labor proposal were rounded up and given radio time.[42] John T. Lyons, Olson's campaign manager, arranged a special luncheon for religious leaders in the Twin Cities, and the all-party headquarters phoned them in advance about the time, place, and subject to be discussed.[43] Endorsements of the plank were secured from educators and public officials, conservative Governor A. C. Ritchie of Maryland obliging at the eleventh hour with a message which described the successful operation of a similar law in his own state.[44]

By the end of October Vince Day could express confidence that the worst was over.[45] However, there was no letup during the remainder of the campaign. The party leaders had been really scared, and election results indicated that the textbook issue did cut into the Farmer Labor plurality, particularly in rural areas.

Other charges against the Olson administration were permeated with a sensationalism difficult to combat. Democrats and Republicans alike accused the governor of building up a gigantic political machine based on graft, corruption, and the misuse of relief funds. They expressed grave fears that unless the voters smashed it immediately, this leviathan would swallow up democratic government and rivet chains of dictatorship on Minnesota.

To support this contention, the Republicans published an indiscreet letter from Budget Commissioner I. C. Strout to county highway supervisors, reminding them that they had been chosen because of their high standing in the Farmer Labor party and would be responsible for winning additional recruits in their territory.[46] The Republicans concluded from this evidence that the high tax rate was a direct result of the padding of state employment lists with Farmer Labor supporters. They also cited the letter as proof that Olson in his position as federal relief administrator would discriminate against the needy in other parties.

The governor had tried to anticipate some of these charges by directing all candidates to resign state positions shortly after the primary. However, his order was never strictly enforced because many Farmer Labor candidates lived a marginal existence and would have become relief cases if deprived of their state jobs. Late in the campaign Olson took the further step of resigning as federal relief administrator. This gesture toward taking politics out of relief only touched off rumors that he had resigned to avoid an indictment for misappropriating federal funds.

This was pure campaign mud, because there could not be the slightest question about Olson's integrity in money matters. Foe and friend alike paid tribute to his rectitude as a public official.[47] He had such genuine contempt for affluence that he lived from hand to mouth, leaving his friends to pay the bills he contracted at the Mayo Clinic. His insurance policies would have lapsed more than once without the vigilance of Ann V. Egan, his personal secretary.

Olson's disregard for money revealed itself in many ways. He loved to gamble it away, though he refused to play pure games of chance, insisting on bridge or poker, where he could exercise some control over his fortunes. He seldom tried to keep track of money, having to fumble through his pockets whenever a bill was needed.[48] When a newspaper reporter quizzed him about switching to a more lucrative profession, Olson replied scornfully, "I never had more fun in my life. Give that up for a few lousy dollars? I'd be a sucker." [49] And during the final days of his life when Charles Ward, overcome by the visible inroads of cancer, burst into tears as he left the sick room, Olson remarked to a friend with obvious relish, "It's a funny thing about Charley. With all of his money he can't do anything about my stomach." [50]

The governor tried to maintain his own high standard of personal honesty in the Farmer Labor administration. When he offered Dave Arundel the post of state liquor commissioner and received the reply that he knew nothing about liquor except how to drink it, Olson was quick to respond: "You don't have to know anything—all that's required is honesty. If you chisel, the information will be back to me in twenty-four hours." [51] And later when the Liquor Commission denied a license to a powerful interest, Olson gave Arundel unconditional support, absorbing pressure of all kinds without complaint.

Nonetheless, Olson's administration suffered from the more common forms of petty graft. Some of it was used to build up a strong Farmer Labor political machine, and the balance found its way into the pockets of strategically placed jobholders. At first Olson's vigilance checked the more questionable activities of his subordinates, but after 1934 he lacked the physical energy to enforce party honesty. Sometimes he affected indifference to dishonest transactions that went on under his nose. When told that one Farmer Labor organizer had collected two thousand dollars and turned in only one thousand, he replied, "We'll be damn lucky if we always get fifty percent." [52]

He was very sensitive, however, to the grafting in the Highway Department. Cheney recalls that an article making veiled allusions to this matter roused Olson to one of his rare displays of anger. Unfortunately, he never made a systematic effort to clean up the state departments, and during his last term the situation rapidly grew worse.

One of John Regan's favorite campaign charges was that Olson permitted relief clients to make purchases at chain stores while loudly proclaiming himself the protector of independent merchants. Inasmuch as W.P.A. Administrator Harry Hopkins forced relief recipients to purchase part of their groceries at chain stores, Olson could do nothing to remedy the situation — with the result that the independent merchants, already unsettled by the March platform, walked out on him.[53]

A final feature of the opposition campaign that made Farmer Laborites nervous was the straw vote conducted with much fanfare by the *Minneapolis Journal*. Based on ballots mailed out to all automobile owners, it showed an increasing plurality for Nelson with each tabulation. The great debacle of the *Literary Digest* poll was still two years in the future, and the role of straw votes in generating bandwagon psychology was as yet undetermined. So, fearing the newspaper victories for Nelson would stampede waverers, the Farmer Laborites made a determined effort to discredit the poll. Olson characterized it as a "fake straw ballot under which any Republican henchman can cast one or one hundred or even one thousand votes for the Republican candidate."[54]

The defensive warfare waged by the Farmer Laborites against their old-party assailants partly obscured an intraparty quarrel that exploded in September when A. C. Townley bolted the party. Dissatisfaction with the Olson patronage policy was the ostensible reason for Townley's defection. However, he did not get along well with Olson and had never acquiesced in the governor's leadership of the reform movement. With a close election in prospect, Townley probably calculated that his support was sufficiently important to warrant his inclusion in the inner circles of the party.

At all events, he jumped squarely into the middle of the always smoldering patronage controversy, and his attacks on all-party jobholders attracted the attention of many sincere people with real or imagined grievances, culminating in a convention at Benson on September 3. Under Townley's guidance the dissidents adopted resolutions denouncing the all-party appointees and demanding their immediate replacement with bona fide Farmer Laborites.[55]

A committee of one hundred was deputized to serve this ultimatum on Olson, and to warn him that rejection would bring Townley into the field as an independent candidate for governor. Olson's effective handling of the committee has already been described.

When Townley subsequently announced his candidacy for governor, Olson's reaction came in the form of a letter to E. P. Paquin, chairman of the committee. Like a father reproving a loved but wayward son, he expressed confidence in the committee's loyalty to the party, suggesting that its members had been misled by A. C. Townley, "a man whom I never have nor do not now consider a Farmer Laborite. For many years as head of the Nonpartisan League, he vigorously opposed the formation of a third party in Minnesota. He has said nothing since the time he so bitterly opposed the formation of the third party to indicate that he has changed from his original theory. . . . The evidence is conclusive that he organized the Benson meeting; that he dominated it; that he did not permit anyone opposed to his designs even to speak; and that his underlying motive was to become a candidate for governor." [56]

By blaming the whole episode on Townley and magnanimously forgiving the committee of one hundred, Olson coaxed many of the dissidents back into the fold. Only fifty-one of the original group attended Townley's St. Cloud strategy meeting on September 16, prompting the governor to remark that all he had lost was Townley's vote.[57]

Subsequent events justified this unflattering appraisal of the old Nonpartisan Leaguer's vote-getting powers. Every leader of consequence in the reform movement denounced him. Even Henry Teigan, his comrade in arms from North Dakota days and constant defender within the Farmer Labor party, broke with him over this latest apostasy. F. B. Ohlquist, secretary of the Benson committee, accused him of selling out to the Republicans and receiving money from Sam Haislet, their publicity director.[58] Whatever the truth of this charge, Farmer Laborites managed to create the impression that Townley was not a bona fide reform candidate but a "hireling of the interests." As a result, he polled an insignificant number of votes, running poorly even in the old League strongholds of western Minnesota.

Much more troublesome than Townley's defection was the sullen refusal of Shipstead to campaign for the Farmer Labor ticket. The abortive effort of the organization to deny him renomination left the senator in an uncooperative frame of mind, and, without allowing himself to be quoted directly, he made it clear that he disliked the candidates, the platform, and the party. He waited until the deadline date before filing in the Farmer Labor primary and steadfastly kept his own counsel throughout the campaign. This aloofness enabled Shipstead to achieve a personal triumph at the expense of the party. His prestige was so high that a reassuring word would have helped to allay fear of the March platform and of state-printed textbooks without impairing his re-election prospects. His silence was taken to imply that he feared the party's radicalism.

In spite of all these obstacles to victory, Olson waged his usual masterful campaign. No outward sign of irritation or physical exhaustion was allowed to show even though he drove himself mercilessly, hitting nearly every hamlet in Minnesota during the last month.

Each oration ran the gamut of political emotions from light-hearted humor to outraged indignation. He dismissed Nelson's awkward attempts to appear liberal as "a bait to catch votes, just as the wolf put on a red shawl to catch little Red Riding Hood." [59] He pointed out that Regan endorsed President Roosevelt but characterized attempts to implement New Deal principles in Minnesota as communistic. With mock solemnity he assured a Mankato audience that Regan would return to live among his neighbors after January 1.

On a level above personalities Olson gave many paragraphs to formulating the aspirations of the common man. Again and again he reaffirmed his loyalty to the fight for better living conditions, nowhere more strikingly than in the October 6 keynote speech: "There is a real issue in this campaign, a very vital issue; and it is not communism . . . nor the Third Internationale . . . nor Russia . . . nor Siberia . . . not even Africa. Precisely stated that issue is: Shall our social and economic order be so changed and so modified as to bring a more equitable distribution of wealth and a decent standard of living?"[60] Then he launched on his familiar plea for a cooperative commonwealth.

To thousands of insecure or unemployed there was something dramatic, courageous, and inspiring in the Olson message. The most frenzied assaults of Democrats and Republicans could not conceal the fact that the governor was their champion. These depressed classes swarmed to the polls in November to extend the Farmer Labor tenure of power. As the returns trickled in on election night, Olson slowly pulled away from his three opponents. The final tabulation showed: Olson 468,812; Nelson 396,359; Regan 176,928; Townley 4454.

Olson's plurality of 72,453 was decisive but fell short of the 188,357 he had piled up in 1932. An analysis of the vote by sections made it clear that labor had re-elected the governor. His margin in heavily urban Ramsey, Hennepin, and St. Louis counties came within a few hundred votes of his margin for the state as a whole. Rural Minnesota voted solidly against him except for the the Red River Valley and the sparsely populated north central counties, indicating that the Republican agitation against the platform and the state printing of textbooks had alienated the farmers.

In a candid post-election statement, Olson attributed the loss of the rural districts "to the fact that in the large population centers we were better equipped to meet the vicious propaganda of the opposition with effective counter propaganda. We found also that in cities the metropolitan press is a discredited institution and hence not believed, while country people still believe to some extent the things they read in newspapers."[61]

This explanation overlooked the possibility that rural Minnesota might reject the Farmer Labor program even if favorably presented. The fact was that farmers began returning to their old orbit in 1934. Never radical in the collectivist sense, they feared the March platform with its threats against the private ownership system and rural independence. Already regretting their spite votes against the Republicans in 1930 and 1932, they were ready to return to the old dispensation now that the economic revival was picking up momentum. Only in the north and west, where drought, heavy mortgage burdens, and poor soil aggravated farmer militance, was there any enthusiasm for the Farmer Labor program.

Thus the election of 1934 foreshadowed the final disintegration of the unstable farmer-worker alliance. Olson's survival in this, his last and hardest election, was primarily due to the steady leftward drift of urban sentiment and his tremendous personal prestige.

Olson's serpentine course during the 1934 campaign deepened the controversy regarding his political and economic creed. The more hidebound conservatives looked upon him as a dangerous demagogue bent upon undermining the very foundations of society. The ultraradicals who had heralded the cooperative commonwealth platform as a sign of his conversion to socialism felt betrayed when he tacitly repudiated the document.

Others, including even Olson's campaign manager, suspected that he had permitted the adoption of an extreme platform to prevent the election of a Farmer Labor legislature and thereby block the enactment of a radical program. Such Machiavellian motivation seems unlikely because it would have involved an exceedingly delicate political maneuver for Olson to reduce the party vote without jeopardizing his own chances of re-election. However, the very fact that persons close to the governor could credit him with this intention suggests widespread doubt regarding his political convictions.

The citizenry shared the feeling of uncertainty. Few even

professed to find a coherent political or economic program in Olson's public utterances. His criticism of the existing system gradually became more extreme, but the remedial measures he proposed were vaguely stated — veering back and forth between a cooperative system of the Swedish type and a public owner-ship program of indeterminate origin. To be sure, Olson proposed concrete solutions for pressing economic problems like farm relief, but these did not dovetail into a pattern consistent enough to counterbalance the baffling effect created by his combination of radical speeches and cautious action.

Olson never pretended that he could accomplish many of his party's objectives.[62] Even worse, he minimized the obstacle of a hostile legislature, saying it spared him the necessity of push-ing the more drastic Farmer Labor panaceas and gave him plenty of fuel for the next campaign. Time after time he dis-illusioned left-wingers by appointing avowed conservatives to key positions. His leisure hours were spent for the most part with members of the class he excoriated so ruthlessly in public speeches. Richard Lilly considered him conservative enough to justify repeated efforts at conversion and always believed that Olson would have joined the Republican party if powerful interests had not blocked his advancement there.

Under the circumstances it was not strange that a substan-tial number of the politically conscious doubted Olson's devo-tion to reform. The more charitable of these dismissed the governor as a muddled thinker uncertain of his goal, while the others looked upon him as a crafty opportunist, seeking power for its own sake.

Harsh judgments become inevitable if Olson's political career is interpreted in terms of theoretical consistency. However, he never evaluated his own activities by such standards. As an eminently practical man, he considered success the principal justification of his policies. Invariably he focused his attention on concrete objectives rather than on nebulous, distant goals. There was not an ounce of the doctrinaire reformer in him. In response to a direct question as to whether he professed communism, he said, "That's what they say. As a matter of fact I haven't read Marx. I'm not interested in names; results count." [63]

Like all realists, Olson distrusted the armchair philosophers who sought to solve all problems by the application of a set formula. He was openly contemptuous of John Strachey, the alleged British communist,* and once diagnosed the trouble with leftists in general as their desire to "ride on a white horse with a pennant flying, hell bent for the barricades." [64] He could not conceal his irritation at the confident enthusiasm of communists who awaited the great day of revolution without any concrete plans. Once when he invited communist demonstrators to use his public address system, an ungrateful zealot shouted into the microphone, "When the revolution comes, Olson, we'll get you." To which the governor replied scornfully, "When the revolution comes, I'll be leading it, and you'll be just a corporal." [65]

He was equally scornful of the editors who criticized his conduct of the Austin strike, characterizing them as "bloodthirsty, swivel chair warriors whose only knowledge of life is gained through travelling from their homes to their editorial sanctuaries." [66] His preference for the company of businessmen stemmed at least partly from the fact that, whatever their limitations, they were at least hardheaded realists.

These numerous manifestations of Olson's pragmatic spirit suggest the futility of judging his deeds by abstract standards. He acted habitually on a practical plane, and generalizations are bound to read into his policies a theoretical unity that never really existed.

If we search for consistency at the operating level, much of the apparent ambiguity in Olson's behavior disappears. No interpretation of the complex forces motivating his actions is entirely satisfactory, but the predominating impulse seems to have been the alleviation of human misery. He had resented

* "The British mind was incapable of appreciating Mr. Strachey, but in the United States he discourses brilliantly at swanky dinners causing delightful shudders to run down the spine of capitalists of both sexes." (Floyd B. Olson, "My Political Creed," *Common Sense*, April 1935, p. 7.)

from early childhood the social and economic arrangements which kept great masses of people on the verge of destitution in a land of plenty. R. L. Norton, a Boston newspaperman, who had a sharp brush with Olson at a Chicago night club, thought his grudge against the existing order stemmed from the fact that he had gone hungry at one period in his life.[67] This was probably an overstatement of the case, but there can be no doubt that Olson felt deeply about the glaring inequalities in society and fought to correct them.

The distinction made earlier, that Olson was more a rebel than a radical, deserves emphasis, because similar surface manifestations tend to conceal important differences between the two. Outward aggressiveness and truculence are characteristic of both types, but the radical usually wants to create a whole new society, whereas the rebel is often content to hack away at specific conditions that irritate him. Sometimes the two attitudes blend indistinguishably in the same person, but this was hardly true of Olson. He was not tormented by apocalyptic visions of a new heaven and a new earth. He had little of the fanatic urge to force a new blueprint on society that characterized the left wing of the Farmer Labor party.

Nevertheless he oozed rebellion from every pore. All his mannerisms and gestures betrayed a dislike of order. He hated discipline and anything that smacked of routine. If he could possibly evade regular hours at the office he did so. Although personally very neat, he delighted to strew clothes and newspapers around hotel rooms. His private finances were always in disorder, and he deliberately cultivated an ostentatious unconcern regarding the accumulation of property in order to shock his middle class associates. His whole viewpoint was colored by a psychological defiance of the status quo, and since it featured economic inequality he objected to it all the more.

Many of the magnificent rebels in politics have been carried to disaster by the very vehemence of their attack on the social order. Olson managed to avoid this danger because of his practical streak and his exceptional ability to analyze human psychology. The desire to do something concrete for the underprivileged prevented his slipping by slow degrees into doctrinaire radicalism, while his understanding of the innate conservatism of the average human being kept him from pressing too rapidly along the path of reform. He knew that the capacity of the people for absorbing new ideas is limited.

Consequently, though he often spoke lyrically of the benefits to be derived from complete socialization, he shied away from endorsement of immediate measures to that end. At the height of the depression he told a Farmer Labor picnic that he was not ready to take such an irrevocable step: "Changes so far reaching come slowly and the change must be especially slow in a social and economic system as complex as this we live in." [68] He had a typically American abhorrence of violent political change. When asked whether he believed in revolution he replied, "I believe in evolution. When we are ten steps ahead of the Bourbons, they will be forced to take one." [69]

Probably Olson's most candid statement of his views on reform was made at a midwestern youth conference where he locked horns with John Strachey. Without equivocation he defended the realistic approach to politics: "I am an opportunist, and I hasten to call myself one before Mr. Strachey does. I do not speak facetiously . . . an opportunist is one who will use any agency he finds at hand — whether he believes in the entire program — to translate into action such part of his own program as is possible . . . I am an individualist in that I will go down the road with any organization that is going my way until I reach the crossroad. The Communists wait for 'the day' and won't tell what they are going to do when it comes." [70]

One of Minnesota's bankrupt farmers summed up Olson's approach to reform with homespun humor: "Floyd is just the kind of leader folks want. He will go as far as any man in the party, and get there first if given a couple of minutes' notice." [71] Olson managed to guide the multitude down the path of reform because he moved slowly enough for the stragglers to tag along. He seldom advanced beyond hearing range of the main column, and he had the flexibility and skill to beat a hasty retreat if necessary.

The veering and shifting that characterized his policy confused his supporters, but this adaptability enabled him to mobilize a gigantic protest movement whose members had nothing in common but their dislike of the existing order. Although this feat necessarily laid Olson open to charges of insincerity and bad faith, the more bewildering discrepancies between his promises and his performance are resolved if we judge the man as a rebel against specific economic ills rather than as a doctrinaire Don Quixote tilting with windmills as a matter of principle.

Even so, no definite answer can be given regarding the motives and objectives of so complex a personality as Olson. Interpretation boils down to thoughtful opinion. Contemporaries could not agree about him. To opponents he seemed a consummate scoundrel and to friends a guardian angel. Between these groups was a vast body of politically conscious citizens less partisan in viewpoint. Perhaps Leif Gilstad expressed the consensus when he characterized Olson as "essentially a sincere crusader for the underdog."[72] Certainly the effort to relieve human misery was the most consistent policy of his political career.

# Chapter XII    DEADLOCK

THE widespread interest in the 1934 gubernatorial campaign partially obscured the spirited contests being waged all over Minnesota for one hundred and ninety-eight legislative seats. The obstructionist tactics of a conservative holdover senate during the 1933 session had emphasized the need for a more tractable membership. Olson gave a preview of party policy when he threatened to visit the districts of reactionaries and acquaint the people with their records.

As the campaign drew near, party leaders worked for the entry of Farmer Labor candidates in as many districts as possible, although the June primary was theoretically nonpartisan. Even loyal all-party members of the Munn coalition like John J. McDonough and E. J. Chilgren faced Farmer Labor opposition. However, the unfavorable effect of the March platform on rural Minnesota, which controlled a disproportionate number of legislative seats, was enough to ruin third-party hopes. Some Farmer Laborites failed to survive the primary and many more were defeated in the general election. Olson was so busy fighting for his own political life that his threatened campaign against reactionary legislators never materialized. He confined himself to general pleas for the election of high-type men who couldn't "be induced into the bars and eating places of St. Paul and persuaded how to vote."[1]

Consequently, when the initial elation over Olson's victory had worn off, Farmer Laborites awoke to the unpleasant reality that they had lost both houses of the legislature. Although the size of the party minority remained unchanged in the senate, the house coalition was wrecked. A few of its members, including Charles Munn himself, had been elected or appointed to better jobs, but the vast majority either failed to secure re-election or slipped through by disavowing their former affiliations. On the other hand, hardly a conservative was unseated.

The prospect of confronting a hostile legislature in January did not bother Olson as much as he pretended. It relieved him of the responsibility for implementing a platform which had bred discord in the party and violated his own standards of practical reform. It permitted him to advocate whatever he deemed politically advantageous without assuming the risks of fulfillment. And it enabled him to transfer the blame for mounting deficits and tax levies to other shoulders.

Hjalmar Petersen, the lieutenant governor elect, got the impression that this arrangement suited Olson. Arguing that real pressure might result in a Farmer Labor senate, Petersen suggested opening up formal headquarters, but Olson rejected this plan in favor of a less ambitious program for personal interviews with uncertain members. So Petersen traveled around the state in Olson's car contacting each newly elected senator.[2]

However, despite his seeming coolness, the governor took to the radio on November 16 for an impassioned denunciation of the forces attempting to organize the house. He branded Roy Dunn, who had directed the conservative campaign, as the chief representative of "invisible government" and challenged him to tell who was financing his many post-election visits with newly elected legislators.[3] This offensive had no appreciable effect, the liberals drawing fifty-three to their house caucus on November 17 and the conservatives seventy-seven a few days later.

The most embarrassing problem for the new house leaders was to find a formula that would justify a legislative organization hostile to a governor who had a fresh mandate from the people. They sought to solve it by noisy avowals of broadmindedness, renaming themselves the "Independent Progressives" and putting forward C. W. Johnson, a Duluth representative with a mixed voting record, as their candidate for speaker. Roy Dunn made a radio address interpreting the election as a rejection of Republican policies rather than an approval of Farmer Labor policies and denying that "the Independent Progressives" were all Republicans.[4]

After the bad showing of the liberal caucus in mid-November, Olson let matters slide until the end of the year. He spent most of December convalescing from a hernia operation, but began to meddle actively in legislative politics just before his inauguration, principally because of rumors about intended investigations of the executive branch. The *Minneapolis Journal* reported that he spent most of the night before the opening session at the Lowry Hotel trying to bring waverers into line.[5] This last-minute intervention proved useless, and the house joined the senate in creating a conservative organization.

There was a good deal of post-election speculation about Olson's biennial message. His victory on a platform that was far to the left of the New Deal, even after cautious interpretation, aroused widespread interest as to his proposals for implementing it. In a candid interview with Marquis Childs of the *St. Louis Post Dispatch* Olson said he thought the public ownership program was dead but that its ends might be achieved by indirect measures. He considered the outlook poor for state printing of textbooks, but believed the legislature would abolish military drill, extend the moratorium on mortgage foreclosures, and enlarge conservation activities.[6]

In spite of this personal opinion on legislative prospects, Olson soon served notice that he would demand enactment of the full Farmer Labor program. The official party organ confidently predicted that his principal recommendations would call for enlarged relief appropriations, a broad social security program, and a constitutional amendment for public ownership of power plants.[7]

Consequently, the legislature was expecting a militant message, but nothing like the sweeping proposals for a new social order which it received. Before he was finished, Olson managed to endorse every radical panacea the Farmer Labor party had ever advocated. Observing at the outset that the legislature's majority would not agree with him as to the hopelessness of a permanent cure of economic ills under capitalism but would concur as to the need for remedial measures, he launched into a series of recommendations ranging all the way from public ownership of key industries to a unicameral legislature.

This declaration of war on the conservatives may have been smart politics from the governor's standpoint, but it provoked a violent reaction in the enemy camp. The legislative clique that had undercut the Olson program in 1933 needed little encouragement to shift from defense to offense. For the most part, its members interpreted the recent election to mean that the benighted voter had at last seen the menace inherent in the Olson program, so that a little more political education along traditional lines would re-establish Republican power in 1936.

The determination of both the governor and the conservative majority to use the legislature as a trial battleground for the 1936 campaign created such an unwholesome atmosphere that no issue could be considered on its merits. Every maneuver was shot through with partisan implications, making it difficult to effect even the clandestine compromises on which politicians set great store. Half the session passed before a major bill reached the governor, and the ensuing weeks were punctuated by petty disputes that ended in mutual recriminations of the bitterest sort. The session was a demonstration of representative government at its worst — unless one assumes that the electorate actually preferred deadlock!

As their first step, the conservatives began a drive to reduce Olson's power over patronage. Bills were introduced to abolish Farmer Labor departments and transfer their functions to the departments beyond the jurisdiction of the governor. Likewise, the senate decided to withhold approval of Olson's interim appointments pending further investigation.

Even more menacing was a bill sponsored by Senator Rockne to outlaw political collections from state employees. Although couched in general terms, it aimed at preventing the notorious three percent contributions by Farmer Laborites to the party

Cartoon by Oscar Cesare, from the Minneapolis Journal,
October 5, 1934

war chest. Since the money was being used to publish the *Farmer Labor Leader* and finance a weekly radio broadcast,[8] the Rockne bill would dry up the major source of funds for favorable publicity. The system of financial exactions from officeholders put the reformers in a bad light, but they had no alternative since the party's economic policy shut off the advertising revenue that made the newspapers of other parties self-sustaining.

The conservatives' trump card was to turn the inquisitorial machinery of the legislature against Olson. Both houses set up investigating committees, but the more thorough job was done by the senate, which appropriated $5000 and put virtually no restrictions on the matters to be probed.

Through some obscure cloakroom deal, Senator James A. Carley, right-wing Democrat from Plainview, became committee chairman. The Farmer Laborites were assigned only three of the eleven places on the committee, and the majority often transacted business in secret, using the daily press to inform the Farmer Labor minority of committee activities.[9] To emphasize still further the partisan spirit of the conservatives, Tom Mouer, a close associate of Senator Schall, was hired as chief prosecutor for the committee at forty dollars a day.[10]

The administration of the state highway and relief departments was subjected to the most sweeping inquisition because these divisions provided employment for many loyal Farmer Laborites. Committee detectives rounded up witnesses willing to testify that there were corruption, bribery, and collusion in the negotiation of highway contracts. They made little effort to check the reliability of these witnesses, requiring only that their charges be sensational enough to hit the newspaper headlines. This standard was easily met by dozens of disappointed job seekers, Townley supporters, and others disgruntled about the Farmer Labor administration for one reason or another.

D. C. Clark, the general manager of a granite firm in St. Cloud, created a major commotion when he testified that C. R. Erickson, the state purchasing commissioner, had demanded

$10,000 for the Farmer Labor party in return for a $245,000 contract. It was difficult for the administration to combat such charges because Carley would not permit the accused to question the witnesses or to testify before the committee. The newspapers increased this handicap by giving smaller space to the denials than to the more dramatic accusations. However, the Clark charges eventually boomeranged when the granite salesman was indicted for issuing worthless checks.

If the committee had not allowed itself to be distracted by irresponsible witnesses, it might well have uncovered evidence of real corruption in the Highway Department. The Farmer Laborites practiced the routine shakedown of contractors for campaign funds and indulged in other forms of petty graft,[11] although it was generally conceded that they lacked the efficiency of their Republican predecessors. Olson never became involved in these unsavory manipulations, but he found it difficult to control his subordinates. The latter escaped in this instance with nothing worse than a bad case of nerves because the committee conducted its probe on a very superficial basis.

The investigation of patronage procedures in the Highway Department disclosed nothing more startling than the predisposition of political parties to reward their friends. I. C. Strout, who wrote the much publicized letter reminding highway foremen of their political obligations, was called to the stand and questioned closely about personnel policies. The senators expressed outraged indignation at his admissions, but Olson made a mockery of the whole episode by offering the committee his letter file of job recommendations with the innocent observation that Farmer Labor policy could be better administered through its friends than its enemies.

When the investigation shifted to the administration of relief, it produced frequent headlines but no evidence that either Olson or his subordinates had misused funds. The record was cluttered with the usual charges of inefficiency and petty graft, ranging all the way from the construction of guest houses with government funds to the purchase of cod-liver oil for relief clients. A St. Paul merchant accused of receiving a contract from the relief administration for five hundred fancy raincoats added a ludicrous touch to the proceedings by roaming the Capitol corridors in search of Senator Carley and informing all who would listen that he had sold exactly two coats to the state.[12]

Other Farmer-Labor-dominated agencies escaped with only a cursory examination. Senator Carley suspended hearings for a week on the pretext of Mouer's illness, but critics were unkind enough to suggest that the investigators had run out of ammunition. Nonetheless, Carley asserted that enough work remained to justify extension of the committee's life beyond the legislative session. Denied this continuance, Carley and his conservative colleagues filed a majority report full of insinuations that the Farmer Labor party was incompetent and dishonest.

The anti-administration propaganda issuing steadily from the senate investigating committee provoked strong retaliatory measures from the Farmer Laborites. Their principal medium was the party newspaper, issued weekly after January 1 under the less partisan title of the *Minnesota Leader*. Effectively supplementing it was the radio campaign conducted by Sylvester McGovern, a journalist with a sardonic tongue, who was carried on the payroll of the Oil Inspection Department at $250 a month.[13] Broadcasting his weekly "Minnesota Merry Go Round" under the pseudonym of Rome Roberts, he twitted the bumbling Carley so mercilessly that the latter denounced him on the floor of the senate and threatened to investigate the program. After the end of the session, McGovern's broadcasts were edited and published in book form with a foreword proclaiming the 1935 legislature to be the best that money could buy.

Olson also took a personal hand in the counteroffensive against the investigating committee. He had made arrangements to write a regular column in the *St. Paul Daily News* during the session, and although he covered a wide variety of questions, the activities of the committee received a generous amount of attention. His observations got under Carley's skin sufficiently to provoke the ill-humored charge that the columns were ghostwritten. Olson replied that the senator was suffering "jitteritis" and went on to admit with mock humility that "as a columnist I am just another governor."[14] In point of fact, the governor wrote all the articles that appeared under his name, and enjoyed the experience thoroughly.

Most of Olson's thrusts at the committee were delivered in a half-satirical vein. He discussed learnedly in his column the disease of "investigatitis," classifying it as a political infection. "Its germ produces the violent desire in the person infected to investigate and thoroughly discredit his political opponent or opponents. The germ is present in the membership of all political parties." Having described the symptoms, "Dr." Olson solemnly assured his readers that the disease becomes active only when a political party has a chance to investigate the record of its predecessors or opponents.[15]

When the committee charged that subversive literature was corrupting the minds of hoboes in the transient camps, Olson suggested that it ought to investigate the Foreign Policy Association of Minneapolis, which had listened to the British radical, John Strachey.

But when, near the end of the session, Olson read the 110-page indictment of his administration prepared by the committee, he was so annoyed that he sponsored a last-minute resolution requesting an investigation of the legislature for bribery and wrote an article in the *St. Paul Daily News* castigating the senate committee in terms almost beyond the bounds of political protocol.

After characterizing the committee as the only tribunal in Minnesota to deny the "meanest man" the right to present his own defense, he went on to say, "I do not mind being called a 'red' . . . I would prefer it to the term 'yellow,' because the term 'yellow' may be applied to those who controlled the legislative investigating committee. I first requested them to call me as a witness and then dared them to call me. The same challenge was made by other people. They were too yellow to do so. If they possessed an atom of courage, they would have welcomed the opportunity to get before them for questioning, the man against whom all of their inquiries were directed." [16]

In view of the steadily mounting tension between the governor and the legislature, it is a wonder the session produced any constructive measures. With the defeat of his reform program a foregone conclusion, Olson focused his attention on relief appropriations and taxation. The conservatives would have liked to sidetrack relief entirely. Public spending for the unemployed ran counter to their social and economic philosophy, and worse, it created Farmer Labor votes, since most of the jobless gave the Olson administration credit for relief.

Public opinion had come to accept relief appropriations as a government obligation, however, and the national administration had established a policy of making its own funds available only if the state supplied a fixed portion of the total outlay. It was one thing to harass Olson by blocking social legislation, but another to refuse appropriations when doing so would shut off federal aid. The most stubborn opponents of the governor knew that such a stand would be political suicide. They dared not withhold relief, and yet their vindictiveness had reached such intensity that they were determined to block Olson as long as possible. Under the leadership of Senator Rockne they gave the voters an exhibition of partisanship gone amuck.

They began by raising all sorts of objections to federal relief procedures on the pretense that they did not emanate from Washington but from Governor Olson. Legislators from the prosperous southern counties protested the requirement that local units contribute on the basis of ability to pay because this would force them to help finance the relief of their bankrupt brethren in the north. They suggested that the whole problem be turned back to the local governments and that all relief appropriations be withheld pending an investigation of the state setup. Lest they alienate their rural constituents whose draft animals were starving for lack of fodder, the conservatives proposed to separate drought relief from the omnibus bill and appropriate $1,000,000 immediately.

Recognizing in this maneuver an effort to buy off the farmers and thereby weaken sentiment for a general relief bill, Olson warned the legislature that a special appropriation for drought relief might cause the federal government to drop the whole relief problem in Minnesota's lap. Nonetheless, both houses passed the $1,000,000 drought relief bill in early February. Final enactment was delayed because the senate version eliminated the state relief administration as a distribution agency. Rockne justified this provision on the ground that "those close to the situation feel that it would be too slow if the funds went through regular channels." [17]

While the two houses were bickering over a compromise plan, definite word was received from Relief Administrator Harry Hopkins that federal aid would be decreased by the amount appropriated in Minnesota. The conservatives suspected that Olson's intervention at Washington was responsible for this decision, but whether this was true or not, Hopkins' ruling torpedoed the plan of separate drought relief.

The house promptly passed the $10,000,000 omnibus bill in the form requested by Olson, but Rockne buried it in the senate Finance Committee and sent two senators to confer with Hopkins in Washington. They returned with assurances of increased federal aid, but congress was so slow in appropriating the necessary funds that the legislature had to pass a stopgap measure making $500,000 available for immediate drought relief.

Despite repeated assurances from the state, regional, and national authorities that the state must contribute $10,000,000 as its share of the relief burden, Senator Rockne continued to sit on the bill for three weeks, stubbornly insisting that he had not been given any definite figures. Whereupon Olson remarked that Rockne was "the only person in Minnesota unaware of the position of the federal government." [18] The senator finally telegraphed to Shipstead for information about Minnesota's relief contribution, and on March 9 Hopkins sent a blunt return wire to the effect that federal relief funds would be shut off unless the state appropriated $10,000,000 immediately.

Forced into action by this ultimatum, Rockne went to the other extreme, putting a bill together so hastily that it reached Olson in a form which would have made millionaires eligible for relief. When the governor returned the bill with sarcastic comments about its unconstitutional features, Rockne replied that the errors were due to Olson's demand for speed.

The senator's capacity for obstruction had not yet been exhausted. His second draft of the bill contained a completely unacceptable clause requiring each county to make relief contributions, and Olson had to reject it once again. In his third effort Rockne accepted the government formula that relief assessments on counties take into account their ability to pay, and Olson signed the measure at last on March 16.

With minor variations, the relief story was repeated in the fight for Highway Department appropriations, where the conservatives were confronted with an identical dilemma: Many Farmer Labor jobholders would be eliminated by cutting off state highway construction, but federal aid would also be eliminated. Senator William Roepke, chairman of the Highway Committee, ignored this danger and reported out a bill cutting the basic rate on automobile license taxes sharply enough to prevent construction of new roads. The house re-enacted the higher 1933 rates, but Roepke refused to yield, deadlocking the conference committee for several weeks.

Finally, on April 9 a compromise slightly below the house rate but still considerably short of the figure requested by the federal government was approved by the legislature. Rural pressure for road construction proved too strong, however, and the conservatives had to capitulate at the last minute, permitting a $12,000,000 bond issue to match federal aid.

Overborne in their fight against relief and highway expenditures, the conservatives sought to avert the final indignity of paying for the Olson program. Both sides agreed that it was unfair for the additional relief costs to be saddled on landed property, where they would automatically fall unless the legis-

Cartoon by John Baer, from the Farmer Labor Leader,
March 31, 1932

lature revised the tax structure. The governor's biennial message recommended that corporations and individual incomes bear the new burden, but the conservatives proposed to distribute it more generally in the form of a sales or turnover tax. Unfortunately, this kind of levy could not be made palatable to the mass of voters. Senator MacKenzie, a strong proponent of the sales tax, could find no better way of concluding a long defense of it than to say it would arouse "tax consciousness." [19]

Doubtless all revenue-raising programs are unpopular, but the universal incidence of the sales tax made it particularly unattractive during the depression. Olson exploited public hostility skillfully by proposing instead to increase taxes on iron ore, utilities, money and credits, inheritances, personal incomes, and chain stores. Since it was commonly believed that big business was chiefly responsible for the depression, the governor's scheme of taxing corporate wealth found favor even among groups who had parted company with him over socialism.

Knowing that he had enough votes in the house to sustain a sales tax veto, Olson played an effective game of legislative blackmail. He demanded a new revenue law loudly and often in the hope that conservatives would be forced to adopt most of his tax program in order to secure even a modified sales tax.

The legislature responded in the same spirit, incorporating some of the governor's tax proposals in an omnibus bill so that he would have to accept the sales levy or else take responsibility for blocking tax revision. But Olson's measures were included in such emasculated form that the governor did not consider a compromise worth while.

Therefore, as the omnibus bill reached the floor of the house on March 20, Olson issued a sharp blast against the sales tax, declaring it "a plan for shifting the burden of taxation from the rich to the poor. That would be vicious enough during normal times, but it is unconscionable during this period of depression." [20] When the conservatives replied that a veto would place responsibility on him for failure to lighten the property tax, Olson promptly retorted, "It is not for the legislature to fix responsibility. It is for the people. The conservatives do not understand that, because they so seldom think of the people. When they do, they think only in terms of a few. Furthermore, the majority of the people are opposed to a sales tax on necessities." [21] He followed up this statement with a series of outspoken articles in the *St. Paul Daily News*.[22]

The legislature refused to be diverted from its course, however. The omnibus bill cleared both houses in mid-April, but the majority fell so far short of the two thirds necessary to override a veto that the conference committee took the painful step of opening negotiations with the governor. By April 20 the *Minneapolis Journal* felt it could safely predict that the adversaries would arrive at a compromise.[23] But forty-eight hours later the conversations collapsed completely. Olson had apparently been willing to accept a sales tax which exempted necessities, but he expected reciprocal concessions on corporate taxation, and these the conservatives were unwilling to grant.

Without wasting any further time, the conference committee reconciled minor differences between the two houses and sent the omnibus bill to the governor. Olson promptly killed it with a veto. Reiterating all his former arguments against the sales tax, he especially condemned the rates levied on amusements: "Those who believe in a low standard of living for the masses contend that amusements come under the head of luxuries. I contend that they come under the head of necessities. Remove amusements from the poor, and their morale is destroyed and their nervous system impaired. In this day of intense nervous strain, relaxation in the form of amusement is almost as necessary as food." [24]

Because of the veto the property tax mill rate had to be raised to an all-time high of 14.95, exposing Olson to outraged protests from conservatives. The president of the Federation of Associations for Tax Reform found it unpardonable that "the will of one man should prevent tax relief in Minnesota," and Rudolph Lee of the *Long Prairie Leader* called the veto "a body blow to the land owners." [25]

The three battles over relief, highway appropriations, and taxation overshadowed a dozen smaller tilts in which Olson lashed back at the legislature regardless of consequences. He even vetoed a nonpolitical bill ratifying the local tax agreement between the village of Hibbing and the Oliver Mining Company because he doubted that the latter would act in good faith without a provision for court enforcement. By mustering a two-thirds vote, the legislature overrode a governor's veto for the first time in the history of the state.

These sharp brushes with the legislature reinforced Olson's outward militance. His frequent addresses from the steps of the Capitol to indignant farmers and unemployed dripped with invectives against the capitalist system. He also condemned the munitions makers, telling University of Minnesota students that the profit motive lay at the root of much war propaganda and urging that steps be taken to eliminate it.[26] Whether he stimulated reform sentiment or was swept along by the current, the governor's uncompromising truculence throughout the legislative session firmly re-established his waning reputation for radicalism.

The dismal record of deadlock reflected little credit on either side. Beyond extending the mortgage moratorium two years, exempting household goods and farm machinery from the personal property tax, and authorizing thirteen new state forests, the legislature accomplished nothing noteworthy. Even the statewide Old Age Pension Act it passed was invalidated through an error of the engrossing clerk, making a special session inevitable. However, by the time Olson convened it very different political problems occupied the center of the stage.

# Chapter XIII THE SPOILSMEN TURN KING-MAKERS

T‌he legislative deadlock on political and economic issues reflected a heightened tempo of class warfare. Drought-stricken farmers set pens of emaciated cattle on the Capitol lawn to dramatize their demands for feed appropriations, and representatives of the unemployed picketed the legislature, denouncing the capitalist system and protesting the inadequacy of relief payments.

These springtime manifestations of unrest were the prelude to widespread industrial conflict in July and August. The wages of unskilled and semiskilled workers lagged far behind commodity prices, intensifying economic distress and driving them to organize for pay increases. This new unionization campaign met with determined resistance from employers. Far from being broken by the truck strike of 1934, they had energetically reformed their lines to prevent an enlargement of the union bridgehead in Minneapolis. The invalidation of the N.I.R.A. suggested that the supreme court might also nullify the Wagner-Connery Act, which was intended to perpetuate the collective bargaining provisions of the defunct Section 7a. The employers were encouraged to return to the congenial task of smashing unions. The consequent breakdown of negotiations for wage increases and the discharge of conspicuous union sympathizers produced a rash of strikes.

The larger conflict between labor and management was complicated by an internal struggle for control of the labor movement. The A.F.L., already fearful of industrial unionism, waged a persistent battle against the militant truck drivers' Local 574; while the communists, for reasons best known to the Kremlin, entered upon a temporary phase of collaboration with orthodox trade union leaders, enthusiastically supporting all strikes and furnishing pickets from the United Relief Workers Association, which they dominated.[1] Their unsolicited aid reinforced worker militance but also gave employers additional excuses for resisting union demands.

The turmoil in the labor movement encouraged political intrigue. Senator Schall stood well with the national A.F.L. hierarchy[2] and urged it to pursue an uncompromising policy in Minnesota. This the A.F.L. leaders were quite willing to do because they had already developed a suspicious attitude toward Olson for his conspicuous services to Local 574. Their chilliness, coupled with the unpredictable zigzags of the communists, kept the Farmer Labor camp in constant fear that these groups would splinter the labor movement and thereby destroy the one solid nucleus supporting the party.

The first serious outbreak occurred in Minneapolis at the Flour City Ornamental Iron Works, where relations between labor and management had been deteriorating steadily for over a year. The workers' basic grievance was a substandard wage scale averaging forty cents an hour. By threatening a strike in July 1934 they had extracted a blanket five-cent increase, but the management stoutly refused further concessions. In grudging compliance with Section 7a, bargaining had been carried on sporadically during the ensuing winter and spring. Then the supreme court invalidated the whole N.I.R.A. on June 3, 1935, and the company abruptly suspended negotiations. With all hope of concessions lost, the workers struck on July 10, throwing a cordon of pickets around the plant.

The company not only refused to arbitrate but made every effort to break the strike. It paved the way for scab operations by securing a suspension of the city ordinance against employees residing at factories, and then slipped through the picket lines two boxcars of strikebreakers equipped to withstand siege.

Clashes between pickets and scabs became so frequent in early September that the company appealed to the new Farmer Labor mayor, Tom Latimer, for police protection. And Latimer, surprisingly, granted the request. By September 11 the police in their efforts to maintain order were handling pickets so roughly that Robley D. Cramer called on the mayor and demanded their removal. Receiving an evasive answer, he urged Olson to exert pressure on Latimer to close the plant.[3] It is not clear whether or not the governor intervened, but Latimer capitulated after a fresh encounter that same night ended with the police firing into the crowd of pickets and killing two bystanders.

Once the plant was closed, the mayor resisted the demands of the business community that it be reopened. His political future had been seriously endangered as a result of the shootings, and he dared not offend labor further. Deprived of police protection, the company could not run enough scabs into the plant to break the strike. Stubbornly the management resisted a settlement for ten more days, but finally gave up the hopeless fight on September 21, granting the employees union recognition, a wage increase, overtime pay, and an arbitration pledge.

In the meantime a second strike had begun at the Strutwear Knitting Mills, also in Minneapolis. Mrs. J. H. Struthers, president of the corporation and a violent foe of organized labor, precipitated the strike by firing eight active members of the Hosiery Workers Union. The knitters, who were indispensable to the operation of the mills, promptly walked off the job on August 15, reappearing in force the next morning to turn back other employees at the entrance.

The Strutwear strike followed the pattern of the earlier dispute, except that Mrs. Struthers proved to be an even more bitter opponent of collective bargaining than the management of the Flour City Ornamental Iron Works. When the mayor turned down her request for police protection, she decided to close the mills rather than deal with "lawless elements." As was so often the case in Minneapolis labor disputes, the energetic participation of communist pickets[4] obscured the wage issue and endowed Mrs. Struthers' unyielding position with a kind of nobility.

When Strutwear had suspended operations for ten weeks without visible effect on the Hosiery Workers Union or the public, the directors began to get nervous. Considerable money was being lost while capital equipment stood idle, and even the elimination of a union hardly justified such heavy sacrifices. The *Minneapolis Journal* indignantly called attention to Strutwear's plight in an October 1 editorial, and a few days later eight company salesmen protested to the mayor that the shutdown was doing Minneapolis irreparable damage. Latimer countered with the point that Strutwear officials refused to negotiate, and he hinted that the Citizens' Alliance was abetting their intransigence: "I don't blame the company as much as somebody else who is telling the officers of the company what to do," he said.[5]

Five more weeks passed. Then a mass meeting of businessmen requested the mayor to work for a resumption of negotiations. But when it became apparent that they sought to reopen Strutwear on company rather than compromise terms, officials of the A.F.L. bluntly told the mayor that the entire Minneapolis labor movement would support the hosiery workers' strike.

Desultory negotiations were continued without result. In late November there was a momentary flare-up of violence when Mrs. Struthers tried to move stock from the mill on a writ of replevin.[6] Union truck drivers refused to haul it out and smashed the windshields of scab operators imported for the job.

After an interval of uneasy quiet, the company abruptly terminated negotiations on December 24 with the announcement that it would forcibly reopen the plant. Latimer promptly requested and secured from Olson a detachment of state troops to keep order. Whereupon three hundred businessmen started action in federal district court to determine whether the mayor and the governor could close a plant on the pretext of averting bloodshed.

There was little doubt as to the outcome. The judges would

welcome an opportunity to rebuke Olson. He had argued the truck strike case in such a way that they could not grant an injunction without assuming responsibility for the probable bloodshed, but in the present instance there was so little likelihood of citywide civil war that they felt free to decide the question in accordance with traditional economic and legal concepts.

Mayor Latimer made matters still simpler for the judges by denying responsibility for the troops. Since there had been no declaration of martial law involving the state, his remarkable assertion created an impossible situation: troops were on duty at Strutwear without any legal commander.

Recognizing the hopelessness of his position in court, Olson ordered the troops withdrawn in the midst of the hearings. But this did not prevent the court from giving him a sharp reprimand. Brushing aside his contention that the shutdown of Strutwear was essential to the preservation of order, the judges declared, "The menace to the liberty and property of the plaintiff arises not from inability of the civil and military authorities to afford the plaintiff protection, but from the uncertainty that those who owe the duty of giving such protection will perform that duty." [7]

The withdrawal of troops failed to break the deadlock. The company could neither reopen the mill by force nor starve the union into submission. Mrs. Struthers instituted a suit to enjoin picketing, but the courts were so leisurely about deciding the question that she finally reopened negotiations with the hosiery workers through a third party. The union's terms had not changed substantially during the seven-months strike, but as it became apparent that the court would not outlaw picketing, she decided to capitulate rather than face bankruptcy. The settlement reached on April 3 called for union recognition, collective bargaining, a wage increase, and arbitration of the cases of the eight employees fired for union activity.

The successful strikes of 1935 consolidated the victory labor had won a year earlier over the Citizens' Alliance. They also, although Olson's part in them was not outstanding, climaxed his long fight for collective bargaining. Increasing certainty that the governor's sympathies and influence would, ultimately at least, be on the side of labor was inevitably a factor of considerable weight in industrial disputes. A consistent defender of the exploited workers, he played a leading role in the revolution that emancipated them from economic bondage.

The perennial patronage question became troublesome again in the summer of 1935. Some of the difficulty stemmed from the sheer impossibility of finding state positions enough for innumerable deserving Farmer Laborites — especially in view of the practice of indiscriminately promising jobs as bait for campaign services. These surface irritants partially concealed the most disruptive force of all: the frenzied struggle within the reform movement for control of the patronage dispensing machinery.

The contest for jobs in 1935 was not so much between individual petitioners as between rival factions. The most openly critical of these came from Ramsey County. Headed by Fred Miller, editor of the *Minnesota Union Advocate*, and W. F. Wright, county chairman of the Farmer Labor Association, it demanded that all appointments be placed on a strictly party basis and cleared through the appropriate county organization. As spokesman for this faction, the *Union Advocate* criticized Olson for building a personal machine at the expense of the party and demanded that he reward those who had elected him.[8]

These simon-pure Farmer Laborites cooperated occasionally with a second and more dangerous faction of professional spoilsmen who had quite different objectives. These men, while paying lip service to Olson, aimed at nothing less than control of the entire party machine. Their machinations were directed by a triumvirate of key figures in the organization: I. C. Strout, the budget commissioner, who had general supervision of personnel in state divisions under Farmer Labor control; Joe Poirier, who directed the distribution of jobs in the Highway

Department; and George Griffith, former Nonpartisan League organizer, who presided over the Oil Inspection Department. Allowed a more or less free hand by Olson during the summer of 1933, they had begun to rebuild the reform movement along traditional political lines, using the undemocratic structure of the Farmer Labor Association to place their friends in key positions.

As early as July 1934, Vince Day took note of the progress of the spoilsmen and denounced the local Farmer Labor clubs as a "political menace," urging that they "be abolished or opened up and made representative of the party." [9] But Olson let matters slide during the fall campaign, and the spoilsmen not only strengthened their position but focused the resentment of disappointed job seekers on the governor.

Even when confronted with such concrete manifestations of hostility, Olson continued to temporize. Ill health and the strain of his battles with the legislature reinforced his constitutional aversion to hasty decisions.

Also, Olson simply could not take the spoilsmen seriously. Their petty scheming irritated and amused him by turns. He was sublimely certain that one well-directed appeal to the people would topple their whole house of cards. Blessed with unusual gifts of leadership which enabled him to build up a devoted personal following, Olson felt only contempt for men who had to rely on artificial supports for power. These rationalizations also reflected a genuine reluctance to fire old friends or political associates. His heart encouraged a passivity which his head should have overruled.

The governor paid even less attention to complaints against his all-party appointments than to the activities of the machine. He conscientiously strove for an improved standard of state administration, and often, even at the lower levels, was loath to part with competent help for political reasons. He shamed critics of his patronage policy for "hunting down some sixty-five-dollar-a-month stenographer who doesn't happen to belong." [10] Time and again he warned Farmer Laborites that the party would never gain its economic objectives if its crusading spirit evaporated in a rush for jobs.

Olson's policy of playing one faction off against another worked after a fashion until midsummer, then an alliance between the professionals and the party purists rapidly brought discontent to a head. The break came on July 13 at a meeting of the Farmer Labor central committee called to consider an exhaustive patronage report compiled by W. F. Wright, one of the Ramsey County dissidents, who proposed to dump all patronage problems in the governor's lap unless he instituted a house cleaning by August 1.[11]

As usual, Olson took his time responding to the ultimatum. He finally made up his mind to fire Strout on August 18. This was an oblique rejection of the Wright report, and the central committee promptly voted to wash its hands of patronage.

The real test for Olson, however, came in the struggle to control the newly created post of director of the Farmer Labor Association. The central committee initially favored Strout, but his appointment would have strengthened the position of Olson's opponents. Vince Day worked feverishly behind the scenes[12] and his efforts bore fruit when the committee withdrew its offer to Strout by a vote of eight to six.

Whereupon Olson, in an effort to split the Ramsey County faction from the professionals, suggested Fred Miller of the *Union Advocate* for the post. When Miller rejected this Greek gift, the governor took full responsibility for patronage. Meeting with the central committee on September 16, he promised to consult the lists endorsed by local Farmer Labor associations, but reduced the value of the concession by reserving the right to make appointments among the 250,000 party supporters outside the association. All groups except the Ramsey County delegation professed themselves satisfied with this direct blow at the machine. So for the moment at least, the governor had succeeded in quelling the revolt.

Although Olson held up his formal announcement until late summer, politicians had assumed from the beginning of 1935 that he would run against Schall for United States senator the following year. As a result, the Farmer Labor leaders were busy with the question of who among them should fall heir to the governorship.

The field was wide open because, as Vince Day pointed out, the party possessed few prominent leaders.[13] Elder statesmen like Magnus Johnson, Knud Wefald, and Victor Lawson were approaching old age or lacked voter appeal, while the younger party leaders suffered from long neglect. For five years Olson had held the center of the stage, completely overshadowing his associates. And like so many able leaders, he had refused to groom a successor, partly for fear of creating a rival. The dangers of this policy became glaringly apparent when the party faced a vacancy in the governorship.

Most prominent among the second-generation Farmer Laborites was Lieutenant Governor Hjalmar Petersen. A country editor and state representative from Askov, he had won early acclaim by piloting the controversial income tax bill through the house virtually unamended. For this service, Petersen was rewarded with the lieutenant governorship in 1934. Many observers interpreted his elevation as a sign of official favor, a view he did nothing to discourage.

If Olson actually intended to build Petersen up as his successor, he soon abandoned the project. The man had genuine qualities of leadership, but his dignified bearing seemed to some to verge on pomposity. This unfortunate manner was coupled with a poorly concealed distrust of urban radicals that impaired his standing with union labor. Also, he seemed to pursue political power with greater frankness than many of his colleagues. There was much to admire in his candid and unaffected desire for public service, but it violated a political tradition that required gestures of disinterestedness from the candidate. Worst of all, Petersen could not forget that he had run several thousand votes ahead of Olson in 1934. It was an achievement of which he had every right to be proud, but it gave him notions of his importance to the movement which others did not share.

With all his faults, Petersen appeared to be the strongest candidate for Olson's mantle early in 1935. Through Abe Harris, the professional politicians approached him and tentatively offered their support.[14] But during the legislative session the lieutenant governor acted with such annoying independence that the professionals began to fear that if Petersen won they would merely exchange one master for another. So they turned to a more pliant candidate, Elmer A. Benson, the forty-year-old commissioner of banks.

Benson had a number of obvious political assets, being an orthodox progressive, a Scandinavian, and an ex-service man. In addition, he had spent most of his adult career as cashier in a small independent bank at Appleton, giving the desirable rural flavor to his background. Most important of all, he had taken so little part in the intraparty feuds over patronage and policy that scarcely anyone really disliked him. He seemed to be a mild-mannered, conscientious administrator with a streak of radicalism in his political philosophy.

Benson's relatively inconspicuous position in the party was a handicap as well as an advantage. Although it had insulated him against factional rancor, it had also prevented him from acquiring rank-and-file support. He was virtually unknown outside the coterie of Farmer Labor jobholders. But in the eyes of the party professionals this drawback was outweighed by the comforting conviction that Benson could be counted on to do their bidding. Accordingly, they undertook the formidable job of winning support for him among the county organizations, which would send the delegates to the nominating convention.

Not all the local units could be stampeded into the Benson camp, but two years of painstaking effort to pack them with state jobholders loyal to the machine paid off in the fall of 1935 when it became apparent that a large block of delegates to the state Farmer Labor convention would be instructed for Benson. A synthetic boom was organized to avoid creating the impression of a dictated nomination. With an unexpected sense of propriety, Strout, Griffith, and Poirier remained unobtrusively in the background, employing as front men Henry Teigan and Abe Harris, who arranged publicity for Benson in official Farmer Labor publications.

The *Minnesota Leader* began to discover news value in the accomplishments of the banking commissioner. Statistics on re-opened banks received enthusiastic treatment, and Benson's accelerated speaking program was given full coverage. By July the purpose had become so obvious that a number of Farmer Laborites criticized Teigan for permitting the *Leader* to take sides within the party.[15] Old Magnus Johnson and A. W. Olson of Shevlin both registered their disapproval publicly. They denounced the machine and said they hoped to purify the party. At the same time, Hjalmar Petersen redoubled his search for supporters.

Through all this, Olson maintained an imperturbable silence. He spoke favorably of Benson in private, but never made him any promise of support. In fact, the only time Olson broached the subject even indirectly was when he urged Benson to speed up the registration of Minneapolis Brewing Company stock on the ground that he might want the beer vote someday. Except for that obscure reference and a casual suggestion about speech lessons[16] he betrayed no interest in Benson's candidacy.

Olson's neutrality probably reflected mixed feelings on the governorship. He had a high regard for Benson's ability and considered him thoroughly reliable. But resentment against the highhanded tactics of the professionals must have made Olson wish at times for the defeat of their candidate. Or it may be that his indifference was unfeigned. Since the spring of 1934 he had waited impatiently for the day when he could lay down the thankless job of mediating endless Farmer Labor disputes. With a six-year senate term in the offing, he was probably willing to accept any gubernatorial nominee with sufficient tact and ability to hold the party together. Benson seemed as well qualified for the job as anybody available, but not outstanding enough to warrant a public endorsement.

In any case, an unexpected event forced Olson to take a

stand. On December 22 Senator Schall was run down by an automobile while crossing a street in Washington and died within twenty-four hours.

His death removed a spiteful foe who had opened the 1936 senatorial campaign against Olson in the fall of 1933 and had spent the next two years attempting to discredit him by every possible means. Olson supporters blamed Schall for editorials by Walter Liggett in the Minneapolis *Midwest American*, which accused Olson of everything from personal immorality to the sale of political appointments.[17] Liggett, although he lived briefly in a house owned by the senator,[18] did not publicly support him politically and likely came by his views of Olson independently. In any case, he preceded Schall to a violent death by two weeks, the victim of an unresolved killing.

Besides the ill-fated Liggett, Tom Mouer, prosecutor for the senate investigating committee in 1935, James Laughlin, originator of an ouster petition against the governor in 1935, and Harold Birkeland, author of the lurid 1934 campaign pamphlets, all worked in the interests of Schall. Indeed, Laughlin and Birkeland were with the senator when he died.[19]

Olson had been systematically gathering ammunition for the coming battle with Schall and had confided to Charles Cheney his intention of releasing material linking the senator with prohibition scandals.[20] All outward signs indicated that Olson was looking forward to the encounter.

So Schall's sudden death created more problems than it solved. By issuing an immediate statement that he would not appoint himself, Olson touched off a frenzied scramble for the vacancy. Scores of politicians thronged into his office pushing the claims of various aspirants. The Democrats even sent Joseph Wolf to speak for John P. Devaney, chief justice of the state supreme court.

The most determined group of petitioners, of course, were the Farmer Labor professionals, who saw in the senatorial vacancy a golden opportunity to build up their gubernatorial candidate, Elmer A. Benson. His appointment to a national post that carried such tremendous prestige would practically ensure his endorsement for governor at the Farmer Labor convention. And the Benson backers had a strong talking point in the fact that the selection of a senator who intended to run for governor would automatically protect Olson from possible opposition by his own appointee.

These arguments were insistently pressed upon the harassed governor in the week following the death of Schall. Christmas Day provided a merciful interlude, but Harris, Griffith, Poirier, and Roger S. Rutchick returned promptly the next day with fresh points for Benson. To reinforce their case, the machine-dominated county organizations had bombarded the governor with dozens of supporting endorsements.

Nevertheless, the professionals departed without anything more definite than a promise that the vacancy would be filled the following morning and permission to print an issue of the *Minnesota Leader* announcing Benson's appointment, for release if the governor decided to name Benson.

Although he talked evasively to these men, Olson bluntly told his new secretary, Herman Aufderheide (Vince Day had been appointed judge of the Minneapolis municipal court on November 8, 1935), that the Benson appointment was impossible. He praised the banking commissioner as an administrator, but declared himself unwilling to appoint a Farmer Laborite of such limited background and experience to the United States senate. Leafing through the stack of Benson endorsements on his desk, he said they came from a lot of jobholders and didn't mean a thing.[21]

Behind the surface objection to Benson was an accumulated resentment against his sponsors. For over a year Olson had managed to tolerate the brash pretensions of the spoilsmen, but their crude effort to dictate the senatorial appointment finally snapped his patience.

Worse than the pressure was the disillusionment. After the 1934 election Olson had told Senator Regnier that the politicians didn't really care for him, only for the man with the big spoon.

This black mood recurred with increasing frequency during 1935 as Olson came to the melancholy conclusion that even boyhood comrades like Abe Harris set a low price on his friendship and were already transferring their allegiance to his successor. Their activity over the senatorial appointment reinforced these misgivings and wounded Olson deeply. Some months later, when Benson, after securing the gubernatorial endorsement, courteously offered to retain any state employees Olson might designate, he received the extraordinary response that they were all worthless except Bill Elsberg, the highway engineer.

During that turbulent day of pressure, the governor could not decide whom he would appoint to the senate. He vacillated between S. A. Stockwell, Victor Lawson, and Henry Arens — all pioneer Farmer Laborites with long records of unselfish devotion to the party. Finally he asked Aufderheide to get Henry Arens up from Jordan by 10 A.M. the next morning, then left the office without giving a clear indication of his intentions.

That same night the little coterie of rebuffed king-makers went into action. Although Olson had not refused to appoint Benson, they considered his evasive manner the equivalent of a negative answer. With feverish haste, they prepared a special issue of the *Minnesota Leader* with banner headlines announcing Benson's appointment and hurried it to distribution points all over the state. C. D. Johnston, editor of the *Leader,* tried three times to reach Olson by phone and secure permission to release the paper. Failing to get in touch with the governor, Johnston distributed the paper on orders from his superiors.

Utterly unaware of this dastardly trick, Olson arrived at his office early the next morning with his former secretary, Judge Vince Day. Encountering General Ellard Walsh in the outer corridor, the governor invited him to come and witness the appointment of a senator. Judge Day was the man Olson had picked to receive the honor.

Day, however, put up unexpected resistance. He protested that the elevation to the bench had fulfilled a lifelong ambition and he was not interested in anything more. He suggested a number of others for the post. But Olson had made up his mind, and in the next fifteen minutes he argued away all Day's objections. Then he dismissed Walsh and the new senator with the reminder that announcement of the appointment should come from his office.

In the meantime, Aufderheide had arrived at work to find a crowd of newspapermen milling around in the reception room. They were angry because the *Minnesota Leader* had been given a scoop on the senatorial appointment. He said he didn't think an appointment had been made, but they jeered at him and handed him a copy of the *Leader*. Dazed, he went on into his office, promising a formal statement at the earliest possible moment.

Shortly thereafter, Olson strode into Aufderheide's office whistling cheerfully. When his eye caught the *Leader* headline he turned white, and paced up and down a full five minutes without uttering a word. Finally, in glacial tones, he said, "Get that son-of-a-bitch on the phone."

Abe Harris and the spoilsmen came over for a series of conferences that lasted most of the day. Eventually Olson gave in and signed the commission appointing Benson, although his personal secretary, Ann Egan, saw him turn the papers over in a last defiant gesture when she brought them to his desk.[22] Actually, the governor had no choice but to acquiesce. If he had repudiated the Benson appointment, he would have split the party wide open. With election year approaching and his stomach insistently demanding attention, Olson lacked the stamina to rebuild the Farmer Labor organization from top to bottom.

Not only did the spoilsmen get away with their insolent challenge to Olson, but they managed to cover up their tracks well enough to mislead the newspapermen. Charles B. Cheney, who suspected foul play, investigated the circumstances surrounding the appointment and wrote a substantially accurate account of the transaction ten weeks later.[23] But by that time interest in the matter had evaporated and the story was dismissed as another Cheney yarn.

The synthetic enthusiasm generated by the *Minnesota Leader* did not ensure the Benson appointment a warm acceptance. J. L. Peterson of Proctor, the Capitol custodian, sounded the tocsin of revolt. Condemning the political control of the jobholders and predicting further manipulations at the state convention, he threatened to enter a ticket of old-time Farmer Laborites in the primary.[24] His protest had little effect, but it foreshadowed the Götterdämmerung that was approaching for the quarreling heroes of reform.

# Chapter XIV THE LAST FIGHT

INTEREST in the Benson appointment was suddenly over-shadowed on December 31 by an announcement that Olson had undergone a major operation at the Mayo Clinic early that morning. This news came to the public without previous warning except for a cryptic statement in the December 28 issue of the *Minnesota Leader* that the governor expected to have a "small but constantly aggravating tumor" removed.[1] The terse bulletin issued by the Clinic was hardly reassuring. It said that an exploratory operation had revealed a polyp, but that the inflamed condition of Olson's stomach made its removal inadvisable.

The bulletin did not say whether the polyp was malignant or benign, but there were disquieting rumors. Even before the public knew an operation had been performed, Charles Cheney was informed that the surgeon had found an incurable cancer, and both Henry Teigan and S. E. Elliott, a Cass County editor close to the administration, suspected a malignant growth.[2] A brash *Fortune* correspondent repeated whispers that Olson would "never run for anything again," and Gilstad of the *Minneapolis Journal* stated flatly that the governor was suffering from an internal growth "far more serious than ulcers."[3]

These depressing statements were plausible. For over a year and a half Olson's health had deteriorated steadily. Senator Regnier, who managed successive Farmer Labor campaigns, was shocked by the governor's loss of physical vitality between 1932 and 1934. During the presidential campaign he had worn out subordinates with his killing pace, but two years later he finished on nerve alone. He looked waxen-faced and ill at his third inauguration. During 1935 his ulcers grew progressively worse, and the intervals of relief which had hitherto made life bearable practically disappeared. Olson later said that he hadn't spent a single day of the year entirely free from pain.[4]

Medical treatment might have afforded some measure of relief, but Olson steadfastly resisted the entreaties of his wife and friends to put himself under a doctor's care. He seemed unable to credit the possibility that a malady could become fatal. Also he had little respect for physicians, and little faith in their curative powers. On the rare occasions when he could be corralled for consultation and treatment, he either ignored the doctors' recommendations or bullied them into prescribing a cure that would not interfere with his accustomed activities.

It was a precipitous drop in weight from 207 pounds in August to 168 pounds at the end of November that alarmed Olson so that he agreed to visit the Mayo Clinic for an examination the second week in December. When tests and radiographs indicated the probability of an internal growth, Dr. Will Mayo convened a formal session of the consulting specialists and with great solemnity informed the governor that he had a polyp which required immediate attention. For once the skeptic was impressed by the medical profession and humbly agreed to return for surgery after the Christmas holidays.

The strain of the next two weeks would have broken most men. In constant pain, under overwhelming pressure about the vacant senate seat, and depressed by thoughts of the impending operation, Olson still managed somehow not to give the public, the politicians, or the newspapermen any intimation of his condition. When he left for Rochester on December 30 Maurice Rose tried to maintain the deception by assuring inquisitive reporters that Olson was to have another routine checkup.

The operation revealed a pancreatic cancer far advanced and inoperable. Dr. Mayo estimated that the governor would not live more than eight months.

With this knowledge, the doctors found it difficult to reconcile their obligation to Olson the public servant with their obligation to Olson the human being. He was the governor of Minnesota, a senatorial candidate, and a presidential possibility on a third-party ticket. The 1936 election plans for the reform movement had been built around him. His attitude on the presidential contest might very well be decisive not only in Minnesota but in the entire Midwest. If they told him what the operation had uncovered and gave him a true estimate of his life expectancy, he could make realistic political decisions, but his will to live might be destroyed.

Rightly or wrongly, the Clinic staff decided not to tell Olson the nature of his malady. As Dr. Will Mayo put it: "The first commandment of the medical profession is not to destroy hope. The governor will find out soon enough himself, and by that time he will have made the mental adjustment."[5] So Dr. Mayo and General Walsh drew up an ambiguous statement for the press, and Olson's attending physicians informed him that the polyp was probably benign.[6]

When the governor had recovered from the effects of surgery, he underwent a long and painful series of X-ray treatments designed to wither up the polyp. He was well enough to return home on February 15, and nine days later left for a three-weeks vacation in Tucson. On the eve of his departure, he talked optimistically about the forthcoming campaign and expressed confidence that his physical recovery would be complete. But his thin, pale face made it difficult for his friends to believe him.

While Olson was convalescing at Rochester, the struggle between the machine politicians and the crusaders for control of the Farmer Labor party burst into the open. The gubernatorial nomination provided the occasion. The senatorial appointment had given the inside track to Elmer Benson, and his opponents were moved to active protest. The most outspoken was the old Litchfield warhorse, Magnus Johnson. A former United States senator and representative, he had served the party faithfully since its inception and resented the effort of professional spoilsmen to convert the reform movement into a patronage machine.

He also disliked the disproportionate influence exercised by all-party appointees on the state administration.

Johnson reacted quickly to the Benson appointment by filing for governor on January 3, saying, "The rank and file of the Farmer Labor party will brook no dictatorship in the control of its policies whether from inside or without the party." [7] But this ringing challenge to the machine fell flat when Johnson foolishly joined forces with A. C. Townley in a protest meeting at Fergus Falls on January 18. Lieutenant Governor Hjalmar Petersen and Attorney General Harry H. Peterson had signed the call for this grass roots meeting, but both of them prudently decided at the last minute not to attend.

Badly discredited by his participation in this futile gesture, Magnus Johnson suffered further misfortune when he was run down by a St. Paul motorist — possibly an all-party Olson supporter, the *Minneapolis Journal* humorously suggested.[8] While recovering from his injuries, he contracted pneumonia and remained in the hospital seven weeks.

The brunt of the anti-Benson campaign, therefore, was borne by Hjalmar Petersen. Fearful that the lieutenant governor, who was a more potent political figure than old Magnus, would split the party in his fight against Benson, Olson invited Petersen down to Rochester for an interview during the first week of February.[9] When their talk finally got around to the gubernatorial race, he ventured the opinion that Petersen had only an outside chance to receive the nomination, but professed interest in a fair test of his popular strength. He suggested as an appropriate precedent for 1936 the 1924 campaign in which the Farmer Labor convention did not endorse anyone. When Petersen indicated that he would favor this procedure, Olson promised "to pass the word along," and the lieutenant governor left Rochester with the happy conviction that he would face Benson in an open primary.

Olson upheld his end of the bargain as he understood it, telling a press conference on February 12 that he would "just as soon" make the senate race without an endorsement and recommending the same procedure for the gubernatorial contest.[10] Senator Victor Lawson of Willmar and other anti-Benson Farmer Laborites enthusiastically seconded the Olson proposal. But W. F. Wright complained that such an arrangement would wreck party discipline, permitting every candidate "to go out and campaign on his own personally written platform." [11] Most of the county conventions, agreeing with Wright, instructed their delegates to endorse somebody even where they were not pledged to a particular candidate.

This development convinced Petersen that Olson was reneging on his pledge "to pass the word along." So Petersen announced his candidacy for governor and began an aggressive campaign for the nomination. In a prepared statement, he promised to give the party badly needed discipline, make department heads toe the mark, and put the Mexican generals in their place. In an oblique jab at Benson, he said he was running because of "the opportunity to serve the party and state rather than because he was urged or begged." [12]

While Petersen was busy condemning inside control "with its patronage fixing and conniving," [13] the professionals quietly and efficiently lined up delegates for Benson. The outcry against dictation scared them out of attempting to instruct the delegates formally,[14] but the great majority were pledged in advance of the convention. No serious contest developed over the question of endorsing candidates because the professionals succeeded in packing the convention with jobholders, some of whom had resided only three or four weeks in the county they represented. These well-disciplined spoilsmen were so numerous that the endorsement of Benson seemed an expression of grass roots sentiment.

The transactions of the convention led to a final but unpublicized split between Olson and Petersen. In a stormy preconvention interview, the lieutenant governor berated Olson for not advising his henchmen to block the endorsement of candidates. And when Olson protested against Petersen's interpretation of the word "advise," he stalked out of the room with the bitter retort that if "advise" was too strong the governor might "suggest." The two men never met again.

Petersen felt grievously wronged because he had assumed that a suggestion from Olson was really a command. This might have been true in the early days of his administration, but irresolution, ill health, and unscrupulous politicians had gradually undermined his position. By 1936 he lacked both the will and the physical strength to challenge the professionals. They had already stolen a senate seat for their candidate and were not likely to sacrifice the convention without an open fight. But Petersen, not yet knowing the story of the senatorial appointment or the seriousness of Olson's physical condition, believed the governor had deliberately broken his pledge and never forgave him for it.

During the three weeks he spent in Tucson, Olson devoted considerable attention to his forthcoming convention speech and received the wise counsel of George Leonard in preparing it. Both men had long advocated the nationalization of key industries and amendments to the Constitution which would increase congressional power over public welfare. Olson gave little attention to this ambitious program as long as he was governor, but his interest revived rapidly as the senatorial election approached. Particularly after the supreme court began striking down New Deal social legislation, he decided to build the Farmer Labor campaign around these dangerous political issues.

Olson had first served public notice of this decision in a speech before the American Commonwealth Political Federation in New York on November 15, 1935. With uncompromising directness, he condemned the five supreme court justices who sought to "stay the march of one hundred and twenty-five million people." [15] Anticipating by a full fifteen months the judicial reorganization program of President Roosevelt, he proposed that the supreme court be brought abreast of public opinion through an increase in the number of judges.[16]

His stomach operation prevented a debate on the Constitution with Governor Eugene Talmadge of Georgia. But he was so irritated by the invalidation of the Agricultural Adjustment Act in January that he devoted his first press conference at the Mayo Clinic to a fresh castigation of the supreme court. After telling the correspondents he had tried "to relax and forget about politics," he pointed out the paradox in a judicial decision that denied the application of the public welfare clause to agriculture when the Constitution had been written by and for agriculturalists.[17] He elaborated these views upon leaving the hospital and announced that he would campaign for senator on a platform advocating constitutional amendments to restrict the power of the supreme court and to enlarge the power of congress. Thus his ideas had actually jelled before they appeared in the militant March 27 address to the Farmer Labor convention.

The party platform also emphasized national questions. Besides raising the supreme court issue, which Roosevelt and the Democrats refused to do, it called for the extension of human welfare measures and for federal ownership of monopolized industries. By major-party standards this was advanced radicalism. It reaffirmed Farmer Labor opposition to capitalism, but in much less provocative terms than those of the 1934 platform. The troubles spawned by that document had taught the party firebrands a salutary lesson. They had no intention of issuing another manifesto. However, just to be on the safe side, Olson sat in with the platform committee and supervised its activities.

The major-party leaders followed the proceedings of the Farmer Labor convention closely, searching for clues on the presidential election. Republican hopes for a national third party to split the liberal vote rose in the spring and summer of 1935 when Farmer Laborites renewed their criticism of the New Deal. Olson, who had issued a blunt post-election statement predicting an agrarian political revolt unless the farmer got prices at least equal to his costs of production,[18] adopted an increasingly hostile line. In a February newspaper article he condemned the A.A.A. program for its restriction of farm production when thousands lacked a nourishing diet, and concluded that neither of the old parties could solve the fundamental ills of the country.[19] About the same time he denounced the McCarran amendment to relief appropriations on the ground that industry would beat down wages if the government paid less than the prevailing rate on its relief jobs.[20] And he told the unemployed that he had "virtually alienated" himself from the Roosevelt administration through opposition to relief wage scales, and on another occasion publicly complained that the President could be "as wrong as any reactionary Republican." [21]

These outspoken criticisms seemed to promise a division of left-wing forces in the 1936 election, but the more realistic Republicans feared there was little flame behind the smoke. Not only did Olson find excuses to avoid attending the Chicago convention of third-party men in July 1935, but when he addressed the American Commonwealth Political Federation, the *Minnesota Leader* announced that participation did not commit him to a national third-party ticket.[22] The real tip-off, however, came in a September newspaper article written by Abe Harris for distribution to Farmer Labor papers all over the state. It explained away Olson's hostile statements and the *Leader* editorials as constructive criticism:

"Reactionary politicians in Minnesota would like to see a break between Olson and Roosevelt but they jumped too hastily to the conclusion that Olson's criticism of some New Deal policies was a step toward alienation. They forget that constructive criticism has never been taboo in Roosevelt's administration. Furthermore, they forget that the New Deal with its far-flung social security program, with its belief in reforming the tax system by narrowing the base and taxing wealth, with its hostility to corporate greed, is far closer to the Farmer Labor program than it is to the hidebound and antiquated notions of Minnesota reactionaries." [23]

Any remaining doubt as to Olson's attitude was dispelled at a November press conference when he predicted that Roosevelt would be re-elected. The *Minneapolis Journal* reluctantly concluded from this statement that Olson had set his sights for 1940: "He would not sacrifice himself as leader of an abortive 1936 national drive against the devils of capitalism. The governor is evidently waiting for President Roosevelt to play out the role of Kerensky before he takes the part of Lenin in the new American revolution." [24]

During the winter local Farmer Laborites like Ernest Lundeen and H. Y. Williams, as well as supporters of the American Commonwealth Political Federation, redoubled their efforts to secure Olson's endorsement of a national third party. They were sure a presidential ticket would fail miserably unless the flourishing Farmer Labor party in Minnesota supported it. They even dangled the nomination before Olson's eyes. But it was all to no avail. He maintained a noncommittal attitude until after the Farmer Labor convention had passed a resolution giving him in effect authority to commit the party. [25]

Even then he threw off the mask by degrees. In mid-April he sat with Joseph Wolf at the Jefferson Day banquet of the Democrats. And two weeks later he instructed the Farmer Labor state committee to boycott the May 30 conference of miscellaneous left-wingers if it took up the question of a presidential ticket. Although he was too ill to attend the conference, he sent the delegates a message warning them that a third-party ticket might defeat Roosevelt and elect a "fascist Republican." [26]

This group of radicals heeded the governor's advice, but in midsummer another faction, which called itself the Union party, nominated Congressman William Lemke of North Dakota for President. By that time Olson lay close to death, but one of his last acts was to telegraph Senator Robert La Follette, Jr. that "liberals must unite in 1936 to re-elect Franklin Roosevelt and to prevent the election of reactionary Alf Landon." [27] This message proved to be Olson's final political testament. His efforts toward committing Farmer Laborites for Roosevelt resulted in a fusion with the Democrats, who supported the third-party state ticket.

During the Olson regime the Democratic-Farmer Labor alliance fell into a two-year cycle, which opened in the odd-numbered years with third-party men criticizing the national administration and closed in the even-numbered years with them praising it. Olson established this unusual relationship with the Democrats by balancing expediency and conviction. He thoroughly disliked the New Deal farm policy based on an economy of scarcity and did not hesitate to speak out against it. He also believed that he could actually drive Roosevelt farther to the left by judicious criticism.[28]

Then, too, as the leader of a party dedicated to basic changes in the social and economic order, Olson could not display consistent friendship for an old-line party without sacrificing part of his left-wing following. Nor could he allow the Democrats to take Farmer Labor support for granted lest they give nothing in return. But when elections approached, Olson based his actions on political realism. Rather than split the left-wing movement for an abortive national campaign, he twice supported a presidential candidate who was going in his general direction.

Olson managed to conceal the seriousness of his illness from the public until late spring. In an incredible display of sheer grit, he spoke for two hours and twelve minutes at the Farmer Labor convention, but thereafter he lost ground rapidly. He spent most of the remaining months at Gull Lake, partly to hide his physical decline and partly because the solitude soothed his aching body. Occasionally he appeared in the Twin Cities or the communities around Gull Lake for a speech.

Wherever he went, Olson was invariably cheerful and optimistic about his health. Leif Gilstad, looking back on the period, wrote: "These closing months of his life were a source of constant amazement to all who knew him. No one could tell for sure whether he actually realized the seriousness of his condition; certainly he never let on by word or act as he proceeded courageously to go on his course."[29] Even intimate associates of Olson never heard him complain. The closest he came to self-pity was when he told General Walsh how much better it would be if he could go off and never come back, so people would remember him in his prime.

This stoicism persisted despite the fact that the truth had begun to dawn on Olson even before he left the hospital in February. Cross-examination of the Mayo specialists gradually enabled him to piece the evidence together, and the steady loss of weight, from 168 pounds in January to 135 in mid-April, confirmed his conclusion. But the final proof came shortly after the Farmer Labor convention when he returned to the Clinic for a checkup. Although the doctors discouraged him, Olson insisted on seeing the X-ray pictures. The growth, which had looked like one thumb in January, was twice as large in April.

Yet somehow he seemed to think that by sheer will power he would be able to overcome the disease. The word *defeat* had never been in his vocabulary. His reassuring statements to the press were not made merely to keep up party morale; they grew out of a desperate belief in the ultimate restoration of his good health.

Toward the end of May, as the cancer grew into his esophagus, swallowing became exceedingly difficult, and he had to be fed intravenously. To relieve his parched throat the nurses would squeeze little watermelon balls in his mouth, hoping that a drop or two would trickle on down. He bore this new affliction patiently, but told General Walsh one day that he would trade his expected senate seat for a glass of crystal cold water.

Throughout June he continued against increasing odds to play the role of governor and senatorial candidate. Although he was literally a walking skeleton, he held a press conference in his office after the primary, expressing pleasure at Benson's three-to-one victory over Magnus Johnson and talking optimistically about plans for the fall campaign.[30]

On June 25 he delivered the principal address at the Paul Bunyan celebration in Brainerd. Scarcely able to stand up, he gave a twenty-minute address — "just to show them a thing or

two," as he confided to his wife. Four days later when he repeated the ordeal at Minnehaha Park in Minneapolis, he got
through the speech but had to have help to reach his automobile afterward.[31] This was his last public appearance.

He returned to the Mayo Clinic on July 9 and underwent a
second operation to get some relief of his pain and nausea. The
night before the operation Leif Gilstad wrote a pessimistic story,
so as soon as Olson recovered consciousness, he told Maurice
Rose to "wire Gilstad that despite his predictions the skipper is
still on deck and the flag at full mast." [32]

Forty-eight hours later he wrote a stouthearted letter to the
members of the Farmer Labor executive committee promising
to be with them "when the battle nears its height" and urging
them not to "heed the voice of gossip nor let the imagination
bring fear." [33] A stranger reading the letter might have thought
the party rather than the governor was suffering from a mortal
illness.

For a time Olson's will to live actually seemed to heal his
ailing body. On August 8 at his own insistence he was driven
to Gull Lake, stopping briefly at Minneapolis, where he held
another optimistic press conference. But he had been at Gull
Lake only a week when the cancer perforated the intestine, and
it seemed unlikely that he would live long enough to get back
to Rochester.

Richard Lilly brought his plane to the Gull Lake airstrip and
General Walsh came with four soldiers from Camp Ripley to
carry the sick man down the stairs and out to the ambulance
that was to take him to the airstrip. Olson protested that ambu-
lances were for sick people, and though the attendants got him
into the conveyance, he objected so vigorously that after only
a short ride they transferred him to Walsh's car and he triumphantly made the rest of the journey sitting up. At the airstrip he was given a strong sedative and did not recover consciousness until after he reached Rochester.

The death watch at the Mayo Clinic lasted a week. As his
life ebbed slowly away, Olson clung to old friends like Maurice

Rose and Ellard Walsh who had served him faithfully in prosperity and adversity alike. Scarcely able to raise his head or talk above a whisper, he shut out the politicians and sycophants who converged on Rochester during the last days. General Walsh acted as a liaison between the governor and the Farmer Laborites who sought admission, although it was generally believed that those entering the outer suite also saw the dying man.

Halfway through the week the governor was visibly cheered by the news that President Roosevelt would make a special trip to Rochester on August 31. Old Paul Olson, who rose from a sick bed to visit his only son, proudly told reporters, "The old fight is in his eyes. I guess he'll make it." [34] Even the Clinic specialists marveled at the tenacity with which he clung to life. But on Saturday, August 22, the struggle drew to a close. Early in the morning Olson complained of intense pain, and by mid-afternoon he was fading fast. He died at 8:29 that night.

Olson's death produced an extraordinary demonstration of public grief. Thousands of the little people for whom he had fought stood patiently in lines more than a mile long to file past his bier in the State Capitol. They jammed the Minneapolis civic auditorium for the funeral oration by Governor La Follette and stood in little clusters along the route to the cemetery. It was a touching tribute to their departed champion.

Death enhanced Olson's reputation because he died before public apathy and the increasing threat of war undermined the reforming zeal of the mid-1930s. As the lesser left-wing leaders who succeeded him wasted their energies in futile skirmishes, Olson's faults were forgotten and his achievements took on legendary proportions. Minnesota came to remember him as a fearless and effective crusader for social justice.

# Notes

Among the collections of personal papers that are cited frequently in the notes that follow, those of Floyd B. Olson (Olson Papers) are filed, with a twenty-five-year ban on their general use, in the vaults of the State Capitol in St. Paul; those of Henry G. Teigan (Teigan Papers) and Vince Day (Day Papers) are available in the manuscript archives of the Minnesota Historical Society in St. Paul.

## Chapter I.  More Rebel than Radical

[1] Olson Papers, Olson to Tom Davis, January 24, 1931.
[2] Teigan Papers, G. H. Bydal to Henry Teigan, May 25, 1924.
[3] *Hawley Herald*, quoted in the *Minneapolis Labor Review*, June 13, 1924.
[4] *Minneapolis Journal*, August 23, 1936.
[5] *Minneapolis Star*, August 24, 1936; also C. R. Walker, "The Farmer Labor Party of Minnesota," *Nation*, March 20, 1937.
[6] *Birmingham* (Alabama) *News*, September 10, 1935.
[7] *Minneapolis Tribune*, August 23, 1936.
[8] Mock, J. R. *Censorship, 1917* (Princeton University Press, 1941), p. 223.
[9] The Birkeland story is told in detail on pages 182–83.
[10] *Minnesota Leader*, August 29, 1936.

## Chapter II.  The Farmer Labor Movement

[1] Bahmer, R. "The Economic and Political Background of the Nonpartisan League" (unpublished Ph.D. thesis, University of Minnesota, 1941), p. 6.
[2] Pingrey, H. B. "The Rise and Decline of Wheat Production in Minnesota" (unpublished M.A. thesis, University of Minnesota, 1930), p. 110.
[3] Smith, B. E. "A Study of the Income of the Minnesota Farmer" (unpublished M.A. thesis, University of Minnesota, 1927), p. 88.
[4] Sulerud, G. L. "Trends in Production in the Red River Valley" (unpublished M.A. thesis, University of Minnesota, 1925), p. 5.
[5] Gaston, H. E. *The Nonpartisan League* (1920), p. 60.
[6] Bahmer, *op. cit.*, p. 443.
[7] Sait, E. M. *American Politics and Elections* (New York, 1939), p. 171.
[8] Bahmer, *op. cit.*, p. 63.
[9] Johnson, E. C., and W. L. Calvert. *Adjusting Farm Debts* (University of Minnesota Special Bulletin 157, December 1932), p. 2.
[10] Holbrook, F. F., and L. Appel. *Minnesota in the War with Germany* (2 vols., St. Paul, 1932), vol. 2, p. 44.
[11] Teigan Papers, "The 1918 Nonpartisan League Platform."
[12] *Minnesota Leader*, February 25, 1932; Hall Papers, newspaper clipping,

July 16, 1922. The Hall Papers are on file in the manuscript archives of the Minnesota Historical Society in St. Paul.

[13] *Minneapolis Labor Review,* January 12, 1923.

[14] George B. Leonard to the author.

[15] *Minneapolis Journal,* March 11, 1924.

[16] *Farmer Labor Advocate,* June 30, 1924.

[17] Charles B. Cheney in the *Minneapolis Journal,* April 30, 1924.

[18] Teigan Papers, Teigan to Olson, May 17, 1924.

[19] *Minneapolis Journal,* May 13, 1924.

[20] *Farmer Labor Advocate,* May 9, 1924; *Minnesota Leader,* June 11, 1924.

[21] *Minneapolis Journal,* June 7, 1924.

[22] *Ibid.,* July 11, 1924.

[23] Teigan Papers, Teigan to H. O. Berve, October 18, 1923.

[24] *Minneapolis Journal,* May 28, 1924.

[25] *Farmer Labor Advocate,* June 5, 1924.

[26] *Minneapolis Journal,* August 14, 1924; *Farmer Labor Advocate,* October 6, 1924.

[27] R. S. Wiggin to the author.

[28] *Minneapolis Labor Review,* September 26, 1924.

[29] *Minneapolis Journal,* October 5, 1924.

[30] Black, A. G., and D. E. Kittredge. *Minnesota Agricultural Index of Prices, Quantities and Cash Incomes, 1910–1927* (University of Minnesota Technical Bulletin 72, December 1930), pp. 34–64.

[31] *Minneapolis Labor Review,* October 10, 1924.

[32] *Ibid.,* November 14, 1924.

[33] C. F. Gaarenstrom to the author.

[34] Teigan Papers, undated article on the 1924 election; *Minneapolis Journal,* February 18, 1930.

## Chapter III.   Victory in 1930

[1] C. F. Gaarenstrom to the author.

[2] *Farmer Labor Advocate,* March 25, 1925.

[3] Teigan Papers, "Constitution of the Farmer Labor Association," 1925.

[4] *Farmer Labor Advocate,* May 13, 1925; *Minneapolis Journal,* February 6, 1933; *Farmer Labor Leader,* October 15, 1933.

[5] *Farmer Labor Advocate,* July 10, 1925.

[6] Teigan Papers, Erling Olson to Teigan, November 12, 1926.

[7] Teigan Papers, Farmer Labor Press Service, May 7, 1928.

[8] *Farmer Labor Leader,* August 15, 1930.

[9] Teigan Papers, Farmer Labor Press Service, October 1, 1929.

[10] *Minneapolis Journal,* January 3, 1930.

[11] Teigan Papers, Bydal to Teigan, December 27, 1924.

[12] In a statement to the Hennepin County grand jury investigating a securities swindle during the Christianson administration. *Minneapolis Journal,* February 10, 1930.

[13] *Minneapolis Journal,* March 28, 1930.

[14] *Ibid.,* March 29, 1930.

[15] Teigan Papers, Farmer Labor Press Service, March 31, 1930.

[16] *Minnesota Union Advocate,* April 10, 1930.

[17] *State News,* April 1930.

[18] *St. Paul Pioneer Press,* March 31, 1930.

[19] *New York Times,* April 13, 1930.

[20] *Minneapolis Journal,* April 23, 1930.

[21] Teigan Papers, Farmer Labor Press Service, June 23, 1930.

[22] *Ibid.,* April 21, 1930.

[23] *Minneapolis Journal,* March 23, 1930.

[24] Teigan Papers, copy of printed letter from C. H. MacKenzie to C. R. Graves, October 10, 1932.

[25] *New York Times,* June 8, 1930.

[26] *Farmer Labor Leader,* August 15, 1930.

[27] *Minneapolis Journal,* September 7, 1930.

[28] Teigan Papers, Farmer Labor Press Service, October 1, 1929.

[29] *Ibid.,* circular letter issued by Ray P. Chase, June 12, 1920.

[30] *Anoka Herald,* June 11, 1918; April 6, 1920; May 25, 1920.

[31] Teigan Papers, Farmer Labor Press Service, July 29, 1930; *State News,* August 1930.

[32] *Minnesota Union Advocate,* August 7, 1930.

[33] *Minneapolis Journal,* September 6, 1930.

[34] *St. Paul Pioneer Press,* September 30, 1930.

[35] *Minneapolis Journal,* October 3, 1930.

[36] See pages 166–69.

## Chapter IV.  Olson's First Legislature

[1] *St. Paul Pioneer Press,* January 7, 1931.

[2] *Minneapolis Journal,* November 11, 1930.

[3] *Ibid.,* November 30, 1930.

[4] *Farmer Labor Leader,* January 24, 1931.

[5] *Hibbing Tribune,* February 10, 1931.

[6] Teigan Papers, T. Pearson to H. Peterson, January 8, 1931; Olson Papers, Magnus Wefald to Olson, January 29, 1931.

[7] Olson Papers, B. H. Farley to Olson, January 12, 1931; Gaarenstrom to Olson, January 8, 1931.

[8] *Biennial Report of the Railroad Brotherhood's State Legislative Board,* 1931, p. 20. (Cited hereafter as *Biennial Report of the R.B.S.L.B.*)

[9] Olson Papers, Olson to Tom Davis, January 24, 1931; Tom Davis to Olson, January 23, 1931.

[10] *Ibid.,* letters to Philip La Follette, Wisconsin; Dan Turner, Iowa; George White, Ohio; Wilbur Brucker, Michigan.

[11] *Rock County Herald,* February 6, 1931; Olson Papers, Fred Keiser to Olson, February 4, 1931.

[12] *Minneapolis Journal,* February 4, 1931.

[13] Black and Kittredge, *op. cit.,* p. 43.

[14] Olson Papers, J. T. Ellison to Olson, April 1, 1931.

[15] *Minneapolis Journal,* March 25, 1931.

[16] Olson Papers, Olson to A. W. Nylone, April 15, 1932; also Floyd B. Olson, "Minnesota Conservation Progress," *Minnesota Waltonian,* May 1932.

[17] Olson Papers, T. Hansen to Olson, March 27, 1931; S. Momb to Olson, April 7, 1931.

[18] *Ibid.,* veto message, April 20, 1931.

[19] *Sewage Conditions in the Metropolitan Drainage District* (pamphlet prepared by civic clubs of St. Paul).

[20] Day Papers, Day to C. H. Ellingson, April 27, 1931.

[21] *Biennial Report of the R.B.S.L.B.*, p. 4.

[22] Olson Papers, undated memo with statistics and marginal comments.

[23] *Ibid.*, F. E. Harrington, commissioner of health, to Olson, April 17, 1931.

[24] *Ibid.*, veto message, April 21, 1931.

[25] *St. Paul Pioneer Press*, April 22 and 23, 1931; *St. Paul Dispatch*, April 22 and 23, 1931.

[26] *Minneapolis Journal*, April 22, 1931.

[27] *Biennial Report of the R.B.S.L.B.*, pp. 33–36.

[28] Olson Papers, Fred Keiser to Olson, April 15, 1931.

[29] *Ibid.*, Fred Keiser to Seth Marshall, April 28, 1931.

[30] *Ibid.*, veto message, April 25, 1931.

[31] *Ibid.*, Henry Arens to Olson, April 28, 1931.

[32] *Ibid.*, George Palinquist to Olson, April 28, 1931.

[33] *New York Times*, May 10, 1931; Teigan Papers, Teigan to William Lemke, April 27, 1931.

[34] *Farmer Labor Leader*, April 30, 1931.

## Chapter V. Slump and Rally

[1] Stevenson, R. A., and R. S. Vaile. *Balancing the Economic Controls* (Minneapolis, 1935), p. 15.

[2] Clark, F. E., and L. D. H. Weld. *Marketing Agricultural Products in the United States* (New York, 1932), p. 622.

[3] Olson Papers, Day to H. Morris, August 31, 1931.

[4] *Long Prairie Leader*, June 25, 1931.

[5] Olson Papers, E. L. Regnier to Olson, June 24, 1931.

[6] Teigan Papers, H. W. Dart to Teigan, August 12, 1931.

[7] Olson Papers, T. W. Walsh to Olson, August 26, 1931.

[8] *Minneapolis Journal*, August 15, 1931.

[9] Teigan Papers, Teigan to M. A. Ulvedahl, October 3, 1931.

[10] Olson Papers, Day to Magnus Johnson, September 9, 1931.

[11] *Appleton Press*, August 7, 1931; *St. Peter Herald*, August 5, 1931.

[12] Olson Papers, F. H. Weiss to C. M. Babcock, August 15, 1931.

[13] *Ibid.*, A. H. Hendrickson to Olson, March 31, 1931; William Bolton to Olson, March 23, 1931.

[14] *Long Prairie Leader*, April 2, 1931.

[15] Olson Papers, Senator George Lommen to Olson, June 29, 1931.

[16] *Minneapolis Journal*, August 13, 1931.

[17] *Ibid.*

[18] *Farmer Labor Leader*, May 14, 1931.

[19] *Deer Creek Mirror*, January 7, 1932.

[20] Teigan Papers, Teigan to R. L. Carver, May 21, 1931.

[21] *Renville County Journal*, September 10, 1931.

[22] *Farmer Labor Leader*, May 14, August 13, October 15, 1931.

[23] Day Papers, memo to Olson, December 16, 1931. See also Teigan Papers, Teigan to J. M. Baar, October 26, 1931, and H. Watts to Teigan, July 4, 1931; Rudolph Lee in the *Long Prairie Leader*, December 10, 1931; Verner Nelson in the *Northern Minnesota Leader*, September 13, 1934.

[24] Teigan Papers, A. H. Hendrickson to Teigan, November 26, 1931; R. A. Trovatten to Teigan, November 11, 1931.

[25] *Long Prairie Leader*, October 29, 1931; *Minneapolis Journal*, November 2, 1931; *New York Times*, October 5, 1931.

[26] Beard, C. A. and M. R. *America in Mid-Passage* (2 vols., New York, 1938), vol. 1, p. 106.

[27] *Farmer Labor Leader*, November 12, 1931.

[28] *Long Prairie Leader*, November 5, 1931; *Minneapolis Journal*, October 29, 1931.

[29] *Minnesota Union Advocate*, February 11, 1932.

[30] Olson Papers, Hay to Olson, November 30, 1931.

[31] *Minneapolis Tribune*, August 23, 1936.

[32] *Minnesota Union Advocate*, November 26, 1931; *Farmer Labor Leader*, December 10, 1931.

[33] Olson Papers, William Mahoney to Olson, December 19, 1931.

[34] *Minnesota Union Advocate*, January 7, 1932; *Farmer Labor Leader*, December 10, 1932.

[35] *Minneapolis Journal*, January 18, 1932.

## Chapter VI.  Capitalism on Trial

[1] *St. Paul Pioneer Press*, March 30, 1932.

[2] *Minnesota Union Advocate*, April 3, 1932.

[3] *Minneapolis Journal*, March 31, 1932.

[4] Teigan Papers, Teigan to S. Ameriger, June 29, 1931; Teigan to Gale Plagman, June 23, 1931.

[5] *Farmer Labor Leader*, May 18, 1931.

[6] Olson Papers, Day to O. E. Neal, March 16, 1932.

[7] *New York Times*, May 31, 1931; Teigan Papers, Teigan to Gale Plagman, June 23, 1931.

[8] Olson Papers, Olson to Roosevelt, June 30, 1933.

[9] *Minneapolis Journal*, April 19, 1932.

[10] *Ibid.*, March 30, 1932.

[11] *Ibid.*, May 17, 1932.

[12] Teigan Papers, Teigan to Regnier, May 20, 1932.

[13] *Minneapolis Journal*, June 19, 1932.

[14] Olson Papers, Olson to Morgenthau, October 11, 1933.

[15] *Minneapolis Journal*, July 23, 1932; *St. Paul Pioneer Press*, July 10, 1932.

[16] *Minneapolis Journal*, July 29, 1932.

[17] Olson Papers, Bouvette to Olson, November 22, 1932; Bennett to Day, January 19, 1932.

[18] Bahmer, *op. cit.*, p. 195.

[19] Olson Papers, H. M. Harden to Olson, August 4, 1932; E. T. Ebbesen to Olson, September 4, 1932.

[20] *Minneapolis Journal*, August 27, 1933.

[21] Olson Papers, Olson to H. G. Gearhart, September 6, 1932.

[22] *Farmer Labor Leader*, September 15, 1932.

[23] Olson Papers, T. W. Curtis, Jr., to Olson, December 22, 1932.

[24] *Ibid.*, Olson to the Reconstruction Finance Corporation, October 11, 1932.

# NOTES

[25] *Ibid.*, speech to the League of Minnesota Municipalities at Red Wing, June 9, 1932.

[26] *Minneapolis Journal*, October 4, 1932.

[27] *Farmer Labor Leader*, August 15, 1932.

[28] *Minneapolis Journal*, October 16, 1932.

[29] E. L. Regnier to the author.

[30] *St. Paul Pioneer Press*, September 5, 1932.

[31] Teigan Papers, Teigan to T. S. Meighan, February 18, 1932; *Minneapolis Journal*, June 1, 1932.

[32] *Minneapolis Journal*, September 21, 1932.

[33] *Farmer Labor Leader*, August 15, 1932; *Minneapolis Journal*, August 28, 1932; Teigan Papers, Farmer Labor Press Service, September 19, 1932.

## *Chapter VII.   The Emergence of a Radical*

[1] *Minneapolis Journal*, August 18, 1932.

[2] Day Papers, memo to Olson, November 14, 1932.

[3] Olson Papers, Day to H. R. Atwood, November 19, 1932.

[4] *Minneapolis Journal*, November 27, 1932.

[5] Olson Papers, Hjalmar Petersen to Vince Day, December 1, 1932.

[6] *Kenyon Leader*, December 16, 1932.

[7] *Minnesota Leader*, August 29, 1936.

[8] Olson Papers, Genevieve Sheldon to Olson, June 21, 1935.

[9] Day Papers, memo to Olson, October 9, 1931.

[10] *Minneapolis Journal*, August 29, 1936.

[11] *Minnesota Leader*, August 29, 1936.

[12] Olson Papers, clipping of interview to *Ah La Ha Sa* ("Voice of Albert Lea High School"), December 9, 1931.

[13] Ford, G. S. *On and Off the Campus* (Minneapolis, 1938), p. 509.

[14] *Minneapolis Journal*, August 23, 1936.

[15] *Ibid.*, January 4, 1933.

[16] Day Papers, minutes of a conference with farm leaders, February 10, 1933.

[17] Olson Papers, Bosch to Olson, January 23, 1933.

[18] *Minneapolis Journal*, January 21, 1933.

[19] Olson Papers, H. Nyclemoe to M. W. Odland, February 6, 1933.

[20] *Minneapolis Journal*, February 25, 1933.

[21] Olson Papers, Henry Nyclemoe to M. W. Odland, February 6, 1933.

[22] *Blaisdell v. Home Building and Loan Association*, 290 U.S. 398.

[23] Stevenson and Vaile, *op. cit.*, p. 37.

[24] Olson Papers, Peyton to Olson, January 7, 1932.

[25] *Ibid.*, F. DuToit to Olson, March 28, 1933; Teigan Papers, S. Ronning to Teigan, May 24, 1932.

[26] Olson Papers, Devaney to Olson, March 4, 1933.

[27] *Minneapolis Journal*, March 5, 1933.

[28] Olson Papers, Olson to Moley, March 9, 1933.

[29] Day Papers, Day to Olson, May 10, 1933.

[30] *Minneapolis Journal*, February 25, 1933.

[31] *Ibid.*, March 6, 1933.

[32] *Farmer Labor Leader*, March 15, 1933.

[33] *Minneapolis Journal*, March 17, 1933.

[34] *St. Paul Pioneer Press*, April 13, 1933.

[35] *Minneapolis Journal*, April 14, 1933.

[36] Teigan Papers, G. W. Robitshek to Teigan, February 21, 1933.

[37] *Ibid.*, W. B. Shay to Teigan, February 20, 1933.

[38] *Minneapolis Journal*, February 25, 1933.

[39] *Farmer Labor Leader*, April 15, 1933.

[40] *Minneapolis Journal*, April 13, 1933.

[41] Teigan Papers, Teigan to W. O. Storlie, January 24, 1933.

[42] *Minneapolis Journal*, January 6, 1933.

[43] Olson Papers, L. D. Coffman to Olson, April 20, 1933.

[44] *Minneapolis Journal*, April 23, 1933.

[45] *Farmer Labor Leader*, April 30, 1933.

[46] *Izaak Walton League Bulletin*, October 1941, p. 7.

[47] Teigan Papers, H. W. Dart to Teigan, September 6, 1931.

[48] Olson Papers, E. V. Willard of the Conservation Commission to Olson, March 16, 1933.

[49] *Princeton Union*, April 27, 1933.

## Chapter VIII.  Toward National Leadership

[1] Maurice Rose to the author.

[2] *Minneapolis Journal*, December 1, 1931.

[3] Olson Papers, Day to J. Y. Aleck, June 3, 1933.

[4] *Minnesota Union Advocate*, November 17, 1932.

[5] Day Papers, memos to Olson, December 10, 1932, May 19, 1933, July 6, 1933. Teigan Papers, G. Kanderlike to Teigan, December 6, 1932; L. W. Martin to Teigan, July 29, 1933.

[6] Day Papers, Welch to Day, June 7, 1933.

[7] *Ibid.*, Day to Olson, July 29 and August 22, 1933.

[8] Olson Papers, Olson to H. H. Peterson, January 10, 1933.

[9] Day Papers, memo to Olson, January 7, 1933.

[10] Olson Papers, manuscript of speech at Eagles' convention, August 4, 1933.

[11] *Minneapolis Journal*, November 23, 1932.

[12] Day Papers, memo to Olson, May 12, 1933.

[13] *Ibid.*, May 11, 1933.

[14] Olson Papers, Olson to Reno, May 12, 1933.

[15] *Farmer Labor Leader*, May 15, 1933.

[16] *Minneapolis Journal*, September 27, 1933.

[17] *Ibid.*, October 21, 1933.

[18] *Ibid.*, November 5, 1933.

[19] John Bosch to the author.

[20] *Minneapolis Journal*, November 5, 1933.

[21] Olson Papers, Olson to Langer, January 10, 1934.

[22] *Business Week*, November 11, 1933, p. 9.

[23] Olson Papers, Senator J. S. McCormick to Olson, November 12, 1933.

[24] *Ibid.*, Olson to Bosch, November 20, 1933.

[25] *Ibid.*, Olson to Roosevelt, March 17, 1934; Roosevelt to Olson, April 16, 1934.

[26] *Ibid.*, Olson to Bosch, September 24, 1934.

[27] *Minneapolis Journal*, August 9, 1933.

[28] Olson Papers, Olson to D. R. Richberg, October 24, 1933.

[29] *Minneapolis Journal,* August 28, 1933.

[30] Olson Papers, Olson to D. R. Richberg, October 21, 1933.

[31] *Minneapolis Journal,* September 17, 1933.

[32] *Austin Daily Herald,* November 11, 1933.

[33] *Ibid.*

[34] Maurice Rose to the author.

[35] *Minneapolis Tribune,* November 15, 1933; *St. Paul Pioneer Press,* November 14, 1933.

[36] *Minneapolis Journal,* November 24, 1933.

[37] Olson Papers, L. K. Williams to Olson, December 1, 1933; Z. L. Begen to Olson, December 1, 1933; V. T. Kolb to Olson, November 24, 1933.

[38] *Farmer Labor Leader,* December 30, 1933.

[39] *Minneapolis Journal,* December 16, 1933.

[40] Olson Papers, manuscript of a radio address over WCCO, Minneapolis, December 21, 1933.

[41] *Minneapolis Journal,* December 27, 1933.

[42] Olson Papers, B. A. Michel to Olson, December 28, 1933.

## *Chapter IX.  A Troublesome Platform*

[1] Olson Papers, E. E. Barness to Olson, January 2, 1934.

[2] *Minneapolis Journal,* August 11, 1933.

[3] *Ibid.,* January 2, 1934. See also *Murray County Herald,* March 1, 1934; *Long Prairie Leader,* January 11, 1934; *Montevideo News,* March 2, 1934; *Faribault News,* February 3, 1934; *Redwood County Sun,* February 2, 1934.

[4] *Mille Lacs County Times,* March 1, 1934; *Minneapolis Journal,* March 22, 1934.

[5] Day Papers, memo to Olson, April 14, 1934.

[6] *Midwest American,* November 3, 1933.

[7] Teigan Papers, Farmer Labor Press Service, February 12, 1934.

[8] *St. Paul Pioneer Press,* February 12, 1934.

[9] *Minneapolis Journal,* February 16, 1934.

[10] *Willmar Daily Tribune,* February 16, 1934; *Askov American,* February 15, 1934; *Mille Lacs County Times,* February 22, 1934.

[11] *Minneapolis Labor Review,* March 2, 1934.

[12] *Minneapolis Journal,* August 27, 1933.

[13] *Ibid.,* February 14, 1934.

[14] *Ibid.,* February 25, 1934.

[15] Day Papers, memo to Olson, March 12, 1934.

[16] *Ibid.,* March 13, 1934.

[17] *Minneapolis Journal,* March 17, 1934.

[18] Olson Papers, Olson to Shipstead, March 23, 1934.

[19] Ellard Walsh to the author.

[20] *Minneapolis Journal,* March 28, 1934.

[21] *Ibid.,* March 29, 1934.

[22] *Farmer Labor Leader,* March 30, 1934.

[23] Day Papers, memo to Olson, May 2, 1934.

[24] *Northern Minnesota Leader,* April 3, 1934.

[25] *Minneapolis Journal,* April 22, 1934.

[26] These opinions and statements come from, in order, the *Minneapolis*

*Journal,* March 31, 1934; *Murray County Herald,* April 15, 1934; *Hibbing Tribune,* April 17, 1934; *Minneapolis Journal,* April 10, 1934; *New York Times,* April 2, 1934.

[27] Day Papers, memo to Olson, April 4, 1934.

[28] *Minneapolis Journal,* April 13, 1934.

[29] Olson Papers, G. H. Asfalg to Olson, April 13, 1934.

[30] Day Papers, memo to Olson, April 14, 1934.

[31] *Murray County Herald,* April 19, 1934.

[32] *Minneapolis Journal,* April 6, 1934.

[33] Day Papers, memo to Olson, April 14, 1934.

[34] *Minneapolis Journal,* April 13, 1934; *Farmer Labor Leader,* April 15, 1934.

[35] *Ibid.*

[36] *Minneapolis Labor Review,* April 20, 1934.

[37] Olson Papers, H. W. Bless to Olson, April 20, 1934.

[38] *Ibid.,* O. J. Rustad to Olson, May 11, 1934.

[39] Day Papers, memo to Olson, May 2, 1934.

[40] To Marquis Childs, *St. Louis Post Dispatch,* quoted in the *Minneapolis Journal,* November 23, 1934.

[41] *Minneapolis Journal,* June 6, 1934.

[42] *Ibid.,* May 21, 1934.

[43] Olson Papers, Day to Hogenson, June 16, 1934.

[44] *St. Paul Pioneer Press,* June 15, 1934.

[45] Olson Papers, A. H. Hendrickson to Olson, April 24, 1934.

[46] *Ibid.,* April 25, 1934.

## Chapter X.  The Truck Strike

[1] Walker, C. R. *American City* (New York, 1937), p. 85.

[2] "The Twin Cities," *Fortune Magazine,* vol. 13, April 1936, p. 193.

[3] Olson Papers, pamphlet entitled "The Citizens' Alliance of Minneapolis," p. 2.

[4] From material captured during the raid on the Citizens' Alliance headquarters and reprinted in the *Farmer Labor Leader,* August 15, 1934.

[5] Walker, *op. cit.,* p. 87.

[6] *Minneapolis Labor Review,* May 18, 1934.

[7] Beard, *op. cit.,* vol. 1, pp. 230–34.

[8] Ross, Anne, "Minnesota Sets Some Precedents," *New Republic,* vol. 80, September 12, 1934.

[9] *Minneapolis Labor Review,* February 9, 1934.

[10] Walker, *op. cit.,* p. 90.

[11] Rodman, Selden, "A Letter from Minnesota," *New Republic,* vol. 80, August 15, 1934, p. 10.

[12] Olson Papers, Olson to D. Richberg, October 24, 1933.

[13] Walker, *op. cit.,* p. 82.

[14] *Minneapolis Labor Review,* May 11, 1934.

[15] *Minneapolis Journal,* May 8, 1934.

[16] *Ibid.,* May 12, 1934.

[17] *Ibid.,* May 16, 1934.

[18] *Duluth Labor World,* September 6, 1924.

[19] *Minneapolis Journal,* October 11, 1933.

# NOTES

[20] Day Papers, Olson to William Bramm, April 13, 1934.

[21] Olson Papers, Olson to Alfred Sessock, December 19, 1934.

[22] *Duluth Labor World*, September 6, 1924.

[23] Olson Papers, Olson to D. Richberg, October 24, 1933.

[24] The strike tactics of Local 574 are described in detail by Walker, *op. cit.*, pp. 99–103; the account is based on interviews with union leaders.

[25] *New York Times*, August 2, 1934.

[26] *Minneapolis Journal*, May 18, 1934.

[27] Olson Papers, Olson to D. Richberg, May 21, 1934.

[28] Walker, *op. cit.*, p. 104.

[29] *Minneapolis Journal*, May 20, 1934.

[30] Walker, *op. cit.*, p. 87.

[31] *Ibid.*

[32] "The Twin Cities," *Fortune Magazine*, vol. 13, April 1936, p. 113.

[33] *Long Prairie Leader*, May 24, 1934.

[34] *Minneapolis Labor Review*, May 25, 1934.

[35] *Chicago Tribune*, May 26, 1934.

[36] Dunne, W. F., and M. Childs. *Permanent Counter Revolution: The Role of the Trotskyites in the Minneapolis Strike* (New York, 1934), p. 19.

[37] *Minneapolis Labor Review*, June 1, 1936.

[38] *Organizer*, July 17, 1934.

[39] *Minneapolis Labor Review*, June 8, 1934.

[40] *Minneapolis Journal*, July 6, 1934.

[41] Olson Papers, Hursh to Olson, July 5, 1934.

[42] *Minneapolis Journal*, July 8, 1934.

[43] Rodman, *loc. cit.*

[44] *Minneapolis Journal*, July 17, 1934.

[45] *Organizer*, July 18, 1934.

[46] *Minneapolis Journal*, July 20, 1934.

[47] *Organizer*, July 20, 1934.

[48] *Farmer Labor Leader*, August 15, 1934.

[49] *Organizer*, July 20, 1934.

[50] *Farmer Labor Leader*, August 15, 1934.

[51] Ellard Walsh to the author.

[52] *Minneapolis Journal*, July 21, 1934.

[53] *Des Moines Register*, November 25, 1934.

[54] *Minneapolis Journal*, July 26, 1934.

[55] Olson Papers, Olson to J. R. Cochran, July 26, 1934.

[56] *Ibid.*, radio address, KSTP, Minneapolis, July 30, 1934.

[57] Walker, *op. cit.*, p. 171.

[58] *New York Times*, July 27, 1934.

[59] *Minneapolis Journal*, July 28, 1934.

[60] Olson Papers, Adams to Olson, August 11, 1934.

[61] *St. Paul Pioneer Press*, July 27, 1934.

[62] *Minneapolis Tribune*, July 30, 1934.

[63] Day Papers, memos to Olson, August 6 and 10, 1934.

[64] *Minneapolis Journal*, July 30, 1934.

[65] *Organizer*, July 31, 1934.

[66] *New York Times*, August 2, 1934.

[67] Walker, *op. cit.*, p. 204.

[68] *Minneapolis Journal,* August 1, 1934.

[69] Day Papers, memo to Olson, August 6, 1934.

[70] Kenneth Haycraft to the author.

[71] Day Papers, memo to Olson, August 3, 1934.

[72] *Ibid.,* August 10, 1934.

[73] *Minneapolis Star,* August 10, 1934; *Farmer Labor Leader,* August 15, 1934.

[74] *Minneapolis Journal,* August 11, 1934.

[75] *Organizer,* August 7 and 9, 1934.

[76] Ross, *loc. cit.,* p. 121.

[77] Day Papers, memo to Olson, August 14, 1934.

[78] Walker, *op. cit.,* p. 217–18.

[79] *Organizer,* August 17, 1934.

[80] Walker, *op. cit.,* p. 218.

[81] Robley Cramer to the author.

[82] Pearson, D., "Washington Merry Go Round" as quoted in the *Farmer Labor Leader,* September 30, 1934.

[83] *Minneapolis Labor Review,* September 28, 1934.

## Chapter XI. The 1934 Election

[1] Charles B. Cheney in the *Minneapolis Journal,* August 23, 1936.

[2] *Minneapolis Journal,* October 29, 1933.

[3] Olson Papers, statement on Judge Nordbye (undated).

[4] *Minneapolis Journal,* February 9, 1936.

[5] Olson Papers, statement to the press, April 26, 1936.

[6] G. B. Leonard in the *Minneapolis Star,* August 24, 1936.

[7] Cheney, C. B., "Cheney's Story," Chapter 30, *Minneapolis Tribune,* November 29, 1946.

[8] Day Papers, memo to Olson, November 23, 1933.

[9] *Ibid.,* January 24, 1934.

[10] Olson Papers, Olson to Lefkovitz, August 17, 1933.

[11] *Windom Reporter,* August 19, 1932.

[12] *Minneapolis Journal,* November 9, 1935.

[13] *Minnesota Leader,* November 16, 1935.

[14] *St. Paul Daily News,* January 28, 1935.

[15] *Minneapolis Journal,* February 15, 1932.

[16] *Ibid.,* August 25, 1936.

[17] Billy Williams to the author.

[18] Morris Hursh to the author.

[19] Maurice Rose to the author.

[20] Olson Papers, Olson to Henry Arens, October 6, 1931.

[21] Ford, *op. cit.,* p. 508.

[22] Cheney to the author.

[23] "Cheney's Story," *Minneapolis Tribune,* November 29, 1946.

[24] Gray, James. *Pine, Stream, and Prairie* (New York, 1945), p. 130.

[25] Maurice Rose to the author.

[26] Herbert Heaton to the author.

[27] Kenneth Haycraft to the author.

[28] Olson Papers, Olson to Elsberg, January 30, 1933.

[29] Hjalmar Petersen to the author.

[30] Ford, *op. cit.*, p. 509.

[31] Olson Papers, Olson to Schmahl, March 4, 1935.

[32] *Minneapolis Journal*, August 31, 1933.

[33] Olson Papers, Lind to Olson, September 12, 1935.

[34] E. L. Regnier to the author.

[35] *Farmer Labor Leader*, October 15, 1934.

[36] Olson Papers, analysis of the Farmer Labor platform.

[37] *Washington Daily News*, September 14, 1934.

[38] *New York Times*, October 7, 1934.

[39] *Minneapolis Journal*, October 27, 1934.

[40] *Farmer Labor Leader*, November 3, 1934.

[41] *Minneapolis Journal*, November 3, 1934.

[42] Day Papers, memo to Olson, October 30, 1934.

[43] *Ibid.*, November 9, 1934.

[44] *Minneapolis Journal*, November 4, 1934.

[45] Day Papers, memo to Olson, November 9, 1934.

[46] *Minneapolis Journal*, October 6, 1934.

[47] "Cheney's Story," *Minneapolis Tribune*, November 29, 1946; *Minnesota Leader*, August 29, 1936.

[48] Ed Goff in the *Minneapolis Journal*, August 23, 1936.

[49] To Donald Grant, *Des Moines Register*, November 25, 1934.

[50] Maurice Rose to the author.

[51] D. R. Arundel to the author.

[52] Elmer A. Benson to the author.

[53] Day Papers, memo to Olson, November 9, 1934.

[54] *Minneapolis Journal*, October 3, 1934.

[55] *Midwest American*, September 7, 1934.

[56] *Farmer Labor Leader*, September 15, 1934.

[57] *Minneapolis Journal*, September 17, 1934.

[58] *Farmer Labor Leader*, October 30, 1934.

[59] *Minneapolis Journal*, October 3, 1934.

[60] *Ibid.*, October 7, 1934.

[61] Olson Papers, undated statement on the 1934 election.

[62] Leif Gilstad in the *Minneapolis Journal*, August 23, 1936.

[63] To Donald Grant, *Des Moines Register*, November 25, 1934.

[64] Gray, *op. cit.*, p. 129.

[65] Janney, John, "Minnesota's Enigma," *American Magazine*, vol. 120, September 1935, p. 47.

[66] *Minneapolis Journal*, November 24, 1933.

[67] *Boston Post*, September 25, 1933.

[68] *Minneapolis Journal*, August 8, 1932.

[69] To Donald Grant, *Des Moines Register*, November 25, 1934.

[70] Olson Papers, memo of speech (undated).

[71] Davenport, Walter, "Just Red Enough to Win," *Colliers*, vol. 94, September 8, 1934, p. 31.

[72] *Minnesota Leader*, August 29, 1936.

## Chapter XII.  Deadlock

[1] *Minneapolis Journal*, October 10, 1934.

[2] *Ibid.*, January 12, 1935.

[3] *Farmer Labor Leader*, November 30, 1934.

[4] *Minneapolis Journal*, November 22, 1934.

[5] *Ibid.*, January 8, 1935.

[6] Reprinted *ibid.*, November 23, 1934.

[7] *Farmer Labor Leader*, December 15, 1934.

[8] *Minnesota Leader*, January 19, 1935.

[9] A. I. Harris in the *Askov American*, February 28, 1935.

[10] Roberts, Rome. *Minnesota Merry Go Round* (1935), p. 130.

[11] "Cheney's Story," *Minneapolis Tribune*, November 29, 1946.

[12] Roberts, *op. cit.*, p. 90.

[13] Olson Papers, Griffith to Olson, October 3, 1935.

[14] *Ibid.*, R. W. Hitchcock to Olson, March 7, 1935.

[15] *St. Paul Daily News*, January 29, 1935.

[16] *Ibid.*, April 26, 1935.

[17] *Minneapolis Journal*, February 6, 1935.

[18] *St. Paul Daily News*, March 1, 1935.

[19] Olson Papers, C. H. MacKenzie, "Minnesota's Staggering Tax Burden," p. 112.

[20] *Minneapolis Journal*, March 21, 1935.

[21] *Ibid.*, March 22, 1935.

[22] *St. Paul Daily News*, March 22, 23, 27, 28, 30, 1935.

[23] *Minneapolis Journal*, April 21, 1935.

[24] *Ibid.*, April 27, 1935.

[25] *Long Prairie Leader*, May 9, 1935.

[26] Olson Papers, speech at the University of Minnesota, April 12, 1935.

## Chapter XIII.   The Spoilsmen Turn King-Makers

[1] Day Papers, Bob Happ to Day, August 23, 1935.

[2] Olson Papers, J. F. McGovern to Olson, May 10, 1935.

[3] Day Papers, memo to Olson, September 11, 1935.

[4] Day Papers, Bob Happ to Day, August 23, 1935.

[5] *Minneapolis Journal*, November 9, 1935.

[6] *Minneapolis Labor Review*, November 29, 1935.

[7] *Minneapolis Journal*, February 6, 1936.

[8] *Minnesota Union Advocate*, November 15, 1934.

[9] Day Papers, memo to Olson, July 17, 1934.

[10] *Minnesota Union Advocate*, June 13, 1935.

[11] *Minnesota Leader*, July 27, 1935.

[12] Day Papers, memo to Olson, August 23, 1935.

[13] *Ibid.*, August 22, 1935.

[14] Hjalmar Petersen to the author.

[15] Teigan Papers, O. H. Behrens to Teigan, July 14, 1935; V. N. Johnson to Teigan, July 25, 1935.

[16] Elmer A. Benson to the author.

[17] *Midwest American*, April 3, April 10, June 29, 1935.

[18] Olson Papers, Emil Leicht to Olson, December 11, 1933; G. A. Totten to Olson, March 7, 1934. Teigan Papers, Andrew Brueberg to Teigan, January 22, 1936.

[19] *Minneapolis Leader*, December 28, 1935.

[20] Olson Papers, Olson to Burton K. Wheeler, December 6, 1935; "Cheney's Story," *Minneapolis Tribune*, November 29, 1946.

[21] Herman Aufderheide to the author.

[22] Ann V. Egan to the author.

[23] *Minneapolis Journal*, March 10, 1936.

[24] *Ibid.*, December 28, 1935.

## Chapter XIV.   The Last Fight

[1] *Minnesota Leader*, December 28, 1935.

[2] *Minneapolis Tribune*, August 25, 1936; also "Cheney's Story," *Minneapolis Tribune*, November 29, 1946. Teigan Papers, Teigan to J. J. Hastings, January 17, 1936; Day Papers, S. E. Elliott to Day, January 10, 1936.

[3] "The Twin Cities," *Fortune Magazine*, vol. 13, April 1936, p. 194; *Minneapolis Journal*, January 7, 1936.

[4] *Minnesota Leader*, August 29, 1936.

[5] Ellard Walsh to the author.

[6] *Minneapolis Journal*, January 13, 1936.

[7] *Ibid.*, January 3, 1936.

[8] *Ibid.*, January 23, 1936.

[9] *Askov American*, February 6, 1935.

[10] *Minneapolis Journal*, February 13, 1936.

[11] *Minnesota Union Advocate*, February 27, 1936.

[12] *Minneapolis Journal*, February 19, 1936.

[13] *Askov American*, March 19, 1936.

[14] Teigan Papers, Teigan to Benson, January 30, 1936.

[15] *Minneapolis Journal*, November 16, 1935.

[16] *New York Times*, November 16, 1935.

[17] *Minnesota Leader*, January 18, 1936.

[18] *Farmer Labor Leader*, November 15, 1934.

[19] *Minnesota Leader*, February 23, 1935.

[20] *St. Paul Daily News*, February 27, 1935.

[21] *Minneapolis Journal*, August 5, 1935.

[22] *Minnesota Leader*, November 16, 1935.

[23] *Askov American*, September 5, 1935.

[24] *Minneapolis Journal*, November 19, 1935.

[25] *Minnesota Leader*, April 4, 1936.

[26] *New York Times*, May 31, 1936.

[27] *Minnesota Leader*, August 22, 1936.

[28] Olson Papers, Olson to B. H. Bowler, August 19, 1935.

[29] *Minneapolis Journal*, August 23, 1936.

[30] *Minnesota Leader*, June 20, 1936.

[31] *Ibid.*, August 27, 1936.

[32] *Minneapolis Journal*, August 23, 1936.

[33] *Ibid.*, July 19, 1936.

[34] *Minnesota Leader*, August 29, 1936.

# Index

156: Rural Credit Bureau controversy, 80; Olson representative in Washington, 89
Game wardens, 63; in patronage question, 79–80
Georgia, 295
Gerrymander, 70–71
Gifford, Walter, 90
Gilbert, A. B., 29–30
Gilstad, Leif, 256, 298, 300
Gleason, ——, in dynamiting case, 25–26
Glenwood, Minn., 23
Goldman, Albert, 219
Goodhue County, 130–31
Gossip about Olson, 5, 36, 147
Governors' conferences: meeting of Roosevelt and Olson, 97–98; midwestern discussions of agricultural problems, 105, 153–54
Grangers, 17, 18
Great Lakes–St. Lawrence Tidewater Association, 64–65. See also St. Lawrence waterway
Great Northern Railroad, 75
Greenbackers, 17
Griffith, George, 46, 63, 175: in 1930 primary, 29–30; as spoilsman, 166–69, 279, 283–85; support of Olson, 267–69
Gull Lake, 5, 78, 80, 144, 213, 298, 300

Haas, Francis J., 208, 220
Haas-Dunnigan plan, 211, 217, 220
Haislet, Sam, 248
Hall, E. G., 23
Harden, H. M., 190
Harris, Abe, 15: boyhood friend of Olson, 7–8; support of Elmer Benson, 282–87; on Farmer Labor attitude toward New Deal, 296
Harrup, R. M., 96
Haugen, John, 93
Hausler, Charles A., 173
*Hawley Herald,* 4
Haycraft, Kenneth, 217
Heffelfinger, F. T., 90
Hendrickson, A. H., 82, 183
Hennepin County, 3, 13, 14, 15, 30, 36, 39, 41, 46, 94, 199, 205, 232,

250: Farmer Labor central committee endorsement of Olson, 28; Dickey-Senn feud, 50
Herring, Clyde L., 226–27
Highway bond issue, 67–68
Highway code, 91: fight for bond issue, 67–68; improvement of working conditions, 81; antagonism of farmers, 82; criticism, 82–83
Highway Department, 233, 246, 278–79: investigation, 263; appropriations, 268
Hitchcock, R. W., 118, 173
Hoidale, Einar, 49–51, 99, 241, 293
Holmberg, N. J., 64, 238
Hoover, Herbert C., 11, 54, 101, 112, 138: attitude toward in Minnesota, 50, 114; attitude toward relief, 90, 107–8; criticism by Olson, 95, 98; defeat, 116
Hopkins, Harry L., 247, 267
Hopper, DeWolf, 9
Hormel, J. C., 160
Hormel strike, 159–60
Hosiery Workers Union, strike, 275–78
Howe, Louis M., 221
Hubbard County, 66
Hurja, Emil, 241

I.W.W., 9–10
Inaugural addresses of Olson: *1930,* 61–62; *1932,* 122–23
Income tax, 96, 122, 139. See also Taxation
*Iconoclast,* 47
Independent Merchants' Committee, 52
"Independent Progressives," 258–59
Indrehus, Edward D., 49, 56, 102
Industrial Commission, 64, 90, 160, 161
Industrial unionism, 204, 273–74. See also Labor; Truck drivers' strike
International Joint Commission, 140, 141
International Teamsters Union, 188, 204
International Workers of the World, 9–10

# INDEX

tude toward Jewish people, 5, 8; auto trip with George B. Leonard, 5–7; enjoyment of conviviality, 5; friendliness, 5, 227–28; humanitarianism, 10, 120–21, 253–55; interest in young people, 15, 121; adaptability, 225, 256; rough manners, 228; power of analysis, 231–32; sense of humor, 232–33; self-imposed isolation, 235; personal integrity, 236–37; disregard for money, 245–46

As county attorney, 14–16, 25–27, 46, 53, 193: investigation of grafting aldermen, 15, 40; dynamiting case, 25–26, 193–94: re-election, 39; Birkeland case, 182–83

As governor: appointment of secretary, 57; inaugural addresses, 61–62, 122; attack on Tidewater Association, 64–65; relations with other governors, 65, 97–98, 105, 153–54, 266–67; attack on Rural Credit Bureau, 66; public works program, 67, 259; relations with legislature, 67–77, 117–20, 130–42, 162–64, 257–72; highway code, 67–68, 81–83; conservation program, 68–69, 141–42, 272; securities legislation, 69–70; vetoes, 70–76, 138, 272; farm conference, 88–89; income tax proposal, 88; relief program, 90–91, 132–35, 163–64, 266–68; Elevator M case, 91; budget difficulties, 115, 137–39; ideas on unemployment insurance, 122–23, 135–36; halting of mortgage foreclosures, 125; attitude toward bank holiday, 128–29; conflict with A. J. Rockne, 131–35, 138, 260, 266–68; advocacy of price fixing, 152–58; sectional viewpoint, 155; in Hormel strike, 160–62; liquor control plan, 162–63; resignation offered, 164; in truck strike, 196, 199, 200–1, 208, 210–12, 215–16, 218–19, 221–22; relationship with reporters, 225; Minnesota-Iowa football incident, 226–27; use of experts, 231; petty graft in administration, 246; *1935*

biennial message to legislature, 259–60; *1935* program, 259–60; fight for Highway Department appropriations, 268; tax program, 139, 270–71; action in Strutwear strike, 276–77; last addresses, 299–300. *See also* Legislatures

As party leader, 3, 40, 41, 234: as speaker, 4, 48, 229; as rebel, 10, 253–56; political beliefs, 10, 251–56; radicalism suspect, 13, 27, 29, 76–77, 95, 251–53; radicalism, 27, 29–30, 35, 89, 108, 116, 119–20, 149, 171, 259–60; sensitivity to public opinion, 34, 229; personal organization, 37, 41–42, 278–80; domination of party conventions, 39, 43–45, 94–96; Republican support, 40, 51; nonpartisan support, 40, 41–42, 46, 52, 113, 228, 244, 279; nonpartisanship, 44, 46, 52, 61, 63, 234, 279; political realist, 45–46, 77, 92, 96–97, 201, 223, 252–53, 255, 298; Democratic support, 49, 51, 101–2, 240–41, 296–98; patronage policy, 62–64, 79–80, 145–48, 278–81; conflict with doctrinaire radicals, 77, 90–91, 96–97, 113, 255; popularity, 78, 165; change of convention tactics, 170–71; modification of *1934* radical platform, 175–80; ruthless attitude toward opponents, 233–34; conflict with spoilsmen, 278–88; attitude toward Elmer Benson, 283, 285–87; split with Hjalmar Petersen, 293

Attitudes: toward gamblers, 15; toward labor, 26, 80–81, 89, 193, 221, 222, 278; toward farmers, 28, 80–81, 88–90, 156–57; toward Communists, 32, 239–40, 253, 255; toward businessmen, 41, 54, 253; toward national third party, 96–97, 296–97; toward Roosevelt, 98, 102, 296–97; toward Farm Holiday Association, 104–5; toward capitalism, 109; toward socialism, 109, 255; toward New Deal, 149, 296, 298; toward N.R.A., 158–59; toward Citizens' Alliance, 193–94; toward

18; Nonpartisan League in, 18; economic conditions, 20; popularity of Olson, 28, 250

Red Wing, Minn., 108

Reform movement, 14, 17, 21, 27, 31, 37, 77, 92, 145, 146, 166, 168, 247, 278, 279, 291: position of Olson in, 13, 25, 27, 29–30, 40, 45–46, 92, 96, 97, 201, 223, 252–53, 255, 298; position of A. C. Townley in, 19, 20–24, 84–85, 91, 102, 113, 124, 230, 247–50, 292; instability, 24–25, 56, 77, 86–88, 91, 94, 113–14, 116, 145, 166–70, 247–49, 291–94. *See also* Farmer Labor party; Nonpartisan League

Regan, John E.: in *1932* campaign, 99, 101–2, 116; character, 111–12; in *1934* campaign, 238–42, 246–47, 249–50

Regnier, Emil L., 79, 100, 172, 235, 289

Relief problem: attitude of farmer, 86, 90; attitude of city worker, 86–87; national funds, 108, 163–64, 266–68; attitude of legislatures, 131–34, 163–64, 266–68; Olson fight for appropriations, 131–34, 163–64, 266–68; investigation of Olson program, 262, 263–64

Reno, Milo, 150, 151

Republican party, 95, 241, 252: charges against the Nonpartisan League, 21–22; in *1924* election, 31–32; whispering campaign, 36, 147; control of Minneapolis, 41; intraparty struggles, 41, 50–51; *1930* Schall-Christianson contest, 48–49; defection of small businessmen, 50; control of legislature, 58–61, 130–42, 163–64, 257–72; control of state departments, 63–64; young Republicans organized, 93; *1932* convention, 93; *1932* platform, 94; *1932* discouragement, 114; legislative leadership of A. J. Rockne, 130–42, 163–64, 266; control of state jobs, 146–47; demoralized, 165; attack on Farmer Labor textbook plank, 242–44; hopes for national third party, 295–96

Campaigns: *1918*, 23; *1920*, 23; *1924*, 34–35; *1930*, 49–52; *1932*, 109–11, 114–15; *1934*, 238–39, 242–47

Primaries: *1918*, 20–22; *1920*, 23; *1924*, 31; *1930*, 43, 48–49; *1932*, 100–1

*See also* Elections

Ritchie, A. C., 244

Roberts, Rome, 264

Rochester, Minn., 221, 284, 290, 291, 292, 300, 301

Rockne, A. J., 67, 137, 164, 165, 260, 262, 267: character, 130–31; conflict with Olson, 131–32; objection to relief program, 132–33, 163–64, 266

Roepke, William L., 268

Roosevelt, Franklin D., 3, 116, 128, 176, 189, 218, 221, 249, 301: meeting with Olson, 97–98; cooperation with Olson, 101, 240–41, 295–97; agricultural program, 149–52, 156–57; attitude toward price fixing, 153–54

Roosevelt, Theodore, 18

"Root Hog or Die Club," 137

Rose, Maurice, 10, 144, 290, 300, 301

Rules Committee of state senate, 60–61

Rural Credit Bureau, 35, 66, 88, 91: Gaarenstrom controversy, 80; elimination, 134–35

Rustad, O. J., 178

Rutchik, Roger S., 285

St. Cloud, Minn., 13, 27, 28, 30, 31, 33, 34, 240, 248, 262; Farmer Labor convention, *1924*, 27–28

St. Lawrence waterway, 45, 64–65, 96

St. Louis County, 250

*St. Louis Post Dispatch*, 259

St. Paul, Minn., 11, 13, 20, 23, 31, 32, 37, 43, 60, 94, 150, 161, 227, 234, 257, 292: third party convention, 31–33; sewage disposal problem, 71–73, 139. *See also* Twin Cities

*St. Paul Daily News*, 264, 265, 271

*St. Paul Pioneer Press*, 45, 167, 213, 225